"This is a brilliant and inspiring collection of studies by three of the leading theologians of our day. It should be on the bookshelf of all Christians."

MATTHEW LEVERING
James N. Jr. and Mary D. Perry Chair of Theology,
Mundelein Seminary

"These basic texts have been the essentials of theological education for centuries and every Christian should know them by heart. This volume makes it possible to carry them around in a user-friendly format that will be of immense help to busy people who need to be inspired again by the basic teachings of our faith."

GERALD BRAY
research professor of divinity,
Beeson Divinity School

"The three pillars of Christian teaching—Decalogue, Apostles' Creed, and the Lord's Prayer—have been the consistent basis of formation in the faith for 1500 years. They represent a foundation shared by Protestants and Catholics alike, built upon across continents and cultures. Lexham's collection of three sterling presentations of each element mines a deep tradition and deploys the wisdom of three superb Christian teachers and scholars. They have offered the 'faith once given' for the people of today in a way that nourishes, illuminates, and challenges. Whether for personal or communal use, this inviting catechism is itself a gift of grace."

EPHRAIM RADNER
professor of historical theology,
Wycliffe College at the University of Toronto

CATECHISM

The Ten Commandments

The Apostles' Creed

The Lord's Prayer

THE COLLECTED
CHRISTIAN ESSENTIALS

CATECHISM

A Guide to
the Ten Commandments,
the Apostles' Creed,
and the Lord's Prayer

PETER J. LEITHART,
BEN MYERS,
AND WESLEY HILL

GENERAL EDITOR, TODD R. HAINS

LEXHAM PRESS

The Collected Christian Essentials
Catechism: A Guide to the Ten Commandments, the Apostles' Creed, and the Lord's Prayer

Lexham Press, 1313 Commercial St., Bellingham, WA 98225
LexhamPress.com

Supplemental prayer material copyright 2023 Lexham Press
Unless otherwise noted, Scripture quotations are from the English Standard Version.

The Ten Commandments copyright 2020 by Peter J. Leithart
Unless otherwise noted, Scripture quotations are from the author's own translation or are from the King James Version.

The Apostles' Creed copyright 2018 by Ben Myers
Unless otherwise noted, Scripture quotations are from the New Revised Standard Version Bible.

The Lord's Prayer copyright 2019 by Wesley Hill
Unless otherwise noted, Scripture quotations are from the New Revised Standard Version.

Page 399 constitutes a continuation of this copyright page.

Print ISBN 9781683597018
Digital ISBN 9781683597551
Library of Congress Control Number 2023930862

Lexham Editorial: Todd Hains, Mandi Newell, Jordan Short, Fanny Gonzalez
Cover Design: Joshua Hunt
Typesetting: Abigail Stocker

CONTENTS

A Guide to

THE TEN COMMANDMENTS

by Peter J. Leithart

A Guide to
THE APOSTLES' CREED
by Ben Myers

A Guide to
THE LORD'S PRAYER
by Wesley Hill

Surely goodness and mercy shall follow me
all the days of my life, and I shall dwell
in the house of the Lord forever.

Psalm 23:6

A LIFE DISCIPLED
BY THE CATECHISM

An Introduction

OUR LORD AND SAVIOR JESUS CHRIST described his word as a seed. A gardener plants a small, unassuming seed in the earth, and he goes to sleep. When he awakes, "the seed sprouts and grows; he knows not how" (Mark 4:27). The seed did its work without any direction or manipulation by the gardener. In the same way God's word is planted in the human heart. We might not feel any different. We might not appear any different. And yet the seed of God's word is doing its work. It sprouts up and grows a harvest of faith, hope, and love.

But what does this harvest of faith, hope, and love look like? The church has defined faith, hope, and love according to the Bible. Faith is defined by the Apostles' Creed, hope by the Lord's Prayer, and love by the Ten Commandments. These three together are known as the catechism.[1] The

---

1. Not to be confused with commentaries on the catechism—like Luther's *Small Catechism* or the Heidelberg Catechism or the Catechism of the Catholic Church—all

catechism is filled with the seed of God's word, which cultivates, catechizes, and interprets us.

The Word That Cultivates Disciples

Making disciples doesn't mean manufacturing disciples; making disciples means cultivating disciples. It's not efficient work. It's not always straightforward work. And, as Jesus' parable of the sower teaches, it isn't our work. It belongs to God, and he's entrusted this work to us by his word and Spirit.

It's hard, faithful work. Patiently we establish a habit of reading and praying God's word, for God's word and prayer make all things holy (1 Tim 4:5). In happiness and in sorrow, in sickness and in health, in rest and in labor, we bring our questions and fears and joys to God's word, and we seed our worries and woes, our thoughts and prayers with God's word. And we wait, we sleep, we work. All the while, we keep bringing ourselves to God's word. We don't know how, but the seed of God's word sprouts up and grows: "He who goes out weeping, bearing the seed for sowing, shall come home with shouts of joy, bringing his sheaves with him" (Ps 126:6).

The Word That Catechizes Disciples

The catechism is a word of God that helps us pray the word of God, read the word of God, and live the word of God. This book is meant to help you make disciples using the catechism, whether that means discipling yourself or discipling others.

---

of which comment on the Ten Commandments, the Apostles' Creed, and the Lord's Prayer as well as the sacraments.

There are four parts to this book: an order of prayer (p. xvii), guides to each part of the catechism (pp. 1–363), individual prayers (or collects) based on each part of the catechism (p. 367), and a daily Bible-reading plan (or lectionary; p. 377). Each part will help you plant the seed of the catechism in your life—in thought, word, and deed.

The great catechists of the church promote a classical method of learning the catechism.[2] First, learn the words of the catechism: memorize the Ten Commandments, the Apostles' Creed, and the Lord's Prayer. Second, learn what the words mean. Third, find new ways and words to state the content of the catechism. Fourth, do it all over again!

"Although I'm indeed an old doctor," the great advocate of the catechism Martin Luther said, "I never move on from the childish doctrine of the Ten Commandments and the Apostles' Creed and the Lord's Prayer. I still daily learn and pray them with my little Hans and my little Lena."[3] He had just as much to learn from the catechism as his children. There's a lifetime of learning packed into the catechism.

The Word That Interprets Disciples

The word of God interprets itself, the world, and us. It shows what we really look like, who we really are, and what we've really done. We are wounded people in need of healing. We

---

2. For example, see Martin Luther's preface to the *Small Catechism*.

3. Martin Luther, "No. 81," in vol. 1 of *D. Martin Luthers Werke, kritische Gesamtausgabe: Tischreden* (Hermann Böhlaus Nachfolger, 1912), 30.26–27, 31.1–2.

are sinners in need of forgiveness. We are lost sheep in need of finding.

Thank God that the word of God does what it says. It confronts and comforts. It tears down and builds up. It kills and brings to life. It plants, sprouts, and grows an imperishable and eternal seed in us: Jesus, with all his gifts of forgiveness, salvation, and life everlasting. And God's word never returns empty:

> As the rain and the snow come down from heaven
>   and do not return there but water the earth,
> making it bring forth and sprout,
>   giving seed to the sower and bread to the eater,
> so shall my word be that goes out from my mouth;
>   it shall not return to me empty,
> but it shall accomplish that which I purpose,
>   and shall succeed in the thing for which I sent it.
>
>   (Isa 55:10–11)

The Lord our God—maker of heaven and earth—has given the flowers of the field and the trees of the wood beauty. And yet their beauty does not last. "The grass withers, the flower fades" (Isa 40:7). But the seed of God's word bears a crop that does not wither and fade. "The word of our God remains forever" (Isa 40:8).

Deep calls to deep at the roar of your waterfalls;
all your breakers and your waves have gone over me.
By day the Lord commands his steadfast love,
and at night his song is with me,
a prayer to the God of my life.

Psalm 42:7–8

AN ORDER
OF PRAYER

With Confession and Forgiveness

W HEN WE'VE RUN OUT OF WORDS—whether because
of sorrow or happiness—God gives us his own words,
because God's word interprets us, our lives, our worries, and
our joys. "The Spirit himself intercedes for us with groanings
too deep for words" (Rom 8:26). And so, since ancient times,
Christian worship has been defined as receiving God's word
and speaking God's word back to him. This order and logic
undergirds the Daily Office: the twin services of Morning and
Evening Prayer (also called Matins and Vespers).

This Order of Prayer is a simplified version of the Daily
Office. The English version of the Daily Office is mediated
through the Book of Common Prayer. The sixteenth-century
English Reformer Thomas Cranmer streamlined the eight
prayer offices of the medieval church into two and rendered
them in common English for common Christians.[1] Thanks

---

1. The Use of Sarum—the order of services at the Salisbury Cathedral—is surprisingly ecumenical. This Roman Catholic rite structures Anglican rites, and it is
approved for use among the Eastern Orthodox. When American Lutherans began
to worship in English, they blended elements of Sarum from the Book of Common

to Cranmer, all are now welcome to enjoy the hallowed tradition of praying psalms and verses.

This simplified Order of Prayer shows the basic structure and logic of the Daily Office. Once you're used to this Order, you should be comfortable with any edition of the Book of Common Prayer (and there are many!) or any of the various traditional prayer offices. If you want to further explore the tradition of the Daily Office, there's a list of prayer books and prayer book resources at the end of the notes section, "Bible References and History of the Order of Prayer," below.

This order of prayer has five parts: (1) INVOCATION, (2) CONFESSION AND FORGIVENESS, (3) THE SERVICE OF THE WORD, (4) PRAYER AND THANKSGIVING, and (5) BENEDICTION. These five parts invite us into God's word, which brings God present with all his gifts of forgiveness, salvation, and life, and they send us out into the world with words of faith, hope, and love.

Prayer begins with the INVOCATION, the speaking of God's name, because God promises to be present in his name and word.

In CONFESSION AND FORGIVENESS, we tell the truth: we have fallen short of God's law by sinning against him and our neighbors; and we hear God's promise of forgiveness and the declaration of forgiveness.

In THE SERVICE OF THE WORD, we hear God's word. God's word calls us to worship, instructs us, comforts us, and

---

Prayer with a slightly different continental tradition (for example, compare the collects, or prayers, of the day during the season of Advent).

gives us hope; we respond in thanksgiving for God's word with God's word.

In PRAYER AND THANKSGIVING, we ask our merciful God for his mercy; we confess who he is and what he has done and continues to do, and we pray as he taught us.

In the BENEDICTION, we praise and thank God, blessing those present with God's name.

This order of prayer can be prayed individually; just read all the text as if you were reading a book. It can also be used by a group—with a leader speaking the plain text, and the group responding with the words in bold. The psalms and songs can be read in unison or in response—with a leader reading up to the asterisk and the group reading the line after the asterisk.

INVOCATION

In the name of the Father and of the Son and of the Holy Spirit.
Amen.

Our help is in the name of the LORD,
who made heaven and earth.   *Psalm 124:8*

I said, "I will confess my transgressions to the LORD,"
and you forgave the iniquity of my sin.   *Psalm 32:5*

CONFESSION & FORGIVENESS

The Confession of Sin

Let us confess our sins to God:

Most merciful God,
**we confess that we have sinned against you
in thought, word, and deed,
by what we have done,
and by what we have left undone.
We have not loved you with our whole heart;
we have not loved our neighbors as ourselves.
We are truly sorry and we humbly repent.
For the sake of your Son Jesus Christ,
have mercy on us and forgive us;
that we may delight in your will,
and walk in your ways,
to the glory of your holy name.
Amen.**

The Forgiveness of Sin

Almighty God have mercy on us,
forgive us all our sins through our Lord Jesus Christ,
strengthen us in all goodness,
and by the power of the Holy Spirit keep us in eternal life.
Amen.

THE SERVICE OF THE WORD

Psalm of Praise

O come, let us sing to the LORD; *
> let us heartily rejoice in the strength of our salvation.

Let us come before his presence with thanksgiving *
> and show ourselves glad in him with psalms.

For the LORD is a great God *
> and a great King above all gods.

In his hand are all the corners of the earth, *
> and the strength of the hills is his also.

The sea is his, for he made it; *
> and his hands prepared the dry land.

O come, let us worship and fall down *
> and kneel before the LORD our maker.

For he is the LORD our God, *
> and we are the people of his pasture, and the sheep of his hand.

Psalm 95:1–7

Glory be to the Father and to the Son and to the Holy Spirit, as it was in the beginning, is now, and will be forever. Amen.

Prayer for Hearing the Word

Blessed Lord, you have caused all holy Scriptures to be written for our learning. Grant us so to hear them, read, mark, learn, and inwardly digest them, that by patience and comfort of your holy word, we may embrace and ever hold fast the blessed hope of everlasting life, which you have given us in our Savior Jesus Christ; who lives and reigns with you and the Holy Spirit, one God, for ever and ever. *Amen.*

Reading of the Word

Here at least one Bible passage is read; see page 377 for a Bible-reading plan.

After a psalm:

Glory be to the Father and to the Son and to the Holy Spirit, as it was in the beginning, is now, and will be forever. Amen.

After other readings:

The word of the Lord:

Thanks be to God!

Response to the Word

In the Morning

Zechariah's Song, *or* The Benedictus

Blessed be the Lord, the God of Israel; *
  he has come to his people and set
  them free.
He has raised up for us a mighty
  Savior, *
  born of the house of his servant
  David.
Through his holy prophets he
  promised of old *
  that he would save us from our
  enemies, from the hands of all who
  hate us.
He promised to show mercy to our
  fathers *
  and to remember his holy covenant.
This was the oath he swore to our
  father Abraham: *
  to set us free from the hands of our
  enemies,
free to worship him without fear, *
  holy and righteous in his sight all
  the days of our life.
You, my child, shall be called the
  prophet of the Most High; *
  for you will go before the Lord to
  prepare his way,
to give his people knowledge of
  salvation *
  by the forgiveness of their sins.
In the tender compassion of our God *
  the dawn from on high shall break
  upon us,
to shine on those who dwell in
  darkness and the shadow of death, *
  and to guide our feet
  into the way of peace.

Luke 1:68–79

In the Evening

Mary's Song, *or* The Magnificat

My soul magnifies the Lord, *
  and my spirit rejoices in God
  my Savior.
For he has regarded *
  the lowliness of his handmaiden.
For behold, from henceforth *
  all generations will call me blessed.
For he who is mighty has done great
  things for me, *
  and holy is his name.
And his mercy is on those who fear
  him *
  from generation to generation.
He has shown strength with his arm. *
  He has scattered the proud in the
  imagination of their hearts.
He has cast down the mighty from
  their thrones *
  and has exalted the humble and
  meek.
He has filled the hungry with good
  things, *
  and the rich he has sent away empty.
He has helped his servant Israel
  in remembrance of his mercy, *
  as he promised to our fathers,
  Abraham and his seed forever.

Luke 1:46–55

**Glory be to the Father and to the Son and to the Holy Spirit,
as it was in the beginning, is now, and will be forever. Amen.**

The Apostles' Creed

God has made us his people through our baptism into Christ.
Living together in trust and hope, we confess our faith:

I believe in God the Father almighty,
    maker of heaven and earth,
and in Jesus Christ, his only Son, our Lord:
    who was conceived by the Holy Spirit,
    born of the Virgin Mary,
    suffered under Pontius Pilate,
    was crucified, died, and was buried.
    He descended into hell.
    On the third day he rose again from the dead.
    He ascended into heaven
    and is seated at the right hand of the Father.
    He will come again to judge
        the living and the dead.
I believe in the Holy Spirit,
    the holy catholic church,
    the communion of saints,
    the forgiveness of sins,
    the resurrection of the body,
    and the life everlasting.
    Amen.

hell: Some English versions of the Apostles' Creed translate this line, "He descended to the dead."

catholic church: The phrase "catholic church" means all Christians throughout time and space who confess the Christian faith.

PRAYER & THANKSGIVING

Lord, have mercy on us.
Christ, have mercy on us.
Lord, have mercy on us.   *Matthew 9:27; Psalm 123:3*

The Lord's Prayer

Lord, remember us in your kingdom,
    and teach us to pray: *Luke 24:42; Luke 11:1*

Our Father who art in heaven,
hallowed be thy name,
thy kingdom come,
thy will be done
    on earth as it is in heaven;
give us this day our daily bread;
and forgive us our trespasses
    as we forgive those who trespass against us;
and lead us not into temptation,
but deliver us from evil.   *Matthew 6:9–13*
For thine is the kingdom and the power
    and the glory forever and ever.
Amen.

The Petitions

O LORD, show us your steadfast love,
and grant us your salvation.   *Psalm 85:7*

Let your priests be clothed with righteousness,
and let your saints shout for joy.   *Psalm 132:9*

O LORD, save your people,
and bless your heritage!   *Psalm 28:9*

Create in me a clean heart, O God,
and renew a right spirit within me.   *Psalm 51:10*

Hear my prayer, O LORD;
let my cry come to you!   *Psalm 102:1*

Prayers of the Heart

God is our loving Father.
He wants to hear our questions, fears, and joys.
Here we offer prayers and thanksgivings
for others and ourselves.

After each prayer:

Thy will be done:
on earth as it is in heaven.

Prayer for the Day

Pray at least one of the following prayers.
One person or all in unison may pray.

Prayer for Anytime

Almighty God, only you can order our unruly wills and desires. Grant to your people that we may love what you command and desire what you promise, that among the many changes and chances of this world our hearts may be fixed where true joys are found; through Jesus Christ our Lord.

Amen.

Prayer for the Morning

Our heavenly Father, we give you thanks through your dear Son Jesus Christ that you have kept us this night from all harm and danger. We ask you to keep us this day also, from all sin and evil, that all our thoughts, words, and deeds may please you. Into your hands we commend ourselves, our bodies and souls, and all things. Let your holy angels be with us, that the evil foe may have no power over us.

Amen.

Prayer for the Evening

Our heavenly Father, we give you thanks through your dear Son Jesus Christ that you have graciously kept us this day. We ask you to forgive us all our sins and the wrongs that we have done and to graciously keep us this night. Into your hands we commend ourselves, our bodies and souls, and all things. Let your holy angels be with us, that the evil foe may have no power over us.

Amen.

BENEDICTION

Let us bless the LORD. *Psalm 103:1*

Thanks be to God.

The grace of our Lord Jesus Christ and the love of God and the communion of the Holy Spirit be with us all.

2 Corinthians 13:14

Amen.

BIBLE REFERENCES
AND HISTORY

Of the Order of Prayer

INVOCATION: Jesus promises to be present in his name and word, and so prayer begins by speaking God's name (Matt 18:20; 28:20; John 14:27).

THE CONFESSION OF SIN: When we confess our sins, we admit that we fall short of the life God describes in the Ten Commandments. We sin against God (the commandments of the first table), and we sin against our neighbor (the commandments of the second table). We sin in what we think, say, and do. In Jesus—who made heaven and earth—our sins are forgiven. By his Spirit we delight in his will and walk in his word. This text is the result of the Joint Liturgical Group in 1968.

PSALM OF PRAISE: God's word calls us to worship, for faith comes through hearing (Rom 10:17). At least since the sixth century, Christians have read Psalm 95 for a call to worship. The psalm may be read responsively or in unison.

Almost all prayerbooks today omit verses 8–11 (some require them to be read during Lent). In 1789 the American Book of Common Prayer omitted these verses of law and judgment and replaced them with Psalm 96:9, 13.

PRAYER FOR HEARING THE WORD: This prayer is based on Romans 15:4 as given in William Tyndale's 1534 translation: "Whatsoever thynges are wrytten afore tyme are wrytten for oure learnynge that we thorow pacience and comforte of the scripture myght have hope." The sixteenth-century English Reformer Thomas Cranmer composed this prayer as the Collect for the Second Sunday in Advent. It was first printed in the 1549 Book of Common Prayer. Every Sunday and feast day has a collect of the day, which is a prayer that goes with the assigned readings of the day.

READING OF THE WORD: There are two general approaches to selecting the readings. The first is the continuous reading of a book of the Bible. For example, a chapter of a Gospel is read until the Gospel is finished; then a new book is selected to read through. The second is a Bible-reading plan or lectionary. For example, there is a Bible-reading plan on page 377 in this book.

RESPONSE TO THE WORD: The reading of God's word ends with a response. Zechariah's Song, traditionally known as The Benedictus from its opening phrase in Latin, is a fitting response in the morning; Mary's Song, traditionally known as The Magnificat, in the evening. Both songs summarize the story and gift of God's word and work for his people. The song may be read responsively or in unison.

THE APOSTLES' CREED: According to ancient tradition, the apostles, under the inspiration of the Holy Spirit, drafted the Apostles' Creed on the day of Pentecost. It expands the succinct biblical logic and confession of the trinitarian formula used in baptism: in the name of the Father and of the Son and of the Holy Spirit. The Apostles' Creed as worded today dates to the fourth century, though its basic form dates as early as the second century.

PRAYER AND THANKSGIVING: The church adapted the cry of beggars in the ancient world—have mercy on us! (Matt 9:27)—as a prayer to the Lord our God who made heaven and earth and who fills the hungry with good things. This cry is called the *Kyrie Eleison* ("Lord, have mercy"). It begins our prayers and thanksgivings: we confess who God is and what he has done and continues to do, and we pray as he taught us.

THE LORD'S PRAYER: This is the traditional English wording of the Lord's Prayer. It is taken from the 1549 Book of Common Prayer, which used William Tyndale's translation of Matthew 6:9–13.

THE PETITIONS: God's word, especially in the Psalms, provides a pattern for our prayers. These verses and responses are adapted from the 1549 Book of Common Prayer. The petitions ask God to sanctify our lives, the church, the world, and those in need with his word and prayer.

The 1549 petitions include a beautiful sixth-century antiphon called *Da pacem*: "Give peace in our time, O Lord; * Because there is none other that fighteth for us, but only thou, O God." This has been omitted in favor of explicit Scripture.

PRAYER FOR ANYTIME: This prayer directs us to find certainty in God's word. It uses Psalm 119 (especially verses 47, 81–82) and Matthew 6:19–21. Dating to the eighth-century Gelasian Sacramentary (an ancient collection of liturgical texts), this collect was typically prayed on the Fourth Sunday after Easter. The 1662 Book of Common Prayer changed the opening line from "whiche doest make the myndes of all faythfull men to be of one wil" to "who alone canst order the unruly wills and affections of sinful men." This change was suggested because of disagreements between the Anglican and Puritan factions of the Church of England; they were not of one will. The 1979 Book of Common Prayer moved this collect to the Fifth Sunday in Lent; the 2019 Book of Common Prayer followed suit.

PRAYERS FOR THE DAY: These prayers beautifully weave together themes from the Psalms: God's gracious providence, protection, and might in our lives. They use Psalm 31:5, Psalm 91:11, and Psalm 41:11 (see also Psalm 121). This version is taken from Martin Luther's *Small Catechism* of 1529. (Luther used the first-person singular; here it's pluralized for use with others.) It has roots in the eighth century—possibly even back to the fourth century. The Collect for the Second Sunday in Lent has a similar sense, and it was used for daily prayer in the middle ages. The 1979 Book of Common Prayer moved it to the Third Sunday in Lent; the 2019 Book of Common Prayer moved it back to the Second Sunday in Lent.

BENEDICTION: The order of prayer ends with praising and thanking God, and then blessing those present with God's name.

Sources for the Order of Prayer

The Gelasian Sacramentary: Liber Sacramentorum Romanae Ecclesiae, ed. H. A. Wilson (Oxford: The Clarendon Press, 1894).

Breviarium ad usum insignis ecclesiae Sarum, 4 vols., eds. Francis Procter and Christopher Wordsworth (Cambridge: Cambridge University Press, 1879–1886).

Martin Luther, *Der Kleine Katechismus*, in *Die Bekenntnisschriften der Evangelisch-Lutherischen Kirche*, ed. Irene Dingel (Göttingen: Vandenhoeck & Ruprecht, 2014), 852–910.

The Book of Common Prayer: The Texts of 1549, 1559, and 1662, ed. Brian Cummings (Oxford: Oxford University Press, 2011).

The 1662 Book of Common Prayer: International Edition, eds. Samuel L. Bray and Drew Nathaniel Keane (Downers Grove, IL: IVP Academic, 2021).

Church Book for the Use of Evangelical Lutheran Congregations (Philadelphia: Lutheran Book Store, 1868).

Common Service Book of the Lutheran Church (Philadelphia: The Board of Publication of the United Lutheran Church in America, 1918).

The Book of Common Prayer 1928 (New York: Church Pension Fund).

The Lutheran Hymnal (St. Louis: Concordia, 1941).

Service Book and Hymnal (Minneapolis: Augsburg, 1958).

Lutheran Book of Worship (Minneapolis: Augsburg, 1978).

The Book of Common Prayer 1979 (New York: Church Publishing).

Lutheran Service Book (St. Louis: Concordia, 2005).

The Book of Common Prayer 2019 (Huntington Beach, CA: Anglican Liturgy Press).

Prayer Book Resources

Marion J. Hatchett, *Commentary on the American Prayer Book* (San Francisco: Harper Collins, 1995).

Carl Schalk, *Living the Liturgy: A Guide to the Lutheran Order of the Divine Service* (St. Louis: Concordia, 2022).

THE TEN
COMMANDMENTS

Peter J. Leithart

AND GOD SPAKE ALL THESE WORDS, SAYING,

I I am **THE LORD THY GOD**, which have brought thee out of the land of Egypt, out of the house of bondage. Thou shalt have no other gods before me.

II Thou shalt not make unto thee any graven image, or any likeness of any thing that is in heaven above, or that is in the earth beneath, or that is in the water under the earth: Thou shalt not bow down thyself to them, nor serve them: for I **THE LORD THY GOD** am a jealous God.

III Thou shalt not take the name of **THE LORD THY GOD** in vain; for **THE LORD** will not hold him guiltless that taketh his name in vain.

THE TEN COMMANDMENTS

IV   Remember the sabbath day, to keep it holy.

Six days shalt thou labor, and do all thy work:

But the seventh day is the sabbath of **THE LORD THY GOD**.

V   Honor thy father and thy mother: that thy days may be long

upon the land which **THE LORD THY GOD** giveth thee.

VI   Thou shalt not kill.

VII   Thou shalt not commit adultery.

VIII   Thou shalt not steal.

IX   Thou shalt not bear false witness against thy neighbor.

X   Thou shalt not covet.

INTRODUCTION

Father to Son

GOD SPOKE THE TEN COMMANDMENTS to Israel at Sinai. Are they for *us*? Are they for us *Christians* who are not Jews, or should Christians live by a "New Testament ethic"? Are they for us Germans or Japanese or Nigerians or Peruvians or Americans? Are they only for Israel or for the nations?

The church has always taken the Decalogue, with modifications, as God's word to Christians.[1] New Testament writers quote it, church fathers appeal to it, Thomas Aquinas comments on it, Reformation catechisms and confessions teach it, prayer books incorporate it into our worship, and church architects carve it on our walls. Christian rulers like Alfred the Great made the Decalogue the basis of civil law.

Has the church been right? Or is this an unfortunate old covenant residue that needs to be purged from the church?

Read in canonical context, the Decalogue presents itself as a Christian text. To see how, we need to examine the text carefully.

COMMANDMENT	LUTHERAN + CATHOLIC
I	No other gods, no images
II	Don't take Name in vain
III	Remember Sabbath
IV	Honor father and mother
V	Do not kill
VI	Do not commit adultery
VII	Do not steal
VIII	Do not bear false witness
IX	Do not covet house
X	Do not covet wife, etc.

REFORMED	ORTHODOX
No other gods	I am Yahweh; no other gods
No images	No images
Don't take Name in vain	Don't take Name in vain
Remember Sabbath	Remember Sabbath
Honor father and mother	Honor father and mother
Do not kill	Do not kill
Do not commit adultery	Do not commit adultery
Do not steal	Do not steal
Do not bear false witness	Do not bear false witness
Do not covet	Do not covet

Scripture doesn't use the phrase "Ten Commandments." Exodus 20 and Deuteronomy 5 record Yahweh's "Ten *Words*" (Exod 34:28; Deut 4:13). These texts contain imperatives, but, like the rest of Torah, they include declarations, warnings, promises. That multiplicity of speech acts is better captured by the phrase "Ten Words" or "Decalogue," which I use throughout this book.

Israel has been in the wilderness for three months when they arrive at Sinai (Exod 19:1). Behind them are the ruins of Egypt, blighted by plagues. They've passed through the sea, received manna and water, grumbled and rebelled. Now the God who revealed his Name to Moses at Sinai (Exod 3:1–12) unveils himself to Israel.

God speaks on the third *day* of the month (Exod 19:16). Yahweh[2] descends with a trumpet blast that summons Israel to assembly. From a fiery cloud, he speaks the Ten Words.

He's spoken ten words before. Ten times Genesis 1 repeats, "And God spoke." At Sinai, God again speaks ten words that, if guarded and obeyed, will form Israel into a new creation. These ten new-creative words present the form of new creation.[3]

Yahweh has spoken on the third day before too. On the original third day, in the seventh of ten creation words, Yahweh called the land to bring forth grass with seed and trees with fruit (Gen 1:11). Speaking from Sinai, he reminds Israel that he brought them from the land of Egypt (Exod 20:2). Israel later commemorates Sinai at Pentecost, a feast of firstfruits. At Sinai, Israel *is* the firstfruits, a people of grain and fruit, the first to rise from the land. God speaks so that the vine brought from Egypt (Ps 80; Isa 5) will become fruitful. He speaks in anticipation of *Jesus'* third day, when the risen Lord becomes firstborn from the dead.[4]

The speaker identifies himself as "Yahweh," who is "*thy* God." At the burning bush (Exod 3), he calls himself "I am who I am." The Hebrew verbs can be translated with any tense: "I will be who I will be; I am who I will be; I will be who I was."[5] The context clarifies. Yahweh sees Israel's affliction and hears their cries. He comes to deliver from slavery. "Yahweh" is the God who will be everything Israel needs and do everything Israel needs done. Everything he is, Yahweh is *for Israel*. "Yahweh" is *Israel's* God, the God of Abraham, Isaac, and Jacob, who makes and keeps promises to his people. He is Yahweh "*thy* God."

To whom is Yahweh speaking? The answer isn't as simple as it seems. When Israel arrives at Sinai, Yahweh designates Moses as his spokesman. After the Ten Words, Moses ascends into the cloud to receive the Lord's word (20:21–22). But Moses is at the foot of Sinai when God speaks the Ten Words (19:25; 20:1). After six speeches to Moses (19:3, 9, 10, 20, 21, 24), God speaks a seventh time to all Israel (cf. 20:18). The Ten Words alone are unmediated, spoken to firstfruits sprung up from Egypt.

But there's a grammatical puzzle. Yahweh speaks to all Israel, but the verbs are in the masculine singular of the second person. The KJV gets it right: "*Thou* shalt have no other gods before me"; "*Thou* shalt not kill"; "*Thou* shalt not steal."[6] It sounds as if God is speaking to an individual man: "You, man, I brought you out of slavery. You, man, don't worship idols, kill, steal, commit adultery, or covet."

Perhaps the grammar indicates that *every* individual must obey. Perhaps God addresses Israelite *men* in particular. Men labor and rule a house, so they have authority to give rest on the Sabbath. Israelite *men* are forbidden to desire their neighbor's wife.

I think something else is going on. We may ask, *Who* was delivered from the house of bondage? Israel, of course, but Israel as *son* of Yahweh (see Exod 4:23). Yahweh's "family" tie to Israel provides a legal basis for his demand to Pharaoh: "Israel is *my* son. You have no right to enslave my son. Let my son go." When Pharaoh refuses, Yahweh cuts off negotiations and takes up the role of a kinsman redeemer, rescuing his son with a mighty hand and outstretched arm. Yahweh's justice is precise: Pharaoh seized Yahweh's firstborn; at Passover, Yahweh takes Pharaoh's.

God gave his first command to Adam, his first son.[7] At Sinai, he speaks to his son, the new Adam. The Ten Words are imperatives, but not merely imperatives. When Father Yahweh speaks to son Israel, he discloses his likes and dislikes. The Ten Words are "a personal declaration"[8] that reveals *Yahweh's* character. Like Proverbs, they're a Father-son talk. The ten new-creative words are designed to form Israel into an image of his Father.

The Decalogue is about Israel's mission. When Israel obeys the Ten Words, his common life becomes a living, filial icon of the heavenly Father among the nations of earth. Hearing the voice from Sinai, Israel takes up Adam's vocation of imitating and imaging his Father.

Many complain about the negativity of the Ten Words. There are two positive commandments—remember the Sabbath day, honor your father and mother. Mostly, it's one "Don't" after another.[9] God says he brought Israel from slavery, but it may seem he just imposed a different slavery.

According to Scripture, Torah is the "perfect law of liberty" (Jas 1:25; 2:12). A community dominated by disrespect for parents, workaholism, violence, envy, theft, and lies isn't free. Besides, *absolute* freedom is impossible. In the world God made, the world that actually exists, things aren't free to do or be anything they please. They're free when they become what they are. An acorn is free to become an oak, not an elephant. The Ten Words guide Israel to grow up to be what he is, the son who rules in his Father's house (see Gal 4:1–7).

Israel cannot listen to the Lord's voice. He asks Yahweh to speak through Moses (Exod 20:18–21). At Sinai, the son's heart is too hardened to hear his Father. But Israel isn't left hopeless. Yahweh *will* have a son who conforms to the Ten Words. The Father *does* have such a Son, the eternal Son who became Israel to be and do what Israel failed to be and do.

The Ten Words are a character portrait of Jesus, *the* Son of God.[10] The Ten Words lay out the path of *imitatio Dei* because they lay the path of the *imitatio Christi*. As Israel kept the commandments, Augustine wrote, "the life of that people foretold and foreshadowed Christ."[11] As Irenaeus said, *Christ* fulfills the law that he spoke from Sinai.[12] The law exposes our sin, restrains the unruly, provides a guide to life. But Jesus is the heart and soul of the Decalogue. The first use of the law is the christological.

Many centuries after Sinai, God returned in the third month, in rushing wind and fire, to pour out his Spirit. At that completed Pentecost, the Spirit began to write "not on stone but on the heart" (see 2 Cor 3:3).[13] He forms a new Israel, a company of sons who share Jesus' Spirit of sonship. By that Spirit, the Father fulfills his ten new-creative words *in us*.

Is the Decalogue for us? We might as well ask, Is *Jesus* for us?

GOD SPAKE ALL THESE WORDS

ALMIGHTY GOD, only you can order our unruly wills and desires. Grant to your people that we may love what you command and desire what you promise, that among the many changes and chances of this world our hearts may be fixed where true joys are found; through Jesus Christ our Lord. **AMEN.**

TWO TABLES

W E KNOW THERE ARE *Ten* Words. Yahweh wrote them with his finger on two tablets of stone (Exod 31:18; 34:1). But the church has never agreed on how to count to ten.

The Bible doesn't give a decisive answer. There are *twelve* negative imperatives in Exodus 20:1–17,[14] and one of the ten ("Honor thy father and mother") doesn't include any negatives. To make ten, Augustine combined the prohibition of images with the prohibition of idolatry and argued there were two commandments against coveting.[15] Origen separated the prohibition of false gods from the command against images and counted only one command against coveting.[16] Roman Catholics and Lutherans follow Augustine; Reformed churches follow Origen (see pages 14–15). I follow the Reformed numbering, with an Orthodox modification: Yahweh's declaration "I am Yahweh your God" is part of the First Word, not a "preface" (as in *Westminster Larger Catechism*, q. 101).[17]

To make matters more confusing, we're never told what was on each of the two stone tablets. Following Augustine, Caesarius of Arles said the first tablet contained three commandments; the second, seven.[18] Origen and others divided the commandments into four and six. Perhaps all Ten Words were on *both* tablets, a double witness to Yahweh's covenant with Israel.[19]

We can sort through some of these debates by paying close attention to the text of Exodus 20. Whatever the two tablets contained, *literarily* the Ten Words aren't divided as 3 + 7 or 4 + 6, but in half, 5 + 5.[20]

Each of the first five has an explanation attached to it. Exodus 20:2 grounds the first word (v. 3): *Because* Yahweh brought Israel from Egypt, Israel should have no other gods. The next four also contain explanations: Don't bow to images, because God is jealous; don't bear the name lightly, because Yahweh punishes; keep Sabbath, because Yahweh kept Sabbath; honor father and mother to prolong your days. By contrast, none of commandments 6–10 is explained.

"Yahweh" appears eight times in the first five words (Exod 20:2–12) but isn't named at all in commandments 6–10. The style of the second half is dramatically different. In Hebrew, the first five commandments contain 145 words; the second five use only 26.[21] In Hebrew, the sixth, seventh, and eighth have only two words each: Not kill, not adultery, not steal.

Why would the Lord speak the Ten Words in two sets of five?[22]

Five is a military number (Exod 13:18, "martial array" is literally "fively"), and the Ten Words are given to Yahweh's "hosts" on their way to conquer Canaan. We have five fingers on each hand; the Ten Words are a two-handed summation of Torah. 5 + 5 patterns appear elsewhere in Scripture.[23] In the inner sanctuary of the temple was the ark of the covenant,

Yahweh's throne, which contained the two tablets with their 5 + 5 words. In the Holy Place were ten lampstands arranged in two rows of five (1 Kgs 7:49) and ten tables of showbread in two rows of five (2 Chr 4:8). Outside in the courtyard, ten water stands in two rows of five formed a gauntlet, a water passage, leading to the temple door (1 Kgs 7:27–37).

The temple architecturally symbolizes the movement of the word from Yahweh's throne, through his house, out into the world. Cherubim guardians flank the ark, each with four faces: ox, lion, eagle, and man. Two cherubim match the two tablets, calling attention to the cherubic character of the law. Like the cherubim, the Ten Words guard the throne. Each cherub face reveals a facet of the law. The Torah is a threshing ox, providing bread. It's a ferocious lion that tears us, and God's enemies, to pieces. Torah offers soaring vistas like an eagle in flight and makes us truly, cherubically, human. Torah is good, but not safe. In the liturgy, you come within range of this cherubic word, a fiery sword that divides and consumes to make you a living sacrifice (cf. Heb 4:12–13).

As the 5 + 5 word proceeds from the cherub throne, it's symbolized by 5 + 5 lampstands. The law is light, illuminating hearts, lighting the community of those who hear, exposing hidden things in dark corners. Ten Words become bread on ten tables, living bread by which we live, for we do not live by bread alone but by the word that proceeds from our Father's mouth. In the Ten Words, Father Yahweh gives light and life to Israel.

Torah wasn't supposed to stay in the house. As the 5 + 5 word feeds and illumines Israel, it becomes a 5 + 5 set of water chariots, a river flowing from the sanctuary to the land and the world. Yahweh's law goes forth from Zion, to draw gentiles, to fertilize creation, until nations beat swords into plows and spears to pruning hooks (Isa 2:1–4). Torah flows out to make the world more like the sanctuary, rich with the light and bread of God.

The Bible is also full of pairs, like the twin tablets of stone. There were two cherubim in the temple (1 Kgs 6:23–28), two pillars at the temple door (1 Kgs 7:15–22), two witnesses in various narratives.[24] One relevant pair is priest and king. The first five words are priestly, focusing on the sanctuary—worship, images, Yahweh's Name, the Sabbath, and honor of parents. The second five commandments are royal, having to do with political life in the land.

Jesus sums up the entire law in a pair of commandments: Love God with all your heart, soul, strength, and mind, and your neighbor as yourself (Luke 10:27; see also Gal 5:14). As Justin Martyr,[25] Irenaeus,[26] Augustine,[27] and many others have said, Jesus' two commandments summarize the two tables of the Decalogue. In the outline I'm using, the first five teach love for God, and the second fill out how we love our neighbor.

Each of the Ten Words addresses an arena of human life: worship, time-keeping, family, violence, sex, property, speech, desire. Yet they overlap and interpenetrate.[28] Each word implies all the others. To obey the First Word, you must also refuse images; bear God's Name; keep Sabbath; honor parents; and refrain from murder, theft, adultery, slander, greed, and lust. We keep Sabbath to honor the one God, to glorify his Name, to give life and protect property, to cultivate contentment and thankfulness. Idolatry is a kind of theft, a form of marital infidelity to the divine Husband, false witness about the living God. Every commandment is a window through which we view the whole Decalogue.

The sequence of commandments isn't arbitrary. As we'll see, Sabbath-keeping (Fourth Word) implies care of parents (Fifth). Dishonor of parents (Fifth) is a kind of murder (Sixth). Murder (Sixth) and adultery (Seventh) are intimately linked, as in the tragedy of David, Bathsheba, and Uriah.

For this same reason, one act of disobedience is infested with others. "No sin comes alone," Luther said, "but it always prompts another one after it." Lust and adultery are quickly followed by lies, "and after that comes manslaughter and bloodshed and finally despair."[29] To offend at one point is to offend in all.

Once again, we see how the Decalogue reveals Jesus, who alone lives as Yahweh's Son, keeping the whole law. He is the Word, Light, and Bread of the Father, whose Spirit flows from the temple of his body to bring life to the world.

COMMANDMENT I

I am the Lord thy God, which have brought thee out of the land of Egypt, out of the house of bondage. Thou shalt have no other gods before me.

TRUE GOD, you are a great God and a great King above all gods. You call us to worship you and you alone. Give us strength and wisdom to recognize and reject all false gods, and to devote ourselves, our souls and bodies, to you as a living sacrifice, holy and pleasing to you. This we pray in the name of Jesus Christ, true God and true man. **AMEN.**

THOU SHALT HAVE NO OTHER GODS BEFORE ME

O N A VISIT TO SOUTH KOREA, I toured a crowded Buddhist monastery. My host told me that university placement tests were approaching and mothers were offering incense and praying for their children. I saw a woman step out of the shrine to take a cell phone call. Then she returned to her idol.

I thought of Isaiah 44: With bits of metal you make your cell phone, and with another bit you make an image and say, "Behold our God."

Idols have mouths, eyes, ears, feet, and noses, but cannot speak, see, hear, walk, or smell. Ominously, the psalmist adds, "Those who worship them shall become like them" (Ps 115). Idolatry produces "sensory organ malfunction."[30] Idols are stupid and make us stupid. They make their worshipers as dead as they are.

Ancient polytheists lived in fear. Their gods were unpredictable, liable to set traps. No one could satisfy all of them.

Somewhere, one would be offended at being neglected and take his gleeful vengeance. In the exodus, Yahweh freed his son Israel from Egypt's thousands of gods (see Josh 24:14), snatching him from deadly idols. The First Word is a summons to walk in resurrection life.

The First Word infuses the Decalogue. Thomas Aquinas said that since God is the end of human life and society, worship is the first commandment.[31] According to Luther, the First Word calls us to faith, and "everything proceeds from the power of the First Commandment."[32] Every sin is betrayal, infidelity to the God who made us his own.[33] The First Word begins with a brief summary of the exodus (Exod 20:2), and that narrative snippet frames the entire Decalogue. Israel has been freed, so they are to live as a free people. They have undergone an exodus, and so are to live as an exodus people.

Literally, the First Word says, in seven Hebrew words, "There shall not be for you another god before my face." "Before my face" means "in my presence," specifically "in my presence in the sanctuary." It doesn't merely refer to ranking (no God higher than me) but to position (no God in my vicinity). Manasseh defiantly violates this commandment when he places a false god in the temple, before the face of Yahweh (2 Kgs 21:7).

Of course, Israel wasn't free to worship other gods *outside* the sanctuary. Yahweh tells Ezekiel (Ezek 14) that Israel's elders built shrines for idols in their hearts. Whenever they come before Yahweh, their idols trundle along with them. The new covenant intensifies this point. Jesus dwells in our hearts by his Spirit, who consecrates our bodies as temples (1 Cor 6). The idols of our hearts are before the face of God as blatantly as Manasseh's.

Perhaps few of you have seen idolatry in practice. None of you, I presume, has a shrine to Baal or Allah in your basement. But we're hardly free of idols. Luther wrote that the First Word requires us to "fear, love, and trust in God above all things."[34] The *Lord* is our Judge, Savior, and Lawgiver. He blesses and curses, bears our sins, speaks a trustworthy, authoritative word. When we tremble before other judges or hope in other saviors, when we pile up our sins on anyone but Jesus, idols occupy our hearts and take control.[35]

Do you fear the opinions of others? Are you paralyzed by worry about how your father or mother will evaluate you? You've set up an idol, a substitute judge—public opinion, a perfectionist father, a hypercritical mother. Have you ever thought: "If only we had a bit more money, our lives would be happy. If only I could get a better job or enjoy a flawlessly decorated home, life would be good." You're looking to a counterfeit savior—money, success, velvety comforts.

When you're cornered, do you lash out and blame others? Do you have so much trouble admitting your sins that you scapegoat your wife or husband, your parents or children? Or do you flagellate yourself for your failures or perceived failures? You're an idolater, dumping sins on scapegoats or treating yourself as a gimcrack Jesus.

Whose imperatives do you obey? Does the voice in your head come from advertisements, popular songs, YouTube or Netflix shows? Who is your *true* Lord—not your *professed*

Lord, but the one who *actually* speaks with authority into your life? If the voice in your head says "Do this," but the voice from Sinai says "Don't," which do you listen to? When you silence the Lord's voice, you've deafened yourself because there's an idol in your ears.

Idols like company. Idolatry is inherently polytheistic. Idols feed off one another, cluster together, transmogrify to keep hold of your heart. Your idols feed off the idols of others. Codependency is more biblically characterized as co-idolatry.

A husband has a drinking problem, which is an idol problem: The sanctuary of his heart is teeming with false gods. He loves a buzz more than God, and seeks a pathetic, temporary salvation in another bourbon or light beer. His bar mates become his judges, as he lives for their approval. Cornered, he pulls another idol out of storage: He rages at his wife's complaints, judging her as if he were the God of Sinai, or piling his sins on her, as if she were the Suffering Servant. Sometimes, whimpering with remorse, he puts himself on the cross. Soon, other gods come back and he's back at the bar for another round.

Meanwhile, his wife's heart is equally infested with idols. She acts out a martyr script, since she's the only one who can save the family and keep everything together. She judges her husband, finds comfort in the approval of friends, stays with her no-good husband because she's afraid of the alternative. Both are slaves. Neither will be free until they smash their co-idols to powder.

At least in *public*, we might think, our secular society has scoured the idols. That's wishful thinking. Modernity manufactures as many idols as any age. Mammon rules the market. We kill to keep ourselves comfortably surrounded by more and new stuff. "Follow your heart" replaces "Thus saith the Lord" as the unquestioned cultural imperative. Nations claim authority over our bodies and souls, demanding patriotic sacrifice on the altar of the nation. Liberal order is a conspiracy to guard public life from God's intrusions. We strip the town square, then genuflect to the nothing.

But for us, there is one God and one Lord, Jesus Christ (1 Cor 8:6). When we worship the one God, our hearts can be single, our desires focused, our lives whole. Idols tear us apart, with their contradictory, shape-shifting demands. We find coherence and integrity in keeping the First Word.

No *society* can be harmonious if everyone worships one's own god. Israel's first freedom isn't freedom to worship anything he pleases. The First Word shouldn't be confused with the First Amendment. "Thou shalt have no other gods before me" is a declaration of independence for a society free of the empty, emptying gods who compete for our love, loyalty, hope, and trust. Politics is constituted in worship, the gesture of homage before an ultimate authority. If we don't honor the living God, we'll bow before some terrible idol, who will devour our souls. A people that keeps the First Word becomes a corporate human image of the one God.

Right from the beginning, Israel prefers idols. Yahweh writes the Ten Words on stone tablets, but Moses has no sooner received them than he rushes down the mountain to shatter the golden calf. Already at Sinai, we get a preview of Israel's history of idolatry, image-worship, blasphemy, and

Sabbath-breaking. Already at the foot of Sinai, we know we need God's Word written on our hearts by the finger of the Spirit. We need a mediator better than Moses, one who can demolish the idols of our hearts.

The promise of the new covenant is *not* that we're liberated from God's word, but that we're liberated to *keep* it. Jesus, the true Son, lives in utter devotion to his Father. He brings no other god before him. His obedience to the First Word gets him killed, but in his life, death, and resurrection he annihilates idols and destroys the works of the devil. God speaks to us who are sons in the Son: "Little children, guard yourselves from idols" (1 John 5:21).

In Christ, the First Word isn't a mere prohibition. It's a call to arms.[36] By it, the Lord enlists us to follow the new Joshua as he purges the planet of every vain imagination (2 Cor 10:5). Jesus has judged the world and triumphed over principalities and powers, and by the Spirit he recruits us as his hosts. The First Word creates a company of subversives who refuse to bow to the thousand-and-one idols of the age. The First Word is a call to mission and a pledge of the Lord's intention: there *will* be a day when every knee will bow, when there *will* be no other gods before him.

COMMANDMENT II

Thou shalt not make unto thee any graven image, or any likeness of any thing that is in heaven above, or that is in the earth beneath, or that is in the water under the earth: Thou shalt not bow down thyself to them, nor serve them: for I the Lord thy God am a jealous God.

JEALOUS GOD, you are great and greatly to be praised. You smash idols and expose the powerlessness of gods who cannot save. Fix our hearts on you and you alone, so that we may flee from idolatry and bow to the one who alone is worthy, Jesus Christ our Lord, to whom every knee will bow and every tongue confess. In his name alone we pray. **AMEN.**

THOU SHALT NOT MAKE THEE ANY GRAVEN IMAGE

I N SOME CHURCHES, THE SECOND WORD is tangled in debates about whether Christians may paint pictures or sculpt sculptures of Jesus or God the Father. Some believe the commandment prohibits art, especially representational art, in a place of worship. Some claim it prohibits representational art as such.

If it forbids *making* images, it prohibits *all* images. The commandment doesn't say, "Don't make images of God." It says, "Don't make graven images of things in heaven, on the earth, or in the waters under the earth." That covers *everything*, because there ain't nothing anywhere except in heaven, earth, or under the earth.

If the commandment prohibited locating images in a place of worship, it would contradict other commandments. Yahweh tells Moses to "make two cherubim of gold" (Exod 25:18), a lampstand with cups "shaped like almond blossoms" (25:33), and pomegranates of blue and scarlet material (28:33). Cherubim are heavenly things, almonds and pomegranates earthly things. If the Second Word prohibits representational art, the Lord didn't stick with his program very long.

The Second Word prohibits making images for a particular purpose—to bow before and serve them. The two verbs in Exodus 20:5 are typical words for worship. "Worship" describes a bodily posture, "prostrate oneself." "Serve" is a general term for the work of Levites and priests. Ancient pagan priests serviced images of their gods. Priests brought meals to the image, cleaned it, bowed before it, praised it. That's the ministry Yahweh forbids in his house.

The commandment forbids certain liturgical *actions*. Yahweh doesn't say Israel is free to use their bodies any way they like, so long as they hold correct thoughts in their head or good feelings in their souls. Of course, bodily actions embody intentions. If a son of Aaron bent before the lampstand to pick up a piece of bread, he wouldn't violate the Second Word. Yet, God cares about what we do with our *bodies*. A good intention doesn't purify a bad action.

Did ancient people think that the image *was* the god? The answer, at least for thoughtful elites, is no. Most understood that the chunk of stone wasn't Athena; the bronze image wasn't Baal, Asherah, or Ra. Ancient priests performed rites to "quicken" divine essence in the statue. Service to the image was service to the god because the quickened image was a "sacrament" of the god's presence.

Yahweh's prohibition of images is more radical than we realize. He's not merely saying, as Clement of Alexandria thought, that we shouldn't confer power on things we make.[37] He isn't saying, "I'm not made of stone, wood, bronze, gold." Everyone *knew* that. He's saying, "Don't think you can serve me by serving an image, or honor me by honoring a likeness." Yahweh's priests served him and cared for his house, but what occupied the house was the living Lord himself, Yahweh's glorious personal *Name* (1 Kgs 3:2; 5:3–5; 8:16–18).

In the judgment of my Reformed Protestant tradition, some churches today are corrupted by the idolatry condemned by the Second Word. No Christian believes an icon is identical to the saint. No one thinks an icon of Christ *is* Christ. Yet some Christians treat icons as "sacraments" of Christ and his saints; they venerate the icon as homage to the one pictured. That's exactly what the Second Word forbids.

Above I used the word "sacrament." Christians *do* have physical signs of God's presence, the water of baptism and the bread and wine of the Eucharist. We know we commune with the body and blood of Jesus because the Lord *promised* to meet us at the table (1 Cor 10:16–17). He hasn't promised to encounter us through pictures. When Christians seek Jesus through an image, they're looking for God in the wrong place.

Honoring God in images isn't just fruitless. It arouses the jealousy of Yahweh. In Scripture, jealousy expresses spurned love. Yahweh addresses Israel as "son," but "jealous" opens a marital perspective on their relationship. Husbands claim their wives' affection, and wives are rightly jealous of their husband's attention. As Origen noted, Yahweh speaks as a jealous bridegroom to warn his bride to flee fornication.[38] Bowing to and serving images is spiritual adultery.[39]

Whatever their intentions, those who serve images "hate" Yahweh (Exod 20:5). Imagine a husband who speaks to digital photos of his wife, fawns on them, kisses them, gazes at them, but never notices his wife. He might say, "I demonstrate my love for my wife *by* loving her picture." But no wife would accept that evasion.

The Second Word implies a contrast between sight and hearing, eye and ear. In Deuteronomy 4, Moses reminds Israel they didn't see any form on Sinai, but heard a voice. When Yahweh tells Moses to carve new tablets, he uses the verb form of "graven image" (Exod 34:1): Moses "graves" tablets. But these graven stones contain *words*, not pictures. Yahweh declares, commands, writes on the tablets. At Sinai, he does *not* show himself. Yahweh is the unseen God who speaks. He is Word.

Eyes are organs of scrutiny and judgment (see Ps 11:4). God sees and judges the creation good (Gen 1:31), Eve sees and evaluates the tree (Gen 3:6), Adam and Eve's eyes are opened after they eat (Gen 3:7). With visible things, we assume a stance of criticism, command, and control. But God is not under our control. We don't judge him, but he us.

Hearing has a different phenomenology. In Scripture, hearing is virtually identical to obedience.[41] To hear is to *receive* commands. Listening puts us in the position of being judged. Hearing opens an uncontrollable future: someone says, for the first time, "I love you," and the world shifts beneath your feet.

Since Sinai, God *has* been seen: The Word tabernacled in flesh and we *saw* his glory (John 1:14). Seeing Jesus, we see the Father (John 14:9). Some Christians say that Jesus' advent changes the Second Word, so that we are now permitted to serve images. But Jesus ascended and is no longer visibly present. We *don't* see his glory as the apostles did. He's with us by his Spirit, the wind who blows where he will, the Spirit whom we hear but cannot see. That Spirit comes to us in sensible forms—in audible words, tangible water, and edible food and drink. Someday we will see Jesus face-to-face. But not yet. To live by the eye is to reach ahead of our time. It immanentizes the eschaton. After the incarnation, we *still* live by ear (2 Cor 5:7), until he comes again.

The twenty-first century is an age of spectacle.[42] Every inch of wall space is filled with flickering screens. Ads entice us with dreams of the good life. A single web image sparks weeks of savage public debate, and leaders lead by projecting an image of power or relatability. Our relations to one another are no longer tangible, mediated through touch, but abstractedly visible, mediated through screens. We create technological miracles and call them tools, then adjust our lives in obedience to their requirements, panting like Pavlov's dog every time we hear a text notification ding. Who's really in charge? The Second Word summons us to resist the temptation to fear, trust, serve, and live by the spectacle. To walk faithfully, we must tune our *ears* to the Word of God.

Some use the Second Word against the Bible. Scripture describes God in human terms, as King, Lord, Husband, Shepherd, Workman, Friend. He's compared to inanimate things: Rock, Sun, Shield. If we're forbidden sculpt or paint images, some philosophers have argued, we should reject the verbal images of Scripture.[43]

That misses the Bible's primary alternative to image veneration. God prohibits veneration of graven images because he's already made his image. The creation account (Gen 1) resembles a temple construction. An ancient temple builder formed the shell, filled it with tools and furnishings, and then, at the climax, placed an image in the inner sanctuary, a sign of the god's presence and his claim on the land. Just so, Yahweh divides earth into three zones, then fills it with plants, heavenly bodies, fish and birds, land animals. The three-story universe is a cosmic temple, with every creatures designed to participate in a cosmic liturgy.

When everything is in place, Yahweh deliberates: "Let us make man in our image, according to our likeness" (Gen 1:26–28). Yahweh works the ground like a potter, forms Adam, and breathes into his nostrils the breath of life (Gen 2:7). Like an image in an ancient temple, Adam and Eve mediate the Creator's presence and lordship. As they fill and subdue the earth, they symbolize Yahweh and his claim on the whole creation. *We* are images of God. When we venerate images, we're not merely exchanging the glory of God for the glory of creation. We give up our own glory. We're alienated from our own vocation.

Idolatry leads to injustice, oppression, the shedding of innocent blood. It's *inherently* dehumanizing because it substitutes senseless wood or stone or metal for *living* images. We keep the Second Word when we keep Jesus' second great commandment, when we do homage to God's image in our brothers and sisters, when we love and serve God in serving and loving our neighbors, when we perform the sacrifices of giving alms, doing good, sharing, and hospitality.

Aroused to jealousy, Yahweh threatens to curse idolaters to the third and fourth generation. Though attached to the Second Word, Luther is right that these words "relate to all the commandments" as a reminder that God is not to be toyed with. He "will not leave it unavenged if men turn from Him." This appendix, Luther says, is a hoop in a wreath that joins the end of the Ten Words to the beginning.[40]

It's a fearful warning, but we shouldn't miss the mercy. Early in the history of the northern kingdom of Israel, Jeroboam I sets up golden calves, violating the Second Word (1 Kgs 12:26–30). All the kings of Israel follow the sin of Jeroboam, but Yahweh arrests each dynasty after three of four generations. He doesn't let liturgical idolatry go on forever.

Besides, Yahweh isn't only a judge of sinners. He also displays his loyal love to those who love and obey him. The love lasts much, much longer than the judgment. He curses to three or four generations but shows love to thousands of generations.

COMMANDMENT III

Thou shalt not take the name of the Lord thy God in vain; for the Lord will not hold him guiltless that taketh his name in vain.

LORD GOD, your name is holy, and you have chosen to be known in Christ alone. Instill in us such reverential fear that we will always honor the grandeur of your name, through lives of obedience and worship, in the divine name of Jesus Christ, who with you and the Holy Spirit is named, worshiped, and glorified. **AMEN.**

THOU SHALT NOT TAKE THE NAME OF THE LORD THY GOD IN VAIN

WHAT'S IN A NAME?

A name is an identifying label. This is Alex, that's Alex Jr.; this is Natalia, that's Peter. Names allow us to address one another. When you see your friend across the street, you call his name to get his attention. At a first meeting, you reveal your name, which gives the new acquaintance power to invoke you. Now he can call you from across the street.

Names are self-revealing. I say "Leithart," and many recognize my German ancestry. My mother named me for Peter Marshall, the twentieth-century Presbyterian chaplain of the US Senate. My name summarizes a family and personal history. Nicknames reveal character traits. "Slim" is obese, "Worm" reads a lot of books, "Springshanks" can dunk a basketball.

The ancient world teemed with gods. You wouldn't ask, "Do you worship God?" You'd ask, "*Which* god do you worship?" The name Yahweh distinguished the God of Israel from other gods. Yahweh isn't "God-in-general." He's "Yahweh Israel's-God."[44] By revealing his Name, Yahweh gave Israel the power to call him. Israel the son called to the heavens "Yahweh, hear us," and Father Yahweh answered.

Like human names, Yahweh's Name has to be revealed, and it is self-revealing. As Origen said, the Name is "the personal character of God."[45] On the mountain, Yahweh calls himself "Yahweh, Yahweh! Gracious and compassionate, slow to anger and abounding in loyal love, yet he by no means clears the guilty" (Exod 34:6–7). Yahweh is the God of compassion and justice, the patient God who won't let us defy him forever. Like human names, "Yahweh" summarizes a history. At the burning bush, Yahweh names himself as the God of Abraham, Isaac, and Jacob, the God who made promises to the fathers and now comes to keep his promises.[46] The Ten Words open with a story: "I am Yahweh your God, who brought you up from the land of Egypt, out of the house of slavery."

Unlike human beings, Yahweh identifies and names *himself*. Moses asks, "What shall I say when Israel asks who sent me?" (Exod 3:13–14). Yahweh doesn't leave him guessing but unveils a Name that Moses couldn't have known otherwise. By contrast, we are *given* names. Surnames come from our parents, their parents before them, and their parents on back to the first someone who received the name. We *receive* our names and identities from others, as a gift. Yahweh, who names himself, shares that Name with Israel. The Ten Words address Israel as Yahweh's redeemed son (Exod 4:23). The Third Word assumes that family connection. As son, Israel has received the family name of Yahweh.

The Third Word is usually translated as, "Do not take the name of the Lord your God in vain," with "take" understood as "speak." Many Christians think the Third Word forbids cussing or oaths. True, the Third Word *does* require us to tell the truth (Exod 23:13; Deut 6:13).[47] When we swear in God's Name, we call him as a witness to the truth of what we're saying. Oaths are self-cursing. Taking an oath, we put ourselves on the line: "If what I say is not true, then may the Lord's curse fall on me." We take the Name of the Lord in vain when we invoke God as witness for false statements. We take his Name lightly when we call down curses without genuine fear of the Lord's judgment. The Lord forbids us to speak as if he doesn't matter.[48] Every word we speak will be brought to judgment (Matt 12:36).

The Hebrew verb, however, isn't "take" or "speak," but "lift up," "carry," or "bear." We bear God's Name on our tongues when we swear, but the Name is also imprinted on our head, hands, and feet. We bear the Name lightly with indifferent or disobedient worship (Exod 20:22–26), with casual sex (Amos 2:7), or when we steal (Lev 6:2–5).[49] Speaking or silent, active or passive, we bear the name *all* the time in *everything* we do.[50] Every sin is a violation of the Lord's holy Name, the Name he shares with us. Do we feel the weight of the Name? Or do we treat it as empty breath? Reducing the Third Word to a command about oaths turns it into a mechanism to preserve social order.[51] That misses the key demand, to honor God's Name. If we give God's Name weight, we might well become abrasive to the social status quo.

In the new covenant, we bear the Name because we're baptized into the Name of Father, Son, and Holy Spirit. With that gifted name comes a new identity, a new history, and membership in a new family. Every Sunday, this Name is re-placed on us, when the minister pronounces the benediction. Aaron "set" the Name of Yahweh on the people by blessing in the Name (Num 6:24–26). When a minister pronounces a triune blessing, the congregation assumes again its baptismal name and is commissioned once again to "bear" the name into the world. The Third Word, like the first two, is a call to mission.

Each age of Israel's history is marked by a characteristic sin, which corresponds to the first three of the Ten Words. During the period of the judges, Israel was tempted to worship the gods of the nations, a sin against the First Word. During the monarchy, Israel broke the Second Word by worshiping Yahweh at high places and through images of golden calves.

During the exile, Israel was scattered among gentiles. They no longer worshiped other gods or erected golden calves. They were called to bear the Name in the midst of the nations and were tempted to compromise and hypocrisy. By the time of Jesus, it was clear that Israel had failed. The Jewish leaders claimed to be children of Abraham, but many were children of the devil, as Jesus said (John 8:44). Jesus condemned the Pharisees and scribes as "hypocrites" who play-acted righteousness. They didn't fill out the robes they wore, nor live up to the family name (Matt 23). Because Israel didn't bear the Name weightily, they "profaned" the Name among the nations (Rom 2:24). Instead of leading gentiles to praise, they sowed blasphemy.

"Name" is a title of the Second Person of the Trinity, the Son. The Father's Name is the Son. The Father is Father only because he has a Son; his reputation is bound up with the Son; he discloses himself in the Son. During the old covenant, the Name dwelt in the temple, sanctifying the temple by his presence. Because the Name dwelt in the house, Israel had to keep the house clean. Sins had to be scoured away, the priests had to maintain the cycle of offerings, trim the lamps on the lampstand, change the showbread on the table. If Israel and the priests failed to maintain the house, it would become polluted and the Name profaned.

As the living Name, Jesus bears the full weight of the Father's Name, bears it until it crushes him and renders him nameless. He suffers our indifference and hypocrisy all the way to the cross, and so the Father raises him and gives him a Name above every Name, that at the Name of Jesus all knees should bow. The living Name goes silent, so that the nations would one day proclaim the Name of the Lord.[52] As Rabanus Maurus and others saw, the greatest sin against the Third Word is denying the Name of Jesus.[53]

Each Israelite was a house, named by the Name, and so each had to maintain the purity of the temple of their body. In the new covenant too, we're named by the Name of the Trinity and indwelt by the Spirit, who consecrates us as his sanctuary. God binds his Name and reputation to us. Whether his name is praised or blasphemed depends on whether we bear his name with the weight it deserves. It is a weighty responsibility to bear the weighty Name of the living God before the world.

COMMANDMENT IV

Remember the sabbath day,
to keep it holy. Six days shalt thou
labor, and do all thy work: But
the seventh day is the sabbath
of the Lord thy God.

TIMELESS GOD, you created the day and the night and divided them one from another, and you appointed lights to govern ordinary time and to signify sacred time. Teach us to number our days, to embrace work and rest, and to reject the injustice and idleness arising from the misuse of time, in eager hope of the heavenly rest that awaits us in Jesus Christ, who worked perfect obedience that we may have perfect rest. **AMEN.**

REMEMBER THE SABBATH DAY

MOST OF THE TEN WORDS are negations: Do not, do not, do not. The prohibited behaviors are like chunks the sculptor chips away to uncover the image of *The Thinker* lurking in the marble. At the center are two positive commandments: "Remember the Sabbath" and "Honor your father and mother." When idolatry and hypocrisy have been eliminated, when violence and infidelity and theft and lies have been chiseled off, *this* is what's left: a day of joy, and harmony among generations. *This* is the gem we discover when the mud is washed away, the beauty at the heart of the new-creative "Do nots." *This* is the life God's son lives before his Father: Israel rejoicing with sons and daughters in the God who "himself is festival."[54]

The Sabbath command is perhaps the most repeated, most expanded-on, and most controverted commandment (Exod 31:12–17; 35:1–3).[55] Sabbaths appear in instructions about other feasts (Exod 12:16; Lev 16:31), and the liturgical calendar of Leviticus 23 is organized around Sabbaths and sabbatical periods. The pattern of 6 + 1 is extended to slavery and manumission (Exod 21:1–11) and care of the land (Exod 23:10–13). Every half century, Israel was to mark Jubilee, an extended super-Sabbath (Lev 25). Sabbath was a perpetual covenant (Exod 31:16), a "sign" between Yahweh and his people (Exod 31:13, 17).

Paul includes the Sabbath among old covenant ordinances that have passed away, fulfilled in Christ (Col 2:16). Augustine,[56] Caesarius of Arles,[57] and others consider Israel's Sabbath as a type of the Christian's spiritual rest, while Augustine[58] and Bede[59] saw it also as an anticipation of eternal rest. These writers are correct that the command requires more than abstinence from work. Christians live continuously in Christ's Sabbath.[60]

Yet most Christians have seen continuing practical relevance in the Fourth Word. Early on, the church began to assemble on the first (eighth) day of resurrection. Some Christian traditions practice a full-day rest, and all traditions recognize the necessity of scheduled time for worship and the wisdom of a rhythm of labor and rest. If we spiritualize Sabbath too quickly or thoroughly, we miss its breadth. The Fourth Word teaches us how to *live*, what we do and don't do.

It begins: "Memorialize the day of ceasing." "Memorialize" is linked to the sign-character of Sabbath. The Bible's first "sign" is the rainbow. When *Yahweh* sees the bow, he "remembers" and keeps covenant (Gen 9:12–17). Similarly, Israel doesn't keep Sabbath merely by recalling it to mind. Israel does something—nothing—on Sabbath to memorialize creation, as an enacted "reminder" to Yahweh to bring creation to fulfillment in a final Sabbath.

Israel memorializes the day by ceasing (*shabat*). Work is good. Human dominion over the world is good. But God requires that we "interrupt" our work to acknowledge him as Lord,[61] as a public confession that our authority over creation is a *derived* authority.[62] Sabbath pauses life's noise. It's the silence that tunes our ears to Yahweh's word.

This dimension of the Sabbath is highlighted in the first instance of human Sabbath-keeping (Exod 16). Israel collects manna for six days but refrains on the seventh, when they trust God's provision. When Israel enters the land, manna ceases, but Israel still keeps Sabbath. Bread from earth, as much as angel bread from heaven, is a gift of God, not a sheer product of human labor. Sabbath serves as a weekly recognition of human limitations and God's generosity. Sabbath is our fundamental stance as creatures, one of receptivity.

Israel's consecration of the day depends on Yahweh's prior consecration (Exod 20:11). But the verb "keep holy" means "sanctify" or "*make* holy." Israel doesn't merely maintain the holiness of a day that is already holy. Ceasing *consecrates* the day of ceasing.

We may clarify the notion of holy time by analogy with holy space. Holy space is space God claims by being present in glory (cf. Exod 29:43). Everything associated with that space is his—people, altars, lampstands, knives, forks, snuffers. Holy things must be used solely for God's purposes. A holy fork can't be used at a barbeque. A priest can't borrow a pinch of holy incense to perfume his home.

Holy time is time claimed by God. The Sabbath is *God's* day as the tabernacle is God's space. On the Sabbath, Israel is on the *Lord's* time. If they use Yahweh's time for their own projects, they commit sacrilege and trespass a holy boundary. We're always on the Lord's time, but the Sabbath embeds that truth in weekly habit.

Israel consecrates the day by worship. At the sanctuary, priests offered extra offerings (Num 28) and throughout Israel the people gathered in local "synagogues" for praise, study of Torah, and prayer. Israel consecrated the day by gathering in the presence of the Sabbath-keeping God (Lev 23:3).

Israel also mimics Yahweh by mimicking Yahweh's *gift* of rest: Yahweh brings Israel from restless slavery; therefore, Israel gives rest to slaves. Most of Exodus 20:10 is a list of seven (!) categories of people who are *granted* rest. Each Israelite takes rest, and each also gives rest. Like Father, like son.

The Sabbath is unparalleled in the ancient world.[63] It spreads out from the seventh day to fill the nooks and crannies of Israel's life. Indentured servants are held for six years, released in the seventh. Debt isn't allowed to become a permanent burden.[64] Land could be sold for fifty years (7 Sabbath years + 1), but reverted to the original owners at Jubilee (Lev 25). At the center of the calendar in Leviticus 23, the Lord reminds Israel to care for the needy (23:22). Torah calls Israel to justice, mercy, and faithfulness, a Sabbath way of life (Isa 58). From this, it's clear that Jesus never broke Sabbath, or made exceptions. Jesus *keeps* Sabbath by giving relief to the distressed. Pulling an ox from a ditch isn't an exception to Sabbath rules (Luke 14:5). It *fulfills* Sabbath by giving rest to a suffering ox.

For these reasons, Joseph Ratzinger calls the Sabbath "the heart of all social legislation." It anticipates "the society free of domination, a foretaste of the city to come" and "the freedom of all the children of God and creation's release from anxiety."[65] In our society, leisure is a monopoly of the rich, while the poor have to work multiple jobs to eke out a subsistence living.[66] Sabbath redistributes and equalizes rest. It treats slaves as persons, not machines. It guards Israel from organizing his time for 24/7 productivity, and so defies the reign of Mammon. As Stanley Hauerwas and William Willimon put it, it's countercultural: one day each week, Christians simply refuse to show up.[67]

Sabbatical sociology is grounded in Sabbatical theology. Sabbath is Yahweh's day of joy, when he delighted in the completed creation.[68] It's socially revolutionary because it's the *Lord's* day, a holy day of worship that opens earthly time to the rhythms of heaven. All Israel, including slaves and animals, mimics the rest of God. We might expect the opposite: because it's *Yahweh's* day of ceasing, human beings *can't* cease. In ancient myths, gods make human beings to serve their divine leisure. The Sabbath, by contrast, is premised on an analogy between God's work and human work: the Creator is himself a craftsman and a manual laborer. The Sabbath highlights an analogy between divine and human rest.

"Analogy" and "mimic" are too weak. By ceasing, son Israel *shares* his Father's Sabbatical. For Israel, this is sheer gift. Yahweh stops working because he's finished (Gen 2:1–4). Israel *hasn't* finished, and neither have we. After rest, we go back to work, but we work with the Sabbath satisfaction of a job done. By keeping Sabbath, we express confidence that the Lord will bring his work to completion and give *us* time to finish. Sharing Sabbath, we participate *already* in the divine pleasure of bringing things to an end, long before things come to their end. We enjoy now what Thomas Aquinas calls "all future blessings."[69] The Lord opens up his day of ceasing to include us, so that we *share* in his rest, like Father, like son.

Yahweh's rest is royal. After battling Pharaoh, the Divine Warrior enjoys victory. Having trampled grapes, he mixes a cup of wine. King Yahweh delivers Israel from deadly service in Pharaoh's house and brings them to Sabbath at Sinai. And so Sabbath theology circles back to Sabbath sociology. By extending Sabbath to Israel and to us, Yahweh raises his son to kingship. We work, but aren't slaves to work. We sit now in heavenly places (Eph 2:6), sharing Jesus' lordship over all. Enthroned in Sabbath glory, we with Israel participate in our Father's rest, and his rest-giving.[70]

COMMANDMENT V

Honor thy father and thy mother: that thy days may be long upon the land which the Lord thy God giveth thee.

HEAVENLY FATHER, you created us and adopted us in Christ. Give us humility to honor our earthly parents, through whom you brought us into being, by speaking well of them and to them, by caring for them in need, and by forgiving them as you have forgiven us, in the name of Jesus Christ, who has made us sons and daughters through faith, and through whom we have received the Spirit of adoption, by whom we cry "Abba, Father." **AMEN.**

HONOR THY FATHER
AND THY MOTHER

T HE FIFTH WORD—"HONOR THY FATHER and thy mother"—seems stuffily conservative. In our topsy-turvy times, it's countercultural.

We late moderns confess the (authoritative?) 1960s creed, "Question authority," applied in the first instance to the family. "Don't trust anyone over thirty," until you cross that threshold yourself. Scripture doesn't treat parental authority as absolute. In some circumstances, parents must be disobeyed.[71] Yet in the Bible, authority is good, and parental authority is the original form of authority.

We believe in equality. We don't defer to our betters because we find it offensive to think we have betters. "Honor," by contrast, indicates a hierarchy. Some *deserve* more attention and respect.

We believe in the self-made man, the buffered self, the isolated individual. Every man is an Adam who has molded himself from the dust, embarrassed by the belly button that bespeaks dependence. Choice is the foundation of all moral action. Nearly any act is sanctified by "consent," the magic word of liberal order. The Fifth Word explodes satanic myths of self-creation by teaching that *un*chosen relationships have moral weight. Christians have long recognized that this principle extends beyond the family.[72] I didn't choose to be born an American or baptized as an infant, yet I should submit to the authority of these given communities.[73]

Today's families are assembled from the blistered shards of broken households. Children are "yours, mine, ours," and grow up with multiple fathers and stepfathers, mothers and stepmothers, a father and a father, a mother and a mother. While most of America's children live with two parents, a quarter of them do not. In some communities, the situation is worse: three-quarters of African American children are born outside marriage. The Fifth Word requires honor of father and mother, *both* in the *singular*, assuming that children have one of each sex as parents, both present.[74]

The Fifth Word assumes that parenthood is inescapable, but our reproductive technologies have eroded that assumption. A couple can have a genetically related child who isn't carried by the mother. Children can be manufactured from donated eggs and sperm and borne by a surrogate, so they have *no* physical connection to parents. Family is detached from biology.

Children in same-sex families *can't* be biologically related to both parents. The relationship between parents and children is legal rather than biological. Adoption is a gift to many children and families, but adoption is necessary because of death or family breakdown. Today, changes in marriage law effectively make adoption the legal paradigm for all parent-child relations. Among other things, this extends the reach of the state, as it takes oversight of all familial relations.

Christians shouldn't be seduced by nostalgia for families of the Victorian age or the 1950s. We live in our age, not theirs. Scripture, not some historical epoch, is our standard. Still, the Fifth Word has an implicit model of family and society. To keep this commandment fully, we must reconstruct the social situation it assumes—two-parent families as a norm, the goodness of authority, the limitations of consent, the preservation of families through a lifelong commitment of a man and a woman.

For Christians, the family's role is limited by the reality of the church. Churches baptize infants to mark them as children of the heavenly Father, nurtured by mother church. In the church, we have multiple fathers and mothers, sisters and brothers (Mark 10:30). Blood relations aren't erased. Peter and Andrew, John and James, were sibling-apostles, and Paul issues commands to fathers and their biological or adopted children (Eph 6:1–4). Yet the church is the Christian's primary brotherhood, our first family and a site of pedagogy and parenting. Due to revolutionary social changes, today's church has a huge mission opportunity. As one of the ten new-creative words from Sinai, the Fifth Word forms a familial counterculture within the family of God, where broken homes can be put back together.

The Hebrew word for "honor" means "glorify," which Scripture uses to speak of honoring God. Your parents aren't God, but they're God's gifts to you, as you are God's gifts to them. The way you treat them should resemble the way you respond to God. As Karl Barth writes, God alone is literally Father because he alone gives life. But he has graciously arranged the world to permit human fatherhood and motherhood. The dignity of parents lies in their capacity to symbolize the heavenly Father.[75]

We can fill out the practical import of this commandment by asking, How do we honor God?

By praising him. Do you speak well of your parents, or do you criticize, grumble, and pretend you know better?

By serving him. The Bible tells us to rise before the hoary head (Lev 19:32). Out of respect for the old, and especially for parents, we adopt a posture of service, like a priest who stands and serves Father Yahweh.

By listening to him. The Hebrew word "glorify" comes from the word "weight." To honor parents is to give weight to their opinions, presence, advice. Whose words weigh more— your parents' or your Instagram friends? Whose voice do you listen to? Parents are called to guide children into mature wisdom. Children honor them when they acknowledge their parents have wisdom they lack, when they allow themselves to be led in the way that leads to life.[76] Children honor parents when they facilitate, rather than inhibit, their parents' mission. The Fifth is the first commandment with a promise (Eph 6:2), and the promise is inherent in the command: as parents fulfill their mission and children respect them, the children are directed toward a long life of blessing in the land.

By trusting him. We trust God to provide for us, do good, have our best interests in view. Children honor their parents by assuming that their rules and curfews and chores are intended to bless them, even if they can't see how. Children honor parents when they ask for what they need and receive what their parents give with thanks.

By submitting to discipline. God proves our sonship by disciplining us (Heb 12). When we resist God's discipline, we're not honoring him. When children fume resentfully about correction, they're disobeying the Fifth Word.

We obey the Fifth Word differently at different stages of life, but the Fifth Word is never superseded. Adult children also must honor parents—praise them, give weight to their words, trust them.

In fact, the commandment is *primarily* addressed to adult children.[77] It requires children to honor parents practically, by caring for them in old age. From this angle, we see how the Fifth Word is intertwined with the biblical vision of a just society. Honoring parents is linked to care of vulnerable orphans and widows (Ezek 22:6–8). Leviticus 19:3 commands: "You shall revere your mother and father,[78] and you shall keep my Sabbaths."[79] Reverence for mother and father, expressed in material support in old age, is a form of Sabbath-keeping. First-century Pharisees avoided this responsibility by vowing money to the temple instead of helping their parents (Mark 7:9–13). Jesus saw through the ruse and condemned them for invalidating the command of God. In Israel, abuse or neglect of parents was a public concern and punished severely.[80]

By my reckoning (see chapter 2), the Fifth Word is in the first table, connected to commandments concerning worship. Addressed to Yahweh's son Israel, the new Adam,

"Honor your father" means "Honor Yahweh your Father, who brought you out of the land of Egypt."[81]

Because the Fifth Word is the heavenly Father's word to his son, it's ultimately about the Father and his eternal Son, who lives as the true Israel to redeem Israel. The Fifth Word not only assumes a certain order in society. It unveils the inner life of God. The Son honors his Father, trusts his Father, submits to his Father, hears his Father, gives the words of his Father weight, submits to his Father's discipline. But this isn't the end of the story. In the same moment, the Father turns the tables to glorify the Son, honor him, listen to his prayers and pleas.

That is the final truth of family life: Young children glorify parents, while parents raise their children to glory. Adult children honor their parents materially, while parents praise their children. In keeping the Fifth Word, family life comes to reflect the mutual honor that is the crenulated communion of the living God.

COMMANDMENT VI

Thou shalt not kill.

LIFE-GIVING GOD, you have formed us from dust and breathed into us the breath of life, and you forbid the unjust taking of life. Make us imitators of Christ, who repaid evil with good, who did not sin in his anger, and who blessed those who cursed him, so that in him we may lay down our lives for others, following the example of him who laid down his life for us. In his name we pray. **AMEN.**

THOU SHALT
NOT KILL

JESUS SUMMARIZES THE LAW WITH two commandments
(Luke 10:27): Love God with all our heart, soul, strength,
and mind; and love our neighbor as ourselves. These commands summarize the Ten Words: the first five commandments are about love for God, and the second five describe
love for neighbor.

The sixth commandment is a suitable heading to the
second half of the Decalogue. The Ten Words don't offer
any rationale for prohibiting murder because the rationale
is given earlier, after the flood (Gen 9:3–7). Yahweh prohibits eating blood and warns against shedding human blood:

> Whoever sheds man's blood,
> by man his blood shall be shed,
> for *in the image of God*
> *He made man.* (Gen 9:6 NASB)

Human life must be protected because human beings are made
in the image of God.[82] The first commandment prohibits worship of any but the God of exodus; the first word of the second
table prohibits assaults on the *created* image of that God.

The first and second halves of the Decalogue match one another: idolatry is a species of murder, murder a kind of idolatry (first and sixth); worshiping images is spiritual adultery (second and seventh); bearing God's name lightly steals his glory (third and eighth); the Sabbath is for renewing covenant vows (fourth and ninth); coveting undermines hierarchies necessary for healthy family, social, and political life (fifth and tenth).[83]

With the Sixth Word, we move from Genesis 3 to Genesis 4. Adam's original sin was idolatry, ignoring God's word (Gen 3). Eve was tempted by the devil, a murderer from the beginning (John 8:44). One of Adam's sons became a satanic murderer himself (Gen 4). The Ten Words forbid both the idolatry of Adam and the fratricide of Cain.

Each of the last five commandments is an extension of the prohibition of murder: Do not assault the image of God by killing another human being. Do not assault the image of God by violating marriage, by seizing another's property, or by defiling his reputation. When we covet, we desire and do not have, and that makes us Cains, envious murderers who attack God through his image.

English translations sometimes translate the Hebrew verb as "murder." That's too specific. The Hebrew verb is used frequently in Numbers 35, which establishes cities where manslayers find refuge from the avenger of blood. The verb often means "murder," the intentional or premeditated killing of a man or woman (Num 35:16, 17, 18, 19, 21, 25, 26, 27). But the same verb describes what we call "manslaughter," unintentional killing or a crime of passion (Num 35:27; cf.

Deut 4:42). Even the just vengeance of the avenger, a form of capital punishment, is rendered with the same verb (Num 35:27; cf. 35:30). Though the word often means "murder," its basic meaning is "manslaying."[84]

Scripture treats different sorts of killing differently. Scripture requires care for animals, but never prohibits killing animals for food. The Lord authorizes civil rulers to execute criminals (Rom 13). Scripture treats the death penalty as just, especially in cases of murder (Exod 21:23; Num 35). As Augustine said, "He does not kill who is the executor of a just command."[85] War is permissible in some circumstances (Deut 20),[86] and Israelites were permitted to kill, under restricted conditions, to defend their homes (Exod 22:2–4).

All shedding of human blood had to be dealt with, either by the confinement of the manslayer, the execution of the murderer, or a rite of cleansing (cf. Deut 21:1–9). Before soldiers went to war, they paid "atonement" money to pre-cover bloodshed (Exod 30:11–16). William Cavanaugh makes the point with provocative sharpness: we moderns gladly kill at the state's behest, but the Bible insists that we may kill *only* in the name of God.[87]

Here we can discern another "perichoretic" connection between the first and the sixth commandment. God determines when killing is permitted because of who he is: Lord of life and death. If we kill at *another's* command, that other has effectively become our God, our Lord of life and death.[88]

You might be feeling some relief right about now. At least here is *one* commandment you've never broken, not *really*, not in any serious way.

Don't let yourself off so easily. If you live in a modern society, you're entrenched in networks of violence. Entertainments thrill us through granular depictions of violence. Scripture calls false witnesses "witnesses of violence." Spend a few minutes on Twitter, and you'll see verbal mayhem. Liberal order presumes that we'll forever disagree about fundamental truths, and thus relies on good violence to counter bad. American greed for more oil, more comforts, more *stuff* drives a foreign policy of perpetual war.[89] Soldiers kill for "a state whose *very ideal* is the separation of violence from the will of God."[90]

Even Christians are happy to separate violence from the will of God. Many Christian soldiers go to war at the command of secular states, without consulting their pastors or considering whether the war is just in the Lord's sight. Few Christians think the church has any authority over a Christian's decision to fight. If God is Lord of life and death, Christians should kill only if he permits it.

Because we don't honor the family as the context for reproduction, because we demand the perfect baby or a right to a child, we've developed technologies of reproduction that create and discard embryos by the thousands. Our disobedience to the Fifth Word feeds a high-tech culture of death, buttressed by legal guarantees.[91] In most "advanced" societies, the murder of unborn babies has been industrialized. Abortion isn't a side issue. As Robert Jenson says, a key mark of civilized society is "the replacement of vendetta by courts and their officers." Legal abortion grants "the most interested party" a license to kill, a privatization of murder that is nothing less than "a relapse to pure barbarism."[92]

We can go deeper by reminding ourselves that the Ten Words are a portrait of the true Israel, the last Adam, the eternal Son, Jesus. Once we get Jesus in view, two things come clear.

First, the *teaching* of Jesus. Addressing the Sixth Word in the Sermon on the Mount, Jesus warns against hatred, anger, and angry words (Matt 5:21–26, 38–48). As Luther put it, the Sixth Word requires a pure heart as well as pure hands, since we can kill with any part of our bodies.[93] Anger can dominate one's life, churning beneath the surface and breaking through at the slightest provocation—a child's embarrassing accident, pressure at work, a traffic jam. You say you're ambitious, but what looks like ambition is envy, a desire to take down the competition. Deep down, you're a murderer. You say you're plain-speaking, but in reality you've turned your tongue into a sword that kills with insults, curses, and frothy outrage. You say you're a leader, but in fact your simmering anger intimidates everyone around you. Anger curves inward into self-hatred, cleverly disguising itself as humility.

We perfect techniques to keep anger under wraps, polish a surface of smooth sociality, most of the time. We even hide our anger from ourselves. The angriest people would be shocked to hear that they're angry, even though they live in continuous defiance of the Sixth Word.

Jesus doesn't forbid anger. Righteous outrage is real, as Jesus' action in the temple demonstrates. Jesus requires a righteousness that surpasses that of the scribes and Pharisees, a righteousness like Jesus' own (Matt 5:17–20). Jesus doesn't merely avoid wrong. His is an active righteousness that triumphs over evil.

What Jesus *commands* is a set of practices to defuse anger and overcome evil with good (Matt 5:21–26). If you're at odds with a brother, leave your offering at the altar and seek reconciliation. Stop the lawsuit; make friends quickly, out of court. Don't seek vengeance; turn the other cheek. The Sixth Word demands we be peacemakers, sons of God like *the* Son.

Second, the Sixth Word describes Jesus' *character and actions*. Jesus' entire life incarnates "Thou shalt not kill." He doesn't assault God's image, but restores it. He doesn't wound, but heals. He doesn't take life, but gives it, abundantly. He doesn't oppress, but liberates. His words, even his harshest ones, are words of life. He uses the sword of his tongue to defend the weak and to call the wicked to a repentance that leads to life.

Jesus has cause to defend himself and to seek vengeance. He has legions of angels at his command. Instead, Jesus gives himself, suffers in silent patience, loves and asks forgiveness for his executioners. He doesn't kill but dies a victim of murder, and so gives life. In the Sixth Word, he calls us to follow, to renounce every form of murder, to be martyrs who give ourselves and so become agents of his abundant life.

COMMANDMENT VII

Thou shalt not commit adultery.

FAITHFUL GOD, you have bound yourself to us as a bridegroom to a bride, and you call us to discipline the desires of the flesh and to flee from youthful lusts. Give us strength to resist temptation so that in any situation, whether single or married, we may be pure and chaste, honoring you in our bodies, in obedience to Jesus Christ, who was tempted in every way we are, yet without sin. In his name we pray. **AMEN.**

THOU SHALT NOT
COMMIT ADULTERY

UNLIKE THE PERMISSIVE GODS OF antiquity and modernity, the God of Sinai is an intrusive God who won't leave us alone. He tells Israel that they must worship and serve him *alone*. He tells them *how* to worship him, without images. Ever the divine Micromanager, he schedules their week. Ever the divine Idealist, he expects us to live in the real world without violence and vengeance. In the tenth commandment, he really steps over the line and intrudes on thoughts and desires.

No commandment prickles more than the seventh. Many live by a creed of sexual autonomy: my body is my own, and my sexual desires, whatever they are, are normal and healthy. How dare the Lord—how dare *anyone*—interfere with my constitutional right to think and do and feel whatever I damn well please? Can I have a *little* privacy, please?

Of course, most are sane enough to acknowledge limits on sexual behavior. Few endorse sex with children, and only extreme progressives say the family should be given a quiet burial, along with the absurd notion of lifelong marital faithfulness. Most know that adultery is a bad deal and agree that society has to guard the family from the acid of infidelity. Adultery breaks up marriages and homes. Men and women suffer trauma and are impoverished by and after divorce. Children watch in horror as their parents battle at home, in court, over *them*, for years. We can't enjoy the goods of marriage if every man is on the prowl for his friend's wife and every wife is looking for a chance to slip away to a motel.

God isn't satisfied protecting the family. He prohibits other forms of sexual activity. Yahweh tells Israel who they can and cannot have sex with—not with one's mother or stepmother, daughter-in-law, sister, or aunt (Lev 18). Yahweh forbids men to lie with men as with women (Lev 18:22), and forbids sexual contact with animals (Lev 18:23). If a man has sex with a virgin, he'll soon have to face her father, who might demand marriage or a dowry (Exod 22:16–17). Yahweh doesn't consider consent the fundamental standard of sexual etiquette but prohibits forms of consensual sex between adults. How *dare* he?

Gentle Jesus makes things worse: "You have heard it said, Do not commit adultery. But I say to you, everyone who looks at a woman to lust after her has already committed adultery with her in his heart" (Matt 5:27–30). Jesus prohibits sexual desires and the habit of "checking out" that fuels desire. If you thought Jesus might leave a loophole, the option of watching porn in the privacy of your bedroom, you're wrong. You watch pornography to do *exactly* what Jesus forbids, to look at a woman or man to arouse lust.[94]

When all is said and done, the Bible demands that men and women channel our mercurial sexuality into a single narrow path: lifelong commitment in heterosexual marriage.

Recently, we've taken sexual autonomy several steps further by making our identity as male or female a matter of choice. Gender dysphoria is a painful burden, but difficult cases don't change the fundamental reality. Each of us has received the gift of being one or another sort of human being, male or female (Gen 1:26–28), a fact inscribed on our bodies. God calls us to be the kind of human being he made us to be. Men are called to the glorious vocation of being men, women to the high calling of being women. Both are called to submit to the order that God established for male and female.

Contrary to our cultural assumptions, there *is* an order to male and female: "The man was not made for the woman," Paul says, referring to Genesis 2, "but the woman for the sake of the man" (1 Cor 11:9). "Adam was first created, then Eve" (1 Tim 2:13). Paul highlights the mutuality of the sexes: Eve originated from Adam, but every man since has originated from a woman. All, male and female, come from God (1 Cor 11:11–12). But mutual dependence doesn't make the sexes interchangeable. Mutuality exists alongside an order of first and second.

Yahweh treats sexual activity as a matter of *public* concern. In ancient Israel, some sexual sins were *crimes*. Adulterers— both the man and woman—are put to death (Lev 20:10). When a man lies with a man as with a woman, both are put to death (Lev 20:13). A man or woman who has sex with an animal is executed, and so is the animal (Lev 20:15–16). A man who sleeps with his mother, stepmother, or daughter-in-law is put to death (Lev 20:11–12).

However these laws apply to other nations, Paul makes it clear that the church publicly enforces sexual norms. The Corinthian man who has sex with his father's wife has to be handed to Satan in a church assembly (1 Cor 5:4). Paul quotes the death-penalty formula from Deuteronomy: "Remove the wicked man from among you" (1 Cor 5:13). The church doesn't use the civil sword. It enforces sexual norms with the far more powerful sword of church discipline.

Societies continue only if they reproduce, and reproduction takes place through sexual union of man and woman. Social order is bound up with bodily differences and sexual intercourse: "What I do in bed is the area of my action in which the community has the most urgent interest." A refusal to legislate here is insane, and dangerous. "No society," Robert Jenson writes, "can endure mere shapelessness." If our sexuality isn't shaped by customary or religious norms, the state will be happy to impose order.[95]

These social and political concerns don't get to the depth of the Seventh Word. Adultery isn't simply a lack of self-control, or unfaithfulness to an oath. The Seventh Word parallels the Second. As veneration of images is spiritual adultery, so adultery is a kind of idolatry. Adultery isn't merely a familial and social catastrophe. It's an assault on God's image.

Sex and marriage are theological realities from top to bottom. Paul wasn't imposing a Christ-and-church paradigm on the neutral natural phenomenon of sexual difference

(Eph 5). Sex is created as a sign of God's love for his Bride. That's what it's *for*. That's why Paul quotes from Genesis 2: The great mystery is that God created man male and female, a differentiated unity and a unified differentiation, as a living sign of his covenant bond with his people.

The account of Eve's creation is an allegory of the covenant God and his people (Gen 2).[96] "It is not good for man to be alone," Yahweh says of Adam. That is: God has chosen not to be alone, but to be God for and with us. "A man shall leave his father and mother and cleave to his wife," Genesis says. Just so, the God of Israel leaves heaven to enter the valley of death to rescue his Bride. Marriage portrays incarnation. "The two shall become one flesh," Genesis says, in a union of life that expresses the one-Spirit union of Christ and the church. A man and a woman aren't married on weekdays and free on weekends, single during the day and married at night. Everything is colored by their marriage, which is as all-encompassing as God's covenant with Israel. "They were naked and not ashamed," Genesis tells us, and so offers hope of future intimacy when, in the new creation, our shame will be removed and we will be forever face-to-face, unveiled, with our Lord.

Every perverse form of sexuality distorts the created design of marriage. Adultery, Clement of Alexandria says, is like the betrayal of idolatry.[97] We seek sexual pleasure without a commitment to a shared life, and so defy the faithful covenant God. We try out multiple sexual partners, and thus live a lie about the God who loves *one* Bride. Homosexual acts shatter the union-in-difference at the heart of God's relation to his people. Sexual sin lies about the Creator. The created order is to be a manifestation of the Lord of the covenant.[98]

This is the logic of the prophetic imagery of sexual unfaithfulness.[99] At times, the prophets condemn the sexual behavior of individuals in Judah. More often, unfaithful Judah is the adulterous wife. Jesus uses the same imagery when he condemns the "evil and adulterous generation" (Matt 12:39; 16:4) that rejects him. James warns his readers not to be "adulteresses," friends of the world who are faithless to the divine Husband (Jas 4:4).

Once we see marriage and adultery in this theological perspective, the "Do nots" fall into place. All are rooted in the fundamental "Do": Be what you are as male and female. As a *married* husband and wife, be the living image of the God of creation and covenant.[100]

Sexual faithfulness in marriage and sexual purity outside of marriage aren't mere demands of law. Sexual faithfulness preaches the gospel. When a husband and wife are faithful to one another, sexually and otherwise, they become a created symbol of the covenant God who keeps his vows to Israel and the new Israel. By keeping the Seventh Word, we dramatize the good news of Jesus, the Bridegroom of the church, who gives himself in utter fidelity to and for his Bride.

COMMANDMENT VIII

Thou shalt not steal.

GIFT-GIVING GOD, you made heaven and earth and all that dwells therein. Help us to remember that every good and perfect gift is from above, and to pursue godliness with contentment, knowing that we brought nothing into the world and can take nothing out of it, so that, satisfied in your grace, we may avoid all unjust gain, through Christ, in the power of the Holy Spirit. **AMEN.**

THOU SHALT
NOT STEAL

A GAIN, THE SIXTH WORD SUMMARIZES the second "table" of the Decalogue, the last five commandments. Like adultery, theft is a variety of murder.

This isn't obvious to us. We own our house, car, furniture, kitchenware, land, the odd family heirloom. But we don't think of them as part of our personality. They're tools, or toys.

There's biblical ground for that distinction. The Torah punishes crimes against persons differently from crimes against property. Murder is punished with a death penalty (Num 35), as is cursing father or mother (Exod 21:17; Lev 20:9). Some sexual acts are capital crimes (Lev 20). But the typical penalty for property crimes is restitution (Exod 22:1–5). You stole $100, so you have to give back $100 plus have $100 taken from you. It's eye for eye: you suffer the loss you imposed on your neighbor.[101]

Perhaps the connection of person and property was stronger when more people sewed their own clothes and built their own homes, or knew the craftsman who made their candlesticks and mixing bowls. In our economy, property is depersonalized. We don't make our own stuff. We dispose of things and buy new things readily, gleefully, greedily. Ring out the old, ring in the new.

Even so, we become emotionally attached to our things. What we *are* includes what we *have*. To own something is to incorporate it into your personality.[102] Think of the pride you take in a new car, home, sofa. Buy a beach house, and you become the sort of person who owns a beach house. Think of your affection for a car or piece of furniture you've owned for a long time. ("We've been through a *lot* together," you whisper when no one is looking.) Think of how you feel when something is stolen. You reassure yourself by saying, "Well, it's *just* a watch." But you can't shake the feeling that you've been violated—not just your stuff, but *you*.

The Bible hints at this connection between persons and property in various ways. In the Torah, the first specific law about theft is a prohibition of kidnapping or "man-stealing" (Exod 21:16). We can steal another person by enslaving him, unjustly imprisoning him, coercing his productivity, manipulating an employee to accept lower-than-reasonable pay.[103] Further, the law demands that we take care of our neighbor's property. If a friend gives you something to keep while he's on vacation, you must protect it as if it's your own (Exod 22:7). If you damage something you borrowed, you must make restitution (Exod 22:14). If you find your neighbor's animal wandering, you must return it or take care of it until the owner reclaims it (Deut 22). If your *enemy's* animal is caught under a burden, you must release and return it (Exod 23:4–5). You can't say, "I love my enemy, but I'm going to trash his stuff."

The Golden Rule encompasses property as well as personal relations: you love your enemy by caring for his property as you would have him care for yours. Protecting your neighbor's things is *part of* love for him.

The connection of person and property is clearest with regard to God's property. Yahweh claims certain things as uniquely his. They are "holy things" or "most holy things" because they belong to God. God himself is holy, and his things participate in his holiness. God incorporates his things into his person. As images of God, the things we own become extensions of our persons.[104] We too have our "holy things" and "holy places."

Once we see the deep bonds we form with our possessions, we feel the full force of Jesus' teaching on wealth. He has no place to lay his head, and he calls disciples from their livelihoods to follow him. He tells the rich young ruler to give away everything. If possessions were loosely fitted add-ons, that would be easy. But it's not easy. Giving away our stuff is like cutting off a limb. Jesus' demand that we be ready to give up our possessions is the same as his demand that we be ready to give up our lives. In both cases, he calls us to *self*-renunciation.

You don't need to put panty hose over your face and sneak into a house to be a thief. You can steal in broad daylight, in the marketplace, whenever you defraud or deceive. Scripture demands honesty in weights and measures (Lev 19:35; Deut 25:15). Over time, ancient metal coins wear thin. A dishonest merchant could shave off layers of a silver coin; he claims the coin contains fifty shekels of silver, when it's only forty-five.

That's theft, and it points to the importance of trust and trustworthiness in economic transactions. Much of our economic activity is mediated through language: promises, contracts, advertisements.[105] You can't say, "I'll be honest in conversation, but my contracts will be blurry around the edges."[106] As Thomas Aquinas said, we break the Eighth Word every time we defraud our neighbor in buying or selling.[107]

The eighth commandment parallels the third. Theft is practical idolatry, service to Mammon, one of our world's most revered idols. More than power, money is the god of Wall Street and K Street and Pennsylvania Avenue. Our polity is organized to maximize GDP. When disaster strikes, we do our patriotic duty by buying more stuff, enabled by smartphones that allow us to shop anytime, anywhere. Advertisements bombard us with enticements to believe, contrary to Jesus, that life consists in the abundance of possessions (Luke 12:15).

Worse, Christians have become utterly comfortable in Mammon's temples, pursuing dreams of unlimited prosperity: "Who's hurt if money molds my life? I'm helping the economy grow, my kids get into the best schools, and I can buy the best dance and piano teachers." We don't recognize that Mammon is as deadly as any idol. Sooner or later, like every idol, it leaves us with speechless mouths, blind eyes, deaf ears.

Christians of earlier ages saw Mammon for what it is. Martin Luther excoriated market fraud with a serrated vehemence that might give Karl Marx pause. He attacked those "who turn the free public market into nothing but a carrion-pit and a robber's den. The poor are defrauded every day, and new burdens and higher prices are imposed. They all misused the market in their own arbitrary, defiant, arrogant way, as if it were their privilege and right to sell their goods as high as they please."[108]

Shatter Mammon. But *how*? Give all your goods to the poor? Join a commune or a monastery? Ultimately, we break Mammon's hold when we acknowledge that all we have is a gift from God. Our property is ours, but in the mode of gift. That's why property "rights" aren't absolute in Scripture. In ancient Israel, land returned to its original owners every fifty years (Lev 25). Farmers weren't allowed to maximize profit from their fields but left the corners of their fields to the landless poor (Lev 19:9; 23:22).[109] Dropped sheaves were left for gleaners, and grapes were reserved for the poor (Lev 19:9–10). Gathering dropped sheaves was stealing from the mouth of the hungry.

The principle holds for Christians: our material goods are like the gifts we receive from the Spirit. They're ours, but we possess them to edify the body. We don't give away everything, but we *do* use everything to bless. We're given material goods to advance God's justice.[110]

Once we reckon with God's universal ownership, we can see the story of fall and redemption shrouded within the Eighth Word. God created Adam to have dominion, to take ownership of creation. The fruit of the tree of knowledge was the one thing that belonged exclusively to God. Adam stole it, and all children of Adam are thieves, stealing God's holy things, assaulting God's image by assaulting the property of others.[111] Above all, we steal *ourselves* from God: We are not our own; we were bought at a price (1 Cor 6:19–20). We bear the Name that marks us as the Lord's property (Third Word), yet we want to be our own god. Every time we disobey, we steal and commit sacrilege, misusing God's holy things.

God didn't imprison Adam's son forever. He sent the Son, who, though existing in the form of God, did not think equality with God a thing to be grasped, seized, or stolen. Instead, he humbled, offered, and emptied himself. Though rich, he became poor that we might share in God's riches. He didn't steal, but gave. He repaid the debt *we* had incurred.

By the new-creative Word, the Spirit of this last, all-generous Adam makes us a new humanity. "Thou shalt not steal" is a character description of Jesus, and obedience to this command is obedience to the gospel, the call to imitate Jesus' labor and self-gift.

COMMANDMENT IX

Thou shalt not bear false witness against thy neighbor.

TRUTHFUL GOD, your word is truth, and in you there is no shadow of turning. Give us courage to always speak the truth and to reject falsehood, knowing that telling the truth is an act of love, for friends as well as for enemies, so that we may know the truth that sets us free, in Jesus Christ, who, with the Father, is worshiped in Spirit and in truth. **AMEN**.

THOU SHALT NOT BEAR FALSE WITNESS

CHRISTIANS SOMETIMES READ THE TEN Words as "moral law," understood as the realm of individual ethics. These commandments do govern the lives of individuals. But Yahweh addresses his son, Israel, so that Israel's *corporate* life will conform to the word from Sinai. The ten new-creative words bring Israel's *social* life under the reign of God. Worship, timekeeping, parental and other authorities, the use of force, sexuality and family life, and property are all integrated into the covenant.[112] With the Ninth Word, courts of justice come into view.

The ninth commandment isn't, "Thou shalt not lie." It's more specific. It requires "witnesses" summoned to testify in court to tell the truth, the whole truth, and nothing but the truth. They must not be "witnesses of violence" (Exod 23:1; Deut 19:15–21). A false witness is a club, sword, and sharp arrow (Prov 25:18) who deploys the bludgeon of state power to murder his neighbor or damage his good name. We speak truth of and to our neighbors because they're made in God's image. To bear false witness is blasphemy against another human, as bearing God's name lightly is blasphemy against him.[113]

Elsewhere, the Torah deals with bribery, intimidation, and other forms of corruption (Exod 23:8; Deut 10:17; 16:19; 27:25). Court decisions shape social life, forcing changes in settled customs[114] and distributing rewards and demerits. If courts are controlled by money or violence, society will be molded by the wealthy, powerful, and malicious. To be just, society must be shaped by truth, centrally by truthful testimony and just decisions in courtroom settings.[115]

The Hebrew verb in the Ninth Word is normally translated as "answer."[116] In context, it connotes "answer a summons" or "answer a question posed in court." But it points to the larger truth that human speech is answering speech. Yahweh spoke to Adam before Adam spoke to Eve. Each of us was born speechless. We learn to speak only as we are spoken to.

That broadens out the Ninth Word. It demands truth-telling in every setting, not merely under the formal procedures of a court of law. As Martin Luther said, it prohibits betrayal, slander, the spreading of evil rumors.[117] True words can destroy, when spoken as gossip. Few themes are more prominent in Proverbs than the wise use of the tongue. Too much speech is dangerous (Prov 10:8). Timing is all the difference between rotten words and verbal apples of gold in settings of silver (Prov 25:11). Sweet speech is dangerously seductive (Prov 5:3), but for the same reason it can persuade kings (Prov 16:21; 22:11). Smooth speech enables the ambitious to steal hearts (see Absalom, 2 Sam 15:6). Deception is a lubricant of social life, from excusable courtesies to self-serving flattery, which has been called the most harmful of lies.[118] We rarely sin without a backup plan in case we get caught: "I can always lie my way out of this."

The Ninth Word is a fitting word for our mediated age. We're spun by a whirlpool of rumor, innuendo, false accusation, slander, libel. People are tried and condemned by online lynch mobs. We like or share Tweets and Facebook posts even though we can't possibly confirm their accuracy. Luther said that the Ninth Word requires us to put "the best construction on everything," to give others the benefit of the doubt. We exaggerate the stupidity or malevolence of ideological adversaries to score points and win honor in Twitter combat. Officially committed to the Ten Words, the church does no better. Christians fire up the digital kindling to burn supposed heretics without due process, humility, or care.

This isn't merely an improper *use* of neutral technology. YouTube gives preference to controversial videos, the more outlandish the better. Twitter is a medium of self-presentation, often self-preening, where every user plays a game of "brand management."[119] Not by accident but by design, social media encourages violations of the Ninth Word.

Lies can become embedded in the foundations of a culture. When a member of the Toraja tribe sets out in his canoe, he tricks the gods by saying, in a loud voice, that he's planning a canoe trip *tomorrow*. No Toraja will compliment a pretty girl, for fear that jealous gods will give her the face of a dog.[120] We smile at the primitive superstition, but in living memory much of Eastern Europe lived under a regime of lies. As Vaclav Havel memorably put it, "Because the regime is captive to its own lies, it must falsify everything. It falsifies the past. It falsifies the present, and it falsifies the future. It falsifies statistics. It pretends not to possess an omnipotent and unprincipled police apparatus. It pretends to respect human rights. It pretends to persecute no one. It pretends to fear nothing. It pretends to pretend nothing." The Soviet bloc crumbled when truth-tellers like Havel and John Paul II uttered the simple, childlike words, "The empire has no clothes."[121]

The Ninth Word parallels the Fourth, the Sabbath command. On the Lord's Day, we confess the Truth that is Jesus Christ, hear the truth from Scripture and sermon, sing the truth. The liturgy trains us in truth-telling. It forms the church as a truth-living people, sons of the Father through the eternal Son.

Truth-telling isn't necessarily "nice." We learn to be truth-tellers when we learn to see clearly and when we break the habit of covering our cowardice with the pious excuse of "love."[122] Immediately after Yahweh forbids Israelites to hate their countrymen (Lev 19:17) and immediately before he tells them to "love your neighbor as yourself" (Lev 19:18), he tells them to "reprove your neighbor" (Lev 19:17 NASB). Prophets like Nathan (2 Sam 12) and Elijah (1 Kgs 17–19) weren't nice. They really performed the cliché: they spoke truth to power. And their blistering words carried divine power, to pluck up and plant, to demolish and build (cf. Jer 1:10). Truthful correction is an expression of love, not hate. If you tell the truth, you will create conflict, and then you are called to be a peacemaker. But true peace can be won only if the truth shatters the false peace of the lie.

Here we stumble on the flip side of today's social disorder. While we gleefully spread gossip on social media, we tiptoe gingerly around the truth. We say we're tolerant and want to avoid triggering. But we're cowards, and hateful cowards to boot. If we can't tell the truth, we cannot identify real evils. If we're forbidden to name problems, we cannot propose solutions.

The second half of the Decalogue deals with love for the "neighbor," but the elusive neighbor comes out of hiding for the first time in the Ninth Word. That tells us something about neighborly relations. We may have a fairly easy time avoiding murder, adultery, theft. Most of us don't get into fistfights with our neighbors or slip a silver fork into our pocket during a dinner party. Most of our interactions with neighbors take place in speech. Wisely, the Lord's first explicit test of our love of our neighbors is, How do we speak about and to them?

The Ninth Word forbids us to answer falsely against our neighbor or "friend." What about enemies? Are we free to answer with false testimony? Augustine was an absolutist: lying is never justified.[123] But Scripture's heroes often deceive their enemies. The Hebrew midwives lie to protect infant boys (Exod 1); Rahab betrays soldiers of her own king to protect Israelite spies (Josh 2; see Jas 2); Jael pretends to offer Sisera a safe tent while intending to split his skull with a tent peg (Judg 4). After a string of female deceivers, we have David, who repeatedly misleads to escape from Saul, Achish, and others. These righteous deceptions all take place in wartime, and typically protect innocent life. They reflect God's justice: At the beginning, the serpent deceived Eve so that she ate from the tree. From that time on, new Eves have turned it back on the serpent's head, eye for eye, lie for lie.

But these are exceptions. Truthful speech is an act of love, and we are to love enemies as well as friends. In all normal circumstances, we speak truth to and about our enemies, refusing to minimize their virtues or exaggerate their faults.

Like the others, the Ninth Word is about Jesus, the true and faithful Witness. He speaks the truth during his life, arousing his enemies' murderous rage. He speaks the truth to skeptical Pilate. As Witness, he summons us as witnesses who answer truthfully about the hope within us, the living Hope that is Jesus himself. He calls us to speak truth no matter what the cost, to love truth more than life. With the Ninth Word, Jesus calls us to martyrdom.[124]

Martyrs aren't losers. Martyrdom is indefeasible. Martyrs speak world-shattering truth on the way to their world-shattering, world-renewing deaths. The Ninth Word is the Creator's command. He is Lord of our tongues. It is also a promise, the Lord's pledge to truthful witnesses: at the last judgment if not before, the truth will out and truthful witnesses will be vindicated.

COMMANDMENT X

Thou shalt not covet.

ABUNDANT GOD, you give us the desires of our hearts when we delight in you. Grant rest to our restless hearts, so that our souls may long for you and you alone, in the name of Jesus Christ, who is our soul's anchor and the desire of all nations, and who, with you and the Holy Spirit, is worshiped, glorified, and treasured as our greatest good. **AMEN.**

THOU SHALT
NOT COVET

S TYLISTICALLY, THE TENTH WORD IS a surprise. In Hebrew, commandments 6–8 consist of two words each, "not" plus a verb. The ninth commandment is loquacious by comparison, with five words. Then the Tenth Word, which has more words (fifteen) than the rest of the second table combined (eleven). It didn't need to be so long. It says "do not covet" twice, and it lists the neighbor's goods in three pairs—house/wife, manservant/maidservant, ox/donkey— and then completes the list with a seventh item, "anything." Why not cut to the chase and say, "Thou shalt not covet anything of your neighbor's"? The doubled verb and the list remind us of the Sabbath command. The stylistic parallel suggests a substantive one: we give Sabbath rest by mortifying our covetous desires.

The Tenth Word is one of two that appears in a significantly different form in Deuteronomy 5. In Exodus 20, the Sabbath command is rooted in creation, while in Deuteronomy Israel keeps Sabbath because Yahweh rescued them from Egypt. The change in the tenth commandment is more subtle. Exodus prohibits coveting the neighbor's house, and then his wife. Deuteronomy reverses the order: "Thou shalt not covet thy neighbor's wife; thou shalt not covet thy neighbor's house" (Deut 5:21). Exodus treats the wife as part of the household; Deuteronomy elevates the wife above the house.

This shift is consistent with the movement of the Torah and biblical history as a whole, an elevation of the bride. The first census in Numbers (Num 1) counts male warriors, but the second, taken after the first Israel has died in the wilderness, numbers according to "families" and includes women and children (Num 26). Numbers ends by reiterating Moses' ruling concerning the inheritance of the daughters of Zelophehad (Num 36). Other covenants have a first "husbandly" phase, then a bridal second phase: first Elijah alone, then Elisha with his company of prophets; first Jesus, then the apostles and the church. Biblical history, and each phase of biblical history, moves from Adam to Adam-and-Eve, from the Last Adam to the Last Adam with his Bride.

The Tenth Word regulates "desire." Covetousness isn't the same as jealousy or envy. Jealousy is a proper protectiveness for what is ours. Distorted, it becomes miserly. Envy is corrosive hatred for another's success or wealth, which seeks an outlet in verbal or physical violence. An envious man may not physically deface his neighbor's stylish home or subvert his business; he'll take every opportunity to defame his neighbor and degrade his house. The jealous hoard, the envious kill, the covetous steal.

Like bodies, societies thrive when different parts contribute to the whole. Eyes serve the body by seeing, hands by grasping, legs and feet by walking. In a healthy society, wisdom, authority, and experience will be honored. The Fifth Word demands that we honor and preserve these hierarchies. Covetousness, envy, and jealousy erode social differentiations. The covetous hand desires the eye's power of sight; the envious ear wants the whole body to be an ear.

Desire is fundamental to biblical anthropology, its understanding of human existence. We think, but we aren't primarily thinking things. We're *desiring* beings. Like the animals, Adam was made a "living soul" (Gen 2:7; cf. 1:20–21, 24, 30). Our souls move us to action, and souls move us by desire (1 Sam 23:20; Job 23:13; Eccl 6:2, 9). Sexual desire is a longing of soul (Gen 34:8), hunger and thirst arise from the soul (Ps 107:9), and the yearning for God's presence is a desire of the soul (Ps 42:1–2; 63:1; 84:2; 143:6; Isa 26:9). Dante was right: everything we do is motivated by proper or distorted love.[125] Desire is the combustible power that moves human life.

Desires are inseparable from evaluations of the desirability of the thing desired. God made trees "desirable to the eyes" (Gen 2:9), and eyes are organs of judgment and evaluation. Eve "saw" the tree was desirable to make one wise, and so she ate (Gen 3:6). Desire moves us to take the object of desire—food, a sexually attractive person, our neighbor's shiny Porsche—and to incorporate it into ourselves.

The Bible acknowledges the disruptive, dangerous power of desire, and Christians developed the notion of seven deadly sins to warn against disfigured desire. But desire isn't evil because it's strong. Desire becomes evil when it's fixed on the wrong objects, when we misevaluate the desirability of something. Eve covets the fruit and takes it, Shechem desires Dinah and seduces her (Gen 34), and Achan covets the treasure of Jericho and steals it from Yahweh (Josh 7:21). Evil desire lays traps (e.g., Deut 7:25). This is why Paul says covetousness is idolatry (Col 3). Our souls impel us to seek satisfactions in things that we *wrongly* judge to be satisfying.

We avoid the trap not by suppressing desire, but by learning to see past the fizzy surface of things. We avoid Lady Folly's trap when we see that her beauty—which is *real* beauty—is a death mask (Prov 6:25). The Bible doesn't teach us to master, control, or kill desire. Our desires are to *mature*, so that our souls, brought to life by the Spirit, move us to pursue *real* treasure and eternal glory *with passion*.

We mimic the desires of others, and sometimes catch their desires as if they were a contagious infection.[126] Desires take cultural, institutional, political forms that shape our souls. Consumer culture is organized to entice desire for all the wrong things. Advertisers try to convince us that this or that food, drink, show, car, vacation is desirable to make one happy. As Ferdinand Mount has pointed out, the seven deadly sins have been given a positive spin: "Covetousness has been rebranded as retail therapy, sloth as downtime, lust is exploring your sexuality, anger is opening up your feelings, vanity is looking good because you're worth it and gluttony is the religion of foodies."[127] What Christians once saw as deadly desires are now the very things that make the world go round.

More subtly, our culture encourages us to think our desires are free. We desire what we desire because we choose to. Or, in an even narrower circle, we desire what we desire because we desire it. Such absolutist notions of freedom are self-contradictory. By our cultural logic, if freedom is limited by anything beyond our known will and desire, then freedom is no longer absolute. But desire is *itself* a limit. When I hunger or thirst, I seek *particular* satisfactions—food and drink. Sexual desire impels toward sexual gratification. Desires can be diverted, repressed, masked, but they retain the same structure. Desire is ordered to ends, tethered to a telos. "Freedom to do whatever I desire" mangles this structure. It leaves desire end-less.

Desire is free only when it's directed toward an object. The Russian poet Vera Pavlova expresses this in an arresting poem:

> I am in love, hence free to live
> by heart, to improvise caresses.
> A soul is light when full,
> heavy when vacuous.
> My soul is light. She is not afraid
> to dance the agony alone,
> for I was born wearing your shirt,
> will come from the dead with that shirt on.[128]

Pavlova links being to freedom: "I am ... hence free." But a specific experience links them: love. Contrary to cynics of all ages, Pavlova insists that love need not be bondage, but can liberate. Liberated by love, she is free to live "by heart" and to "improvise caresses." Her spontaneity isn't spontaneous. It bubbles up as a by-product of love's bond.

As the poem continues, "heart" modulates into "soul," and the poet introduces a paradox of soul and body. Full bodies are heavy, empty bodies light. Souls, by contrast, are not weighed down by being full; rather, the fuller they are, the lighter, airier, and more ethereal they become. Love lightens the soul, freeing it to live by heart, while a loveless soul is as heavy and earthbound as an overstuffed stomach. Even the prospect of death doesn't weigh down the lover's soul. Love will bring her from death wearing her lover's shirt.

Desire is liberating not *in spite of* its fixity but *because of* its fixity. "Follow your heart" is paralyzing advice to someone whose eyes are dazzled by every passing beauty, whose vacuous soul is blown about by the most recent Tweet. Living by heart is freeing *only* for someone whose heart is already taken. Lovers alone are free to act spontaneously without risk that spontaneity will collapse into the absolute freedom that is indistinguishable from nihilism.

We're in Augustinian territory, where the key is to order desires *rightly*, to direct our loves at lovable things that deserve our fixed love. From this Augustinian perspective, we are genuinely free only if our desires are trained, only if we have been brought out of the Egypt of self-love to embrace proper objects of love.

Yahweh liberated his son Israel, and he wants his son to live in freedom—free from tyrannical gods, free from idols, free to rejoice, free from fear of violence, seduction, theft, rumor, and gossip. These freedoms are achieved, however, only if the *souls* of Israel are free, free from evil desires and fixed on true riches.

This the law cannot give. It cannot grant the freedom it commands and commends. Augustine, alluding to Paul

(Rom 7), notes that the law provokes a desire to break it. We don't even know that our desires are evil until the law brings them to light: "You started to make an effort to overcome what was inside, and what was hidden came to light."[129]

To be true sons, we need another Pentecost beyond Sinai, when the Spirit writes on human hearts. Then we'll fulfill Jesus' teaching: "Where your treasure is, there will your heart be also" (Matt 6:21 KJV). That describes Jesus' life of filial freedom, his soul hungering and thirsting for his Father's pleasure. In the Tenth Word, he calls us to the same freedom. Life is a treasure hunt. We seek a place to place our hearts, where we find the weighty treasures that lighten our souls.

ENDNOTES

For *The Ten Commandments*

1. See Christopher R. Seitz, "The Ten Commandments: Positive and Natural Law and the Covenants Old and New—Christian Use of the Decalogue and Moral Law," in *I Am the Lord Your God: Christian Reflections on the Ten Commandments*, ed. Carl E. Braaten and Christopher R. Seitz (Grand Rapids: Eerdmans, 2005), 18–38.

2. "Yahweh" transliterates God's name, which is also represented by YHWH. It's often rendered as LORD or LORD. Since it's a personal name, not a title, I have chosen to transliterate it.

3. Clement of Alexandria (*Stromata* 6.16) links ten to creation, listing "Decalogues" of heaven, earth, and human nature.

4. Origen links Sinai's third day to Jesus' resurrection in *Homilies on Genesis* 8.4.

5. Victor P. Hamilton, *Exodus: An Exegetical Commentary* (Grand Rapids: Baker Academic, 2011), 64.

6. In sixteenth-century English, "thou" was singular and "you" or "ye" plural.

7. Yahweh's command to Adam was also delivered on a mountain, Eden (Ezek 28:13–14).

8. Edward L. Greenstein, "The Rhetoric of the Ten Commandments," in *The Decalogue in Jewish and Christian Traditions*, ed. Hennig Graf Reventlow and Yair Hoffman (London: T&T Clark, 2011), 11. See Stanley M. Hauerwas and William H. Willimon, *The Truth about God: The Ten Commandments in Christian Life* (Nashville: Abingdon, 1999), 19.

9. Thomas Aquinas points out that denials are more open-ended than affirmations. If you say, "It's white," you deny it's black. If you say,

"It's not black," it could be white, red, blue, yellow, or orange (*Summa Theologiae* I–II, q. 100, art. 7).

10. John Wesley applies the words of Hebrews to the law: Like Jesus, the law is "the express image of his glory." Wesley concludes that the law is "divine virtue and wisdom in a visible form." Quoted in D. Stephen Long, "John Wesley," in *The Decalogue through the Centuries: From the Hebrew Scriptures to Benedict XVI*, ed. Jeffrey P. Greenman and Timothy Larsen (Louisville: Westminster John Knox, 2012), 174. Clement of Alexandria offers an imaginative numero-alphabetic interpretation: *yod* is the tenth letter of the Hebrew alphabet and the first letter of "Jeshua." Hence: the Ten Words speak of Jesus the Word (*Stromata* 6.16).

11. Augustine, *Against Faustus* 22.24.

12. Irenaeus, *Against Heresies* 4.16.6.

13. Augustine, *Sermon* 155.6.

14. See my discussion in "Don't Do, Don't Desire," Theopolis Institute, January 7, 2019, https://theopolisinstitute.com/leithart/dont-do-dont-desire.

15. Cited in Thomas Aquinas, *Summa Theologiae* I–II, q. 100, art. 4. Thomas agrees with Augustine.

16. Origen, *Homily 8 on Exodus*.

17. For a defense of Augustine, see Jason S. DeRouchie, "Counting the Ten: An Investigation into the Numbering of the Decalogue," in *For Our Good Always: Studies on the Message and Influence of Deuteronomy in Honor of Daniel I. Block*, ed. Jason S. DeRouchie, Jason Gile, and Kenneth J. Turner (Winona Lake, IN: Eisenbrauns, 2013), 93–125. See my response: "Counting to Ten," Theopolis Institute, February 18, 2019, https://theopolisinstitute.com/leithart/counting-to-ten.

18. Caesarius of Arles, *Sermon* 100a.

19. Meredith G. Kline, "The Two Tables of the Covenant," *Westminster Theological Journal* 22 (1960): 133–46.

20. So Philo, *De Decalogo*, cited in Paul Grimley Kuntz, *The Ten Commandments in History: Mosaic Paradigms for a Well-Ordered Society* (Grand Rapids: Eerdmans, 2004), 16–17.

21. In Hebrew, each letter has a numerical value. A gematria is the numerical sum of the letters of a word. Twenty-six is the gematria of "YHWH."

22. The first five words form a chiastic unit of their own: Peter Leithart, "Chiasm of Five Words," Theopolis Institute, November 29, 2018, https://theopolisinstitute.com/leithart/chiasm-of-five-words.

23. See Eduard Nielsen, *The Ten Commandments in New Perspective* (Naperville, IL: Alex R. Allenson, 1968).

24. Two angels visit Sodom, Moses and Aaron witness before Pharaoh, Elijah and Elisha call Ahab to repentance, two witnesses appear in the city where the Lord was crucified (Rev 11).

25. Justin, *Dialogue with Trypho the Jew* 93.10.

26. Irenaeus, *Against Heresies* 4.16.3–4.

27. Augustine, *On Faith and Works* 11.17.

28. Bernd Wannenwetsch speaks of the "perichoretic" character of the Decalogue, each commandment indwelt by the others ("You Shall Not Kill," 148). See also John M. Frame, *The Doctrine of the Christian Life* (Phillipsburg, NJ: P&R, 2008), who sees each individual commandment as a "perspective" on the whole.

29. Martin Luther, Lecture on Genesis 39:15 (WA 44:369.5–6), quoted in Wannenwetsch, "You Shall Not Kill," 162n46.

30. The phrase is from G. K. Beale, *We Become What We Worship: A Biblical Theology of Idolatry* (Downers Grove, IL: IVP Academic, 2008), 41.

31. Thomas Aquinas, *Summa Theologiae* I–II, q. 100, art. 6.

32. Luther, *Large Catechism*, in *The Book of Concord*, ed. Robert Kolb and Timothy J. Wengert (Minneapolis: Fortress, 2000), cited in Timothy J. Wengert, "Martin Luther," 109. See also Luther, *Freedom of the Christian*: "Not by the doing of works but by believing do we glorify God and acknowledge that he is truthful. Therefore faith alone is the righteousness of a Christian and the fulfilling of all the commandments, for he who fulfils the First Commandment has no difficulty in fulfilling all the rest" (LW 31:353).

33. Moshe Halbertal and Avishai Margalit's *Idolatry*, trans. Naomi Goldblum (Cambridge, MA: Harvard University Press, 1992), stresses the personal-relational element of idolatry.

34. Luther, *Small Catechism*, explanation of the first commandment.

35. The following paragraphs are indebted to David Powlison, "Idols of the Heart and 'Vanity Fair,'" *Journal of Biblical Counseling* 13, no. 2 (1995): 35–50.

36. David Bentley Hart, "God or Nothingness," in *I Am the Lord Your God: Christian Reflections on the Ten Commandments*, ed. Carl E. Braaten and Christopher R. Seitz (Grand Rapids: Eerdmans, 2005), 57–58.

37. Clement, *Stromata* 6.16.

38. Origen, *Exhortation to Martyrdom* 9.

39. Thus the Second and Seventh Words match each other, a hint that the first table of Five Words matches the second table. Moshe Halbertal and Avishai Margalit observe that adultery is the main biblical image for idolatry (*Idolatry*, trans. Naomi Goldblum [Cambridge, MA: Harvard University Press, 1992]). In the ancient world, images also had political uses. In prohibiting images, Yahweh forbids Israel to enter alliances with idolaters. See Gary North, *The Sinai Strategy: Economics and the Ten Commandments* (Tyler, TX: Institute for Christian Economics, 1986), 29–38.

40. Luther, *Large Catechism* in *Book of Concord*. According to the enumeration Luther follows, this blessing and curse is attached to the first commandment.

41. Luther even called the ear *the* Christian organ. Lecture on Hebrews 10:5 (LW 29:224).

42. Guy Debord, *Society of the Spectacle*, trans. Ken Knabb (London: Rebel Press, 2004).

43. Halbertal and Margalit, *Idolatry*, 37–66.

44. "God of Abraham, Isaac, and Jacob" is nearly Yahweh's surname.

45. Origen, *On Prayer* 24.2–3.

46. Eusebius (*Proof of the Gospel* 5.16.243) sees a hint of the Father-Son relation in the Ten Words. Yahweh first speaks of himself as "I Yahweh," then of his name in the third person. Eusebius writes, "The second Lord is here mystically instructing his servant about the Father."

47. See Patrick D. Miller, *The Ten Commandments*, Interpretation: Resources for the Use of Scripture in the Church (Louisville: Westminster John Knox, 2009), 65, 68.

48. Hauerwas and Willimon, *Truth about God*, 47.

49. Miller, *Ten Commandments*, 82, 87, 97.

50. The verb "bear" is used in Exod 19:4, where Yahweh says he "carried" Israel to Sinai on eagle's wings. Because he bore them, they are to

bear him. Elsewhere in Exodus, the verb means "forgive" or "pardon" (Exod 32:32; 34:7). Yahweh has carried away Israel's sins, and for that reason they bear his name.

51. Ephraim Radner has explored this shift in "Taking the Lord's Name in Vain," 77–84.

52. I'm riffing on Ephraim Radner, "Taking the Lord's Name in Vain," 84–94.

53. Rabanus Maurus, *Commentary on Exodus*, cited in Radner, "Taking the Lord's Name in Vain," 92.

54. The phrase is from Ramon Lull, *De proverbiis moralibus, tertia pars caput VIII–Caput XVII, tome II*, in *Opera omnia* 42 (Mainz, 1721; repr., Frankfurt am Main: Minerva, 1965), quoted in Kuntz, *Ten Commandments in History*, 53.

55. Miller, *Ten Commandments*, 118.

56. Augustine, *Sermon* 8.6; *Letter* 55; *Tractate on John* 20.2.

57. Caesarius of Arles, *Sermon* 100.4.

58. Augustine, *Sermon* 179a.

59. Bede, *Homilies on the Gospels* 2.17.

60. See Karl Barth, *Church Dogmatics* III.4, §53.1 (p. 72): "He who has a self-renouncing faith on Sunday will have it also on a week-day. In the week he may and will work conscientiously and industriously, but neither as the lord nor as the slave of his work. ... In the week he will have to fix his eyes on one aim after another, yet not fall under the dominion of any material or spiritual, individual or collective Mammon. As he is busy on the everyday, he will also rest; as he fights on the everyday, he will also be at peace; as he works on the everyday, he will also pray."

61. "Interrupt" is from Barth, *Church Dogmatics* III.4, §53.1 (p. 50). Miller says that service of God is "routinized" by the Sabbath (*Ten Commandments*, 131).

62. Samson Raphael Hirsch, *Horeb: A Philosophy of Jewish Laws and Observances*, trans. I. Grunfeld, 2 vols. in 1 (New York: Soncino, 1962), 76–77.

63. David L. Baker, *Tight Fists or Open Hands? Wealth and Poverty in Old Testament Law* (Grand Rapids: Eerdmans, 2009), 294.

64. Miller, *Ten Commandments*, 138.

65. Joseph Ratzinger, *Collected Works*, vol. 2, *Theology of the Liturgy: The Sacramental Foundation of Christian Existence*, ed. Michael J. Miller, trans. John Saward et al. (San Francisco: Ignatius, 2014), 198–99.

66. Stanley Hauerwas and William Willimon, *The Truth about God: The Ten Commandments in Christian Life* (Nashville: Abingdon, 1999), 59.

67. Hauerwas and Willimon, *Truth about God*, 64.

68. Abraham J. Heschel, "A Palace in Time," in *The Ten Commandments: The Reciprocity of Faithfulness*, ed. William P. Brown (Louisville: Westminster John Knox, 2004), 214–22.

69. Thomas Aquinas, *Summa Theologiae* I–II, q. 100, art. 5.

70. Miller puts it nicely: The ethic of response is also an ethic of correspondence (*Ten Commandments*, 125).

71. Miller, *Ten Commandments*, 202.

72. According to the *Westminster Larger Catechism* (q. 124), "father and mother" represents "not only natural parents, but all superiors in age and gifts; and especially such as, by God's ordinance, are over us in place of authority, whether in family, church, or commonwealth." Luther agrees that the commandment refers to "parents and other authorities" (*Small Catechism*).

73. This implies also that civil, social, church, and economic leaders should rule with quasi-parental solicitude.

74. "Father *and* mother" is a biblical refrain (Exod 21:15; Prov 1:8; 6:20; 15:20; 30:17). If the father is king, the mother is queen.

75. Barth, *Church Dogmatics* III.4, §54.2 (p. 245).

76. Barth, *Church Dogmatics* III.4, §54.2 (pp. 255–59).

77. Patristic writers commonly assume that the commandment addresses adults. Honoring parents, Origen says, includes sharing "the necessaries of life, such as food and clothing" (*Commentary on Matthew* 11.9). See also Ambrose, *The Patriarchs* 1.1; Jerome, *Letter* 123.6; Augustine, *Sermon* 45.2. See Miller, *Ten Commandments*, 170–74; Hauerwas and Willimon, *Truth about God*, 71.

78. Note the order!

79. See Miller, *Ten Commandments*, 172–73.

80. Miller, *Ten Commandments*, 184.

81. Who is Israel's mother? Israel is "son," but also "bride" of Yahweh and "mother" of her children. Honoring the mother means honoring the traditions, habits, reputation of the people of God. Specifically,

it means honoring leaders, who serve as "nursemaids" to the people (Num 11:12). Moses asks: Did I conceive and bring forth this people? (Num 11:12). The answer is no, and the implication is that Yahweh is "mother" as well as Father of Israel. Clement of Alexandria suggests that Wisdom is Israel's mother (*Stromata* 6.16).

82. Samson Raphael Hirsch writes that human beings are temples of the living God, and we dare not attack God's holy house (*Horeb*, 224). Philo too saw murder as sacrilegious theft "from its sanctuary of the most sacred of God's possessions," cited in Kuntz, *Ten Commandments in History*, 19.

83. James B. Jordan, *Studies in Exodus: Lecture Notes* (Niceville, FL: Biblical Horizons, 1992), 65.

84. See Miller, *Ten Commandments*, 224–31.

85. Augustine, *On Lying* 13.23. Thomas Aquinas agrees (*Summa Theologiae* I–II, q. 100, art. 8): The commandment prohibits undue killing, but the death penalty is *not* undue killing.

86. See Miller, *Ten Commandments*, 234–38.

87. Cavanaugh, "Killing in the Name of God," 127–47, esp. 131.

88. Hauerwas and Willimon, *Truth about God*, 80.

89. Hauerwas and Willimon, *Truth about God*, 87. See also the searing analysis in various books by Andrew Bacevich.

90. Cavanaugh, "Killing in the Name of God," 147.

91. Bernd Wannenwetsch, "You Shall Not Kill," 168–69.

92. Robert W. Jenson, *Systematic Theology*, vol. 2, *The Works of God* (Oxford: Oxford University Press, 1999), 88.

93. Cited in Wannenwetsch, "You Shall Not Kill," 152–53, 156.

94. As John Paul II put it, pornography detaches desire for the body from the "spousal" meaning of the body. Our bodies are designed for personal union, not for masturbatory pleasure.

95. Jenson, *Works of God*, 88–91.

96. The following paragraph depends on Karl Barth, *Church Dogmatics* III.4.

97. Clement, *Stromata* 6.16.

98. Jenson, "Male and Female He Created Them," 187.

99. Adultery is mentioned in the prophets far more than in the Torah (Isa 57:3; cf. Jer 3:8–9; Ezek 16, 23).

100. According to Thomas Aquinas, this is the deep rationale for the Bible's prohibition of premarital sex. An adulterous man doesn't give a body that belongs to his wife to his mistress. He gives "the body of Christ" that was given at baptism. If a man must not betray his wife, "with much more reason must he not be unfaithful to Christ?" (Thomas, *Catechetical Instructions* 102, cited in Hauerwas and Willimon, *Truth about God*, 94).

101. This is preferable to imprisonment. If I go to prison for stealing $100, the victim never gets his $100 back, and I pay far more than $100 in time, loss of reputation, despair, criminalization. I pay "debt to society," but I never pay what I owe to the victim. Restitution punishes the criminal in proportion to his crime *and* protects the rights of victims.

102. Hirsch, *Horeb*, 233.

103. Miller, *Ten Commandments*, 319.

104. We get a glimpse of this in the laws of purity. A person becomes unclean because of various bodily functions (Lev 15), or by contact with an animal carcass or a dead body (Lev 11; Num 19). A person's *clothing* also becomes unclean, so that when he cleanses himself, he has to wash his clothes as well as his body. Houses can also be defiled by mold or "leprosy" (Lev 14). Clothing and living spaces are extensions of persons, and share in the state of purity or impurity.

105. Did you read the fine print when you signed up for Facebook?

106. Hirsch, *Horeb*, 236, emphasizes the necessity of truthful words in economic life.

107. Thomas Aquinas, *Summa Theologiae* II-II, q. 66. Cited in Hauerwas and Willimon, *Truth about God*, 106.

108. Quoted in Wengert, "Martin Luther," 116.

109. Miller, *Ten Commandments*, 322, 329.

110. Hirsch, *Horeb*, 249.

111. Clement of Alexandria accused the astrologers of his day of theft because they stole control of fortune from God and gave it to the stars (*Stromata* 6.16).

112. Brueggemann, "Truth-Telling," 292.

113. Miller, *Ten Commandments*, 344–45.

114. Think of the dramatic effect of America's civil rights laws and court decisions, especially in the South.

115. Brueggemann, "Truth-Telling," 293.

116. A point made by Hirsch, *Horeb*, 265. See my exploration of the usage at "False Answer," Theopolis Institute, December 7, 2018, https://theopolisinstitute.com/leithart/false-answer.

117. Martin Luther, *Small Catechism*.

118. Hirsch, *Horeb*, 251.

119. The notion that social media use is "brand management" comes from my Theopolis colleague Alastair Roberts.

120. This is from the work of A. C. Kruyt, cited by J. Douma, *The Ten Commandments: Manual for the Christian Life*, trans. Nelson D. Kloosterman (Phillipsburg, NJ: P&R, 1996), 322–23.

121. Vaclav Havel, "The Power of the Powerless," history.hanover.edu/courses/excerpts/165havel.html.

122. Hauerwas and Willimon, *Truth about God*, 120.

123. Augustine, *On Lying*. See his statement, e.g., in 5.6. Paul J. Griffiths defends and updates Augustine's position in *Lying: An Augustinian Theology of Duplicity* (Eugene, OR: Wipf & Stock, 2010). In contrast, Jerome distinguished lying into three categories (malicious, useful, humorous), only one of which was wrong (malicious). See Augustine, *Letter* 28 to Jerome and Jerome's commentary on Gal 2:11–14.

124. Hauerwas and Willimon, *Truth about God*, 124.

125. Dante, *Purgatorio*, canto 17.

126. The modern prophet of "mimetic desire" is René Girard.

127. Ferdinand Mount, *Full Circle: How the Classical World Came Back to Us* (New York: Simon & Schuster, 2010).

128. Vera Pavlova, "I am in love, hence free to live," trans. Steven Seymour, *Poetry*, January 2010, https://www.poetryfoundation.org/poetrymagazine/poems/53191/i-am-in-love-hence-free-to-live.

129. Augustine, *Sermon* 26.9.

THE APOSTLES' CREED

Ben Myers

PREFACE

THE CHRISTIAN FAITH IS MYSTERIOUS not because it is so complicated but because it is so simple. A person does not start with baptism and then advance to higher mysteries. In baptism each believer already possesses the faith in its fullness. The whole of life is encompassed in the mystery of baptism: dying with Christ and rising with him through the Spirit to the glory of God. That is how the Christian life begins, and to seek to move beyond that beginning is really to regress. In discipleship, the one who makes the most progress is the one who remains at the beginning. And that is where theological thinking comes in handy. Theology does not have all the right answers, but it can help us to contemplate the reality of baptism and to penetrate more deeply into its meaning for life.

That is why I wrote this book. Not because anyone needs to be told what to believe but because Christ's followers have everything they need already. "All things are yours," says Paul: "all belong to you, and you belong to Christ, and Christ belongs to God" (1 Cor 3:21–23). We are not beggars hoping for scraps. We are like people who have inherited a vast estate: we have to study the documents and visit different locations because it's more than we can take in at a single glance. In the same way, it takes considerable time and effort to begin to comprehend all that we have received in Christ. Theological thinking does not add a single thing to what we have received. The inheritance remains the same whether we grasp its magnitude or not. But the better we grasp it, the happier we are.

So this small book is an invitation to happiness. I have written it with a glad heart, and I hope it will be helpful for others who want to comprehend the mystery of faith in all its "breadth and length and height and depth, and to know the love of Christ that surpasses knowledge" (Eph 3:18–19).

The book began life as a series of sermons on the creed at Leichhardt Uniting Church in Sydney. I am grateful to the Rev. Dr. John Hirt and to the Leichhardt congregation for their friendship and hospitality on that occasion. To them this book is affectionately dedicated. The sermons were long, and the book is short. In both cases I take comfort from the words of Irenaeus: "Since the faith is one and the same, the one who says much about it does not add to it, nor does the one who says little diminish it."[1]

I. **I BELIEVE IN GOD THE FATHER ALMIGHTY,**
maker of heaven and earth,

II. **AND IN JESUS CHRIST, GOD'S ONLY SON, OUR LORD:**
who was conceived by the Holy Spirit,
born of the Virgin Mary,
suffered under Pontius Pilate,
was crucified, died, and was buried.
He descended into hell.
On the third day he rose again
from the dead.

He ascended into heaven and is seated

at the right hand of the Father.

He will come again to judge

the living and the dead.

III. **I BELIEVE IN THE HOLY SPIRIT,**

the holy catholic church,

the communion of saints,

the forgiveness of sins,

the resurrection of the body,

and the life everlasting.

AMEN.

INTRODUCTION

The Ancient Catechism

O N THE EVE OF EASTER Sunday, a group of believers has stayed up all night in a vigil of prayer, scriptural reading, and instruction. The most important moment of their lives is fast approaching. For years they have been preparing for this day.

When the rooster crows at dawn, they are led out to a pool of flowing water. They remove their clothes. The women let down their hair and remove their jewelry. They renounce Satan and are anointed from head to foot with oil. They are led naked into the water. Then they are asked a question: "Do you believe in God the Father Almighty?" They reply, "I believe!" And they are plunged down in the water and raised up again.

They are asked a second question: "Do you believe in Christ Jesus, the Son of God, who was born of the Holy Spirit and Mary the virgin and was crucified under Pontius Pilate and was dead and buried and rose on the third day alive from the dead and ascended in the heavens and sits at the right hand of the Father and will come to judge the living and the dead?" Again they confess, "I believe!" And again they are immersed in the water.

Then a third question: "Do you believe in the Holy Spirit and the holy church and the resurrection of the flesh?" A third time they cry, "I believe!" And a third time they are immersed. When they emerge from the water they are again anointed with oil. They are clothed, blessed, and led into the assembly of believers, where they will share for the first time in the eucharistic meal. Finally they are sent out into the world to do good works and to grow in faith.

That is how baptism is described in an early third-century document known as the *Apostolic Tradition.*[2] It points to the ancient roots of the Apostles' Creed. The creed comes from baptism. It is a pledge of allegiance to the God of the gospel—a God who is revealed as Father, Son, and Holy Spirit; a God who is present to us in the real world of human flesh, creating, redeeming, and sanctifying us for good works.

It is often said that creeds are political documents, the cunning invention of bishops and councils who are trying to enforce their own understanding of orthodoxy. In the case of the Apostles' Creed, nothing could be further from the truth. It was not created by a council. It was not part of any deliberate theological strategy. It was a grassroots confession of faith. It was an indigenous form of the ancient church's response to the risen Christ, who commanded his apostles to "make disciples of all nations, baptizing them in the name of the Father and of the Son and of the Holy Spirit" (Matt 28:19–20). The Nicene Creed is a different matter, since it was formulated by two church councils in the fourth century. But even that creed is essentially an enlargement and clarification of the ancient baptismal confession.

Later generations of believers sometimes said that each of the twelve apostles had written one line of the creed—hence the name "Apostles' Creed." It is a charming legend that conveys a deep truth: that the baptismal confession is rooted in the faith of the apostles, and ultimately in the word of the risen Christ himself.

By the second century, the basic form of the creed can be found in widely dispersed Christian communities. Irenaeus, a pastor in second-century Gaul, speaks of a threefold "rule" or "canon" that defines the faith of all Christians throughout the world:

> The church, indeed, though disseminated throughout the world, even to the ends of the earth, received from the apostles and their disciples the faith in one God the Father Almighty, the creator of heaven and earth and the seas and all things that are in them; and in the one Jesus Christ, the Son of God, who was enfleshed for our salvation; and in the Holy Spirit, who through the prophets preached the economies. ... The church ... carefully guards this preaching and this faith which she has received, as if she dwelt in one house. She likewise believes these things as if she had but one soul and one and the same heart. She preaches, teaches, and hands them down harmoniously, as if she

possessed but one mouth. For though the languages throughout the world are different, nevertheless the meaning of the tradition is one and the same.[3]

This rule of faith had two functions. First, it was educational. It formed the basis of catechesis for new believers. In the period of preparation for baptism, new adherents to the Christian faith would memorize the creedal formula and would receive instruction in its meaning. The threefold confession of faith was to be written on the heart so that it could never be lost or forgotten. That way, all believers would have a basic guide to the interpretation of Scripture, and even illiterate believers would be able to retain the substance of the biblical story. They would see Scripture as a unified witness to one God—Father, Son, and Holy Spirit. And they would see the created world as the domain of God's activity: God creates our world, becomes incarnate in it, and will ultimately redeem it fully in the resurrection of the dead. That is how the Christian mind was formed by the ancient catechism.

Second, the rule of faith was sacramental. It was not only used as a catechism in preparation for baptism but was also part of the baptismal rite itself. A person becomes a disciple of Jesus and a member of his community by making the threefold pledge of allegiance. Baptism is a threefold immersion into the life of God. "The baptism of our regeneration takes place through these three articles, granting us regeneration unto God the Father through his Son by the Holy Spirit."[4] The creedal words are words of power. They are words that perform: like naming a yacht, or making a bet, or speaking a marriage vow. In baptism, something is brought into being as the words are spoken. It is the words, just as much as the water, that make a baptism. By these words a person becomes a disciple of Jesus and a member of his community.

So the creed is both informative and performative,[5] both educational and sacramental. It is a summary of Christian teaching as well as a solemn pledge of allegiance. These two functions of the creed can be distinguished but not separated. Catechesis is necessary so that we can make the baptismal declaration with understanding and with genuine commitment. And in turn the baptismal confession orders our thinking about God and the world.

Even today the creed provides a framework—strong yet surprisingly flexible—for Christian thinking and Christian commitment.

ARTICLE I

I believe in God,
the Father Almighty,
maker of heaven and earth

ALMIGHTY FATHER, you have made heaven and earth by the power of your Word, and you have created faith in us by the power of that same Word. Instill in us deep and abiding trust, so that in believing we may come to understand, and in understanding we may more perfectly love you and your Son, Jesus Christ, who, with you and the Holy Spirit, is worthy to be trusted and glorified, now and forever. **AMEN.**

I

THE FIRST WORD IS PERHAPS the strangest part of the whole Apostles' Creed: "I." Who is this I? Whose voice is speaking in the creed?

I have been to wedding ceremonies where the couple write their own vows. It is a recent custom that reflects wider cultural changes. In the past, one of the things that made a wedding special was the fact that you got to say exactly the same words that everybody else said. When a couple said their vows, they weren't just expressing their own feelings. They didn't use their own words; they used the same words that their parents and their ancestors had spoken, and they made those words their own.

But today we are skeptical about the past. We are skeptical about anything that is merely handed down to us. We assume that the truest thing we could ever say would be something we had made up ourselves.

In the same way, Christians today are often suspicious of creeds. Many churches are more comfortable with mission statements than with creeds. The thing about a mission statement is you always get to make it up for yourself. It's like writing your own wedding vows.

But here's the paradox. It is the individualized confession, like the personalized wedding vow, that ends up sounding like an echo of the wider society. What could be more conformist than expressing your feelings of love through your own specially crafted wedding vow? The wedding is a grand occasion, so you want to make it special: but the more you try to personalize it, the more it degenerates into triviality and cliché. The ceremonial quality evaporates. Or again, what could be more conformist than a mission statement? Every company has one. And although each one is unique, they all sound eerily similar, as if all the companies in the world were out to achieve the same blandly generic aims. I think there is a similar dynamic at work in many churches today. The harder they try to be special and unique, the more they seem exactly like everybody else.

By contrast, to confess the creed is to take up a countercultural stance. When we say the creed we are not just expressing our own views or our own priorities. We are joining our voices to a great communal voice that calls out across the centuries from every tribe and tongue. We locate ourselves as part of that community that transcends time and place. That gives us a critical distance from our own time and place. If our voices are still echoes, they are now echoing something from beyond our own cultural moment.

"I believe." Who is the "I" that speaks when we make that confession? It is the body of Christ. It is a community stretched out across history, "terrible as an army with banners" (Song 6:10). The whole company of Christ's followers goes down into the waters of baptism, crying out the three-fold "I believe!" In baptism nobody is invited to come up with their own personal statement of belief. All are invited to be immersed into a reality beyond themselves and to join their individual voices to a communal voice that transcends them all.

The truest and most important things we can ever say are not individual words but communal words. Most of the words of my life are trivial and fleeting. They fall from my lips and drift away like dead leaves. But in the creed I am invited to say true words. In confessing the faith of the church, I allow my own individual "I" to become part of the "I" of the body of Christ.

It is then that I am saying something of deep and lasting importance. It is then that my words have roots.

BELIEVE

WHEN POLITICIANS MAKE PROMISES, WE don't really expect them to keep their word. We understand that promises are motivated by self-interest, that words are tactics to achieve other aims. And we're not just cynical about other people's promises. We lack confidence in our own words too. We make solemn promises of lifelong commitment—after signing the prenuptial agreement. Our ability to trust has been eroded by the sad experience of broken promises, if not by a deeper cynicism about the capacity of words to bear truth.

Nevertheless, when we say the Apostles' Creed we are reminded that life itself is founded on trust. Christians in the ancient church went naked to the waters of baptism. The second birth is like the first. We are totally dependent. We bring nothing with us except life. The birth cry of baptism is the threefold "I believe" of the creed, a cry of total trust in the Triune God.

In North Africa toward the end of the fourth century, Augustine pointed out that life would be impossible without trust. Most of the things we know about the world are really things we believe on the basis of someone else's word. We can't verify for ourselves if events in world history have really happened. But we accept testimonies that have come down to us from the past. We can't visit every location on a map to verify that they all really exist. But we accept the word of others who have been to those places. Closer to home, the family is knit together by trust. I wasn't there to witness the moment of my own conception. If I want to know who my father is, I will have to take my mother's word for it. And I gladly accept her word: I would prefer to trust her than to seek independent verification. It would diminish me as a person if I went around trying to verify everything. Only by adopting an attitude of trust am I able to live and flourish as a human being. Without trust, Augustine says, "we would be unable to do anything in this life."[6]

Obviously not every family is an exemplar of loving trust, and not every parent proves to be trustworthy. But Augustine's point is that we don't have the resources to verify everything for ourselves. Social life is woven together by threads of trust. If I really wanted to live without trust I would need to remove myself from society and live in total isolation. But even then, I would need to rely on tools and technologies that I did not invent and that I do not fully understand. I would need to trust the work of others.

The tragic quality of life comes partly from the fact that human beings are not always trustworthy, yet still we cannot live without trust.

The gospel holds out to us the promise of a totally trustworthy God. Can we verify that promise? Augustine's answer, surprisingly, is yes. Over time we learn that God's promise is worthy of our trust. God's trustworthiness is verified by experience. But we don't start with verification. We start with trust: this leads to experience: and experience leads to knowledge of God's trustworthiness. Augustine says, "If you can't understand, believe, and then you'll understand."[7]

That doesn't mean that Christian belief is an irrational leap into the dark. It is more like tasting a dish that you have never tried. You have seen other people enjoying it; you have read the reviews; the chef swears you'll like it. There are good grounds for trusting, but you will never know for sure until you try it. "Taste and see that the LORD is good," sings the psalmist (Ps 34:8). The first act is an act of trust that gives rise to ever-increasing certainty, which in turn nourishes a deeper and a more knowledgeable trust.

The creed is full of mysterious things. It speaks of things that I can't immediately observe or verify for myself. I believe in God the Creator. I believe in Jesus Christ, God-become-flesh in the midst of creation. I believe in the Holy Spirit, God invisibly transfiguring creation from within. How could I prove the truth of these statements? How could I know for sure? When I take the first step, I start to see the whole world through the eyes of God's promise. I start to live in an environment of trust. And then I learn from experience that God is good—"as good as his word," as the saying goes.

IN GOD THE FATHER

WHAT DO WE BELIEVE ABOUT GOD? Right away the creed uses the language of Scripture: God is "Father." It is an echo of revelation when Christians use this word. It is not an idea based on speculation or philosophical reasoning. Jesus reveals God as his "Father." He relates to God as his own Father and invites his followers to share in the same relationship. He calls God "my Father and your Father" (John 20:17), and "your heavenly Father" (Matt 6:14). He teaches his disciples to pray, "Our Father" (Matt 6:9)—that is, to stand alongside Jesus and to address God in the same way Jesus does.

Jesus' relationship to God is unique but also inclusive. His followers stand on the inside of Jesus' unique relationship to God. Jesus calls God "Abba, Father" (Mark 14:36), and his followers are empowered by the Holy Spirit to pray in the same way (Rom 8:15–16). That is what it means to be baptized into the Triune God. By the Spirit we are immersed into the life of Jesus so that we come to share in his position before God.

We speak to God, and God listens to us, as if we were Jesus. Jesus is God's child by nature, and we become God's children by grace. Jesus is born of God; we are adopted. So when we confess that God is "Father," it is not a theological idea but a confession of the defining relationship of our lives. We call God "Father" because that is what Jesus calls God, and because Jesus has invited us to relate to God in the same way. In other words, we call God "Father" because of revelation.

Today many Christians are uneasy about this word. Doesn't it give a privileged place to masculine language? Doesn't it imply that there is gender in God? Doesn't it reinforce the picture of an old bearded man in the sky? These might sound like contemporary concerns. But early Christian teachers were already very sensitive to these problems. They took pains to explain that the Bible uses the word "Father" without any connotations of gender. In fact, this was one of the things that distinguished Christian belief from ancient pagan ideas about the gods. There was a colorful cast of Greek and Roman gods. Some were male; some were female. They could be passionate, hot-headed, lustful, unpredictable. They could change their minds.

Early Christian teachers were careful to differentiate the God of the gospel from the gods of Greek and Roman culture. The pagan gods are many, but the God of Israel is One. The pagan gods can fly into a rage, but the true God is unchangeable and therefore totally reliable. The pagan gods can be inflamed with lust, but the true God seeks the good of humanity without any self-interest. The pagan gods can arbitrarily turn against human beings, but the true God consistently seeks our good. There was a special word for this in early Christian teaching: God's *philanthropia* (literally "love of humanity"). And while the pagan gods can be male or female, the true God totally transcends gender and the body.

When the fourth-century theologian Athanasius wanted to distinguish Christian belief from the pagan gods, he pointed out that the true God is "by nature incorporeal and invisible and untouchable."[8] In a sermon preached in Constantinople toward the end of the fourth century, Gregory of Nazianzus explained that the words "Father" and "Son" should be used without having any "bodily ideas" in our minds. Otherwise we would be back in paganism, imagining a God who physically procreated in order to bring forth a son. We use the words "Father" and "Son," Gregory says, "in a more elevated sense." We "accept the realities without being put off by the names." Ordinary family connotations cannot be applied to God, much less connotations of gender. "Do you take it," Gregory asks his congregation, "that our God is a male because of the masculine nouns 'God' and 'Father'? Is the 'Godhead' a female because in Greek the word is feminine?" Such crude biological thinking would be pagan, not Christian.[9]

What then does the word "Father" mean? For Christians, the word describes a relationship and nothing more. Here is Gregory again: "'Father' designates neither the substance nor the activity, but the relationship, the manner of being, which holds good between the Father and the Son."[10] The Father is the source, the origin, the wellspring of divine life. And the

Son derives from that source. So there is a relationship of origin between Father and Son. According to early Christian teaching, that is all we are meant to think of when we say the word "Father." We purify our language of all thoughts of gender—otherwise we would be projecting our own assumptions onto God instead of listening to God's self-revelation. "Every bodily thought must be shunned in these matters,"[11] says Athanasius—not because Christians have an aversion to the body but because we have an aversion to the pagan gods!

If the word "Father" refers to a relation of origin within God, then we can draw one important conclusion: God is not only Father but also Son. These words, "Father" and "Son," are relational terms. Neither would make sense without the other. Writing in the second century, Tertullian was the first to develop this simple but important insight: "Father makes son, and son makes father. … A father must have a son to be a father, and a son must have a father to be a son."[12] When we confess that God is eternally Father, we always have in mind as well the eternal reality of the Son.

ALMIGHTY

"**P**OWER" IS NO LONGER A nice word. It has a decidedly sinister ring to it. When we speak of power we tend to think of dangerous relationships or of wider systems of domination and control.

But that is not how "might" or "power" is understood in Christian teaching. The early Christians often compared God to a breastfeeding mother: it is a favorite image in numerous sermons and writings from the ancient church. We relate to God not like loyal subjects submitting to a powerful ruler, but like infants drawing nourishment from a mother. God's power is not only above us but also alongside us, beneath us, and within us. It is not the power of subjection and control but a power that frees and enables. Augustine described the divine power as "maternal love, expressing itself as weakness."[13]

This is not like the power of the pagan gods who intervene in the world from time to time. God's might is everywhere present in creation. It is the underlying mystery of everything that exists. It is not just a solution to problems in this world. It is the reason there is a world at all.

We could not really trust in God if God's power were limited, sporadic, or unpredictable. A God who exercised that kind of power would be a pagan god: not the world's sustainer but its invader, or perhaps a distant ruler whose wishes have to be imposed by force.

That is the problem with trying to place any limitations on God's power. If God's power were just one power among others—if God were "mighty" but not "almighty"—then divine power would end up being another form of manipulation or control. Only a God who is totally free and totally sovereign can relate to the world with total love, patience, and generosity. There is power elsewhere in creation: each living thing has its own unique power and energy. But God does not have to compete with these other powers. God's power is their source, the reason why they exist at all. God's power is what sustains and nourishes the power of creatures.

True power is not the ability to control. Controlling behavior is a sign of weakness and insecurity. True power is the ability to love and enable without reserve. God's power, like the power of a good parent or teacher, is the capacity to nourish other agents and to help their freedom to grow. Without the "sovereignty" of a good parent, children have a diminished sense of their own worth and their own agency. In the same way, God's sovereignty is what secures human freedom, not what threatens it.

In the creed we confess the three great movements of God's power: God lovingly brought the world into being; God lovingly entered the womb and became part of the world in Jesus Christ; and God the Holy Spirit is lovingly transfiguring the world in the lives of the saints.

At every point, God's power is hidden. It is a "gentle omnipotence,"[14] as the British theologian Sarah Coakley has said. God is invisibly almighty in the act of creation, invisibly almighty in the womb of the Virgin, invisibly almighty in the darkness of the tomb, invisibly almighty in the company of believers and in the communal life they share.

The world lives because of this gentle but all-embracing power, and we are free because of it.

MAKER OF HEAVEN
AND EARTH

IN THE SECOND CENTURY, CHRISTIAN teachers struggled to define their beliefs and commitments in opposition to popular rival teachings. The prevailing cultural mood was one of deep spiritual pessimism. Members of the educated class took it for granted that the physical world was inherently evil and irredeemable. They yearned to escape from the world of the flesh and to experience spiritual enlightenment.

Marcion, a charismatic teacher of the second century, had said that the material universe was created by a wicked and incompetent god. Marcion was especially disgusted by the human body, "flesh stuffed with dung" as he called it. Like some of the gnostic teachers of the same period, he was horrified by sex. He viewed procreation as a monstrous evil. Marcion's followers had to adapt their lives to an austere renunciation of sex, marriage, and childrearing. Natural bonds were dissolved; only spiritual bonds were of any value.[15]

Marcion's doctrine was not the only challenge to the emerging Christian movement. The second century witnessed the proliferation of spiritual sects whose adherents were known as gnostics (literally "knowers"). Gnostic teachers claimed to have secret knowledge about the cosmos and the soul. They taught that the physical world was created by an inferior deity and that salvation consisted in escaping from the material world by means of esoteric wisdom. Such teachings were very diverse, but what they had in common was a dualism that divided the (bad) creator from the (good) redeemer and the (bad) world of flesh from the (good) human spirit.

The Christian baptismal confession developed, in part, in response to such world-denying doctrines and the wider culture of despair that had engendered them. Right from the start, Christians were marked by their positive stance toward creation. The Gospel of John begins by retelling Israel's creation story: "In the beginning ..." (John 1:1; Gen 1:1). The followers of Jesus believed that in him they had encountered the enabling source of creation. They had come to know the one through whom "all things were made" (John 1:3). Looking into the face of Jesus, they had seen the blueprint of reality and had come to understand God's good plan for the whole creation.

It was spiritually countercultural to be baptized into this world-affirming faith. The ancient Christians refused to see anything in the world as inherently evil. They confessed that everything in this world has been made by the good and wise God whom they had come to know in Jesus.

Part of the appeal of Gnosticism lay in its response to the problem of evil. Why is there so much evil and suffering in this world? It is, the gnostic teachers reasoned, because the world is the product of an evil god; the very stuff of creation is deficient. That is an elegant solution to the problem of evil. But it raises even worse problems. If previously I had been tormented by experiences of suffering and injustice, after accepting the gnostic doctrine I come to see my very existence as an intolerable injustice. Previously I had been at home in the world and had protested against the disagreeable parts of life. But now I find that the world is no longer my home at all. I am radically alienated from life—the life of all creatures, the life of human society, and my own life. My spiritual existence is a lonely spark of goodness in an overwhelmingly hostile world from which I want to flee and whose destruction I yearn for.

That is how it felt to be a gnostic in the ancient world. I start out wanting a solution to the problem of evil and end up experiencing the whole creation, including my own body, as a vast satanic prison. The gnostic is like a person who sees a red wine stain on the carpet and cannot think of any solution except to cover the rest of the floor in wine. The stain is no longer visible: but at what cost? Gnosticism solves the problem of evil only by transforming everything into evil.

In response to such world-denying visions, early Christian teachers argued that everything in creation is good. Evil, properly speaking, does not exist at all. There are no evil entities, only good ones created by a good God. When a creature fails to be properly itself, when it turns away from its own nature and purpose, then it becomes a deficient version of itself. It is evil to the extent that it now lacks something essential to its own nature. A guitar makes an evil sound when it goes out of tune; its "evil" is not a positive quality but only a deficiency. Or to use the favorite illustration in the ancient church, evil is the absence of good qualities just as darkness is the absence of light. The upshot of all this is that evil cannot be attributed to the Creator. The fourth-century Cappadocian teacher Gregory of Nyssa put it like this: "If a man in broad daylight freely chooses to shut his eyes, it is not the sun's fault when he fails to see."[16]

This is not to say that evil is insignificant. Its consequences are real and devastating. But when we experience those consequences we are experiencing the effects of a deprivation of goodness. Imagine if I were to murder someone by striking them with my reading lamp. The lamp is good when it is used well, and the strength of my arm is a gift of God, but these good things become evil when they are used for the wrong purpose. The consequences of that murder would be very real. There are moral problems here about the way creatures use their freedom, but these are not metaphysical problems about whether creation is good or evil.

Though many evil things happen in this world, Christians confess that we are still living in God's good creation. It is a sick world that needs healing, not an evil world that needs destruction. That is the difference between Christianity and Gnosticism.

It is often said that creeds are narrow and intolerant. But in the ancient world the truth was exactly the opposite. It was the Christian creed that took a stand on behalf of creation. It was the creed that said "no" to those doctrines that condemned creation, disparaged the body, and sought escape from the world of the flesh. Gnosticism was the most comprehensive intolerance imaginable. It was intolerance of the universe and of life and of whatever it means to be human. In saying "no" to Gnosticism, the church says "yes" to the whole material universe.

ARTICLE II

And in Jesus Christ, God's only Son, our Lord: who was conceived by the Holy Spirit, born of the Virgin Mary, suffered under Pontius Pilate, was crucified, died, and was buried. He descended into hell. On the third day he rose again from the dead. He ascended into heaven and is seated at the right hand of the Father. He will come again to judge the living and the dead.

OUR LORD JESUS CHRIST, in the virgin's womb you were made flesh for our salvation by the power of the Holy Spirit. Pour upon us that same Spirit, so that faith, hope, and love may be born in us, and that we, like Mary, may be ever receptive to your holy will. This we ask in your holy name. **AMEN**.

AND IN JESUS CHRIST, GOD'S ONLY SON, OUR LORD

W E TEND TO THINK OF creeds as cold didactic sum-
maries of doctrine. But the real centerpiece of the
Apostles' Creed is not a doctrine but a name.

Even before the ancient baptismal confession had taken
shape, perhaps the earliest Christian confession consisted of
just two words: *Kyrios Iēsous*, "Jesus is Lord" (Rom 10:9; 1
Cor 12:3). That early statement remains the spiritual heart-
beat of the baptismal creed. Everything else in the creed
radiates like the spokes of a wheel from that hub: personal
attachment to Jesus; total allegiance to him.

At the center of the Christian faith is not an idea or a
theory or even a vision of life but the name of a person, Jesus
Christ. Our faith centers on personal attachment to him. A
much later Christian confession, the Heidelberg Catechism
(1563), gives eloquent voice to the personal center of faith
when it begins with the question and answer: "What is your
only comfort in life and in death? That I am not my own, but

belong—body and soul, in life and in death—to my faithful Savior, Jesus Christ."

Attachment to Jesus is personal, but that is not to say that it's a private matter. Paul reminds the Philippians that one day all worldly powers and authorities will speak the name of Jesus and will confess that "Jesus Christ is Lord" (Phil 2:9–11). To confess Jesus as Lord means to acknowledge him as the one who shares the identity of Israel's God. In the Old Testament Scriptures God is named YHWH, *Kyrios*, Lord; and in the New Testament Jesus is revealed as the one who bears that name. So to confess Jesus as Lord is to set him above all other loyalties. It is to make a universal claim. If Jesus truly shares the identity of YHWH, then he is the hidden truth of creation, of history, and of every human life (Col 1:15–17). I confess him as *my* Lord only because I recognize him as *the* Lord.

Such a universal claim might sound insensitive or even oppressive to modern pluralistic ears. And it is true that Christians have at times used the universality of the gospel to justify oppression and injustice. Rightly understood, however, the message of Jesus' lordship is a word of comfort and hope for all people.

In the ancient church, the confession of Jesus' lordship began to change the way Christians thought about slavery. Christianity took root in societies that were rigidly stratified and hierarchical. There were clearly marked distinctions between men and women, rich and poor, Jews and gentiles, slaves and free. But the Christian community did not accept that people were defined by those social distinctions. All came to the same baptismal waters and confessed the same Lord. When they entered naked into the waters of baptism, no one could tell the difference between rich and poor, slave and free.

So even when the Christian movement had barely begun, we find Paul urging a believer to regard his Christian slave as "no longer a slave … but a beloved brother" (Phlm 16). By the fourth century, Gregory of Nyssa issued a scathing denunciation of the institution of slavery. Gregory didn't have access to modern ideas of individual rights and liberties. As he saw it, the problem with slavery was that it creates a false lordship. By making one person the master of another, human beings claim an authority that belongs only to God. As Gregory says to the slave owner, "you have forgotten the limits of your authority." The world has only one Lord—and this Lord "does not enslave," but "calls us to freedom."[17]

Because Jesus is the universal Lord, all worldly power is limited and provisional. Because he is Lord, social distinctions are relativized and will ultimately be set aside completely. All people owe their allegiance not to any other person but to Jesus. Before him they are able to recognize one another as sisters and brothers. And so the logic of universal lordship gives rise to an egalitarian ethic.

The ancient institution of slavery didn't vanish all at once. But when slaves and free persons stood side by side and confessed that Jesus is Lord, the days of slavery were numbered. When early believers entered the waters and took the name of Jesus on their lips, the tectonic plates shifted. The slow revolution had begun.

WHO WAS CONCEIVED BY THE HOLY SPIRIT

AT THE BEGINNING OF LUKE'S Gospel, the angel visits Mary and tells her that "the Holy Spirit will come upon you, and the power of the Most High will overshadow you" (Luke 1:35). This opening act of Jesus' story is meant to remind us of another beginning: "In the beginning God created the heavens and the earth. Now the earth was formless and empty, darkness was over the surface of the deep, and the Spirit of God was hovering over the waters" (Gen 1:1–2 NIV).

Creation occurs when the Spirit of God broods over the formless abyss and brings forth life out of nothing. Elsewhere the Old Testament writers speak of the divine Breath or Spirit as the source of creation: "When you send forth your spirit, they are created" (Ps 104:30). When God forms Adam from the ground in the second creation story, the man is at first a lifeless clay sculpture. But then God breathes spirit into the clay, and it becomes a living being (Gen 2:7).

So when the Spirit broods over the womb of Mary, we see a picture of God's creative work happening all over again. Jesus is brought into being by the creative breath of God's Spirit. A Christian pastor in the second century, Hippolytus, said that in the Virgin's womb the Son of God "refashioned the first-formed Adam in himself."[18] The first Adam led the human race astray. But here is a new Adam, a new beginning for the human family, a new ancestor who will lead us into life and joy.

In the third century, Origen of Alexandria came up with a striking image to illustrate the way Jesus' humanity was united to the eternal Son of God. He pictured a piece of iron placed in a fire until it is glowing with heat. This iron, he says,

> has become wholly fire, since nothing else is discerned in it except fire; and if anyone were to attempt to touch or handle it, he would feel the power not of iron but of fire. In this way, then, that soul [that is, Jesus' human soul] which, like iron in the fire, was placed in the Word forever, in Wisdom forever, in God forever, is God in all that it does, feels, and understands.[19]

Jesus is truly human: nothing but iron. He is truly divine: nothing but fire. Jesus is so permeated by the divine presence that every part of his humanity is filled with divine energy. He is born of a woman: he is conceived by God's Spirit. He is human: he is divine. He is iron: he is fire.

This way of thinking about Jesus' humanity and divinity is really just an attempt to make sense of the complex things that are said about Jesus in the Gospels. The Gospels portray

Jesus as someone whose life is drawn directly from the source of God's own creative energy. Even in his mother's womb, he is already the bearer of the Holy Spirit. In Luke's Gospel, the same Spirit that brooded over Mary's womb is always flashing out and touching the lives of those who come into contact with Jesus. When Mary greets her cousin Elizabeth, the baby in Elizabeth's womb leaps for joy and Elizabeth is filled with the Holy Spirit (Luke 1:41). In the sixth century, the Syrian preacher Jacob of Serug described the scene like this:

> The Son of God sent forth the Spirit … and the boy was baptized by the Holy Spirit while he was still in his mother's womb. At once the confined babe began preaching to prepare the way for the King who came from the house of David. A new message was heard from within the womb, a babe who leaps and exults and hurries to prepare the way.[20]

It is the same Spirit who flashes out when the woman with the flow of blood touches the hem of Jesus' clothes and is instantly healed (Matt 9:20–22). It is the same Spirit who, when Jesus lies dead in the tomb, breathes life into his body so that death is dissolved and the grave is emptied (Rom 8:11). And it is the same Spirit that flashes out on the day of Pentecost so that tongues of fire descend on Jesus' friends and they are transformed from a lifeless rabble of frightened followers into fearless witnesses of the resurrection (Acts 2:1–4). The same Spirit who rested on Jesus in his mother's womb now rests on the whole company of Jesus' followers.

Jesus is the bearer of the Spirit and the sender of the Spirit. In him, the Spirit creates a new beginning for the whole human race. That is what the church proclaims in the concise but astonishing words of the ancient catechism: "conceived by the Holy Spirit."

BORN OF THE
VIRGIN MARY

"I can't believe that!" said Alice.

"Can't you?" the Queen said in a pitying tone. "Try again: draw a long breath, and shut your eyes."

Alice laughed. "There's no use trying," she said: "one *can't* believe impossible things."

"I daresay you haven't had much practice," said the Queen. "When I was your age, I always did it for half-an-hour a day. Why, sometimes I've believed as many as six impossible things before breakfast."[21]

THERE ARE CHRISTIANS TODAY WHO take a similar view of the virgin birth. To them, the idea of the virgin birth is a relic of bygone days when people were simpler and found it easier to believe in impossible things. We can handle the rest of the creed, but the virgin birth stretches credulity too far.

The trouble starts when we take this line of the creed and view it in isolation. It would be like finding a bicycle chain if you had never seen a bicycle. You would struggle to make sense of the strange object: what is it for? Is it a weapon? Or an uncomfortable piece of jewelry? To understand the bicycle chain you have to see it in its proper context. It's the same with the virgin birth. If we take it in isolation we might conclude that it's just a spectacular miracle or even a logical absurdity. And then it becomes a sheer effort to try to believe it—as if saying the baptismal creed were the same as trying to believe six impossible things before breakfast.

To understand the virgin birth we need to see how it fits into the whole story of Scripture—a story in which miraculous births play a starring role.

Israel's story begins with a promise to Abraham and Sarah (Gen 12–17). A couple who cannot conceive are chosen by God and told that they will have a great family. Sarah laughs at the promise. But later, when she has given birth in her grand old age, the child is named Laughter (Hebrew: Isaac) because of the astonished joy of his parents. Sarah can hardly believe her own body: and yet it's true. She has given birth to the promise.

The next great turning point in Israel's story is the arrival of Moses (Exod 2:1–10). Although Moses' conception is not a miracle, his infancy is marked by a miraculous escape from danger. He is snatched away from the murdering hand of Pharaoh. He is placed in a basket and set adrift on the river, where he is found and adopted by a member of the royal household, an Egyptian princess who then appoints the baby's biological mother to be his nursing maid. The whole story portrays an amazing providential design by which Moses is spared and, as it were, smuggled right into the heart of Egyptian power. All this is meant to anticipate the great miracle to come when God will deliver the people of Israel from slavery.

When Israel has come to the promised land, before the establishment of the monarchy, God raises up judges to lead the people. The greatest of the judges is Samson, and his story begins with another miraculous birth (Judg 13:1–25). Samson's mother is unable to conceive. But she is visited by an angel who tells her that she will give birth to a savior who will triumph over the Philistines.

After the age of the judges comes the age of the prophets and kings. It begins with Hannah, a woman full of grief because she cannot bear children (1 Sam 1:1–20). In answer to her prayer, Hannah becomes miraculously pregnant and her child Samuel becomes the prophet who will anoint the first kings of Israel. With the miraculous birth of Samuel the whole line of Hebrew prophets comes into being.

That is how it goes in the Old Testament: at the great turning points of history, we find a woman, pregnant, and an infant child brought into the world by the powerful promise of God. Israel's story is a story of miraculous births.

Later the people of Israel were taken from the promised land and led away into Babylonian captivity. It was the darkest hour of their history. Out of the depths of despair, the promise of God was heard again through the prophet Isaiah. The prophet compared the coming deliverance to the joy of a miraculous pregnancy:

Sing, O barren one who did not bear;
burst into song and shout,
you who have not been in labor!
For the children of the desolate woman will be more
than the children of her that is married, says the LORD.
Enlarge the site of your tent,
and let the curtains of your habitations be stretched out;
do not hold back; lengthen your cords
and strengthen your stakes.
For you will spread out to the right and to the left,
and your descendants will possess the nations
and will settle the desolate towns. ...
All your children shall be taught by the LORD,
and great shall be the prosperity of your children.

(Isa 54:1–3, 13)

It is as if Israel, in her exile, has been a poor woman in a small tent with room for only one. But now it's time to make alterations on her home, to prepare the space for a bustling family. The one who has never been in labor is about to give birth. That is what the promise of God looks like.

It is not hard to see why pregnancy and childbirth played such an important role in the history of God's covenant with Israel. God's overarching plan is to bring blessing to all the nations through the descendants of Abraham. If ever the Hebrew women ceased to bear children, the promise would have failed: the whole world would be lost. Pregnancy and childbirth are the means by which God's promise makes its way through the crooked course of history. Every newborn child is a reminder of the promise. Every male child was physically marked by circumcision: a potent reminder that their bodies were not merely their own but had been scripted into a bigger story.

Against this backdrop it should come as no surprise to find Israel's Messiah entering the world by means of a miraculous pregnancy. In the Gospel of Luke, the first character we meet is another faithful Jewish woman who can't conceive: Elizabeth. Like Samson's mother, Elizabeth was promised that she will bear a child (Luke 1:5–25).

After Elizabeth has become pregnant, we meet her cousin Mary. An angel tells Mary that she too will miraculously conceive and that her child will be the fulfillment of all God's promises to Israel. Mary responds with simple trust and gladness. The joy of her Magnificat (Luke 1:46–55) is the same joy that made Sarah laugh when she gave birth to Isaac. It is the same joy that wiped away Hannah's tears when she gave birth to Samuel. Israel's joy—the joy of God's promise, the joy of salvation—is all summed up in that startling experience of the birth of a miraculous child.

The confession that Jesus Christ was born of a virgin isn't just a bit of theological eccentricity. It's not a random miracle story. It's a reminder that our faith has deep roots in Israel's story and Israel's Scriptures. The coming of the Savior wasn't just a new thing. It was the culmination of the whole great story of God's loving faithfulness to the people of Israel. When we confess that Jesus is "born of the Virgin Mary," we see him silhouetted against the backdrop of God's promise to Abraham, the exodus from Egypt, the rule of the judges, the coming of the prophets, and the promised deliverance from exile.

The meaning of history is not power and empire, but promise and trust. The secret of history is revealed when a woman, insignificant to the eyes of the world, responds in joy to God's promise and bears that promise into the world in her own body.

SUFFERED

U NTIL NOW, YOU WOULD THINK the creed was describing a perfect world. It has spoken of the God who creates the world and then enters into that world through the womb of a woman. So far there is no hint that anything is wrong. The Apostles' Creed makes no mention of the fall or original sin. But now we hear ourselves confessing the word "suffered," and with a painful jolt we realize all is not well.

When God comes into the world in the person of Jesus, God is met with violent resistance. The creatures have turned against their Creator. The loving Creator of the world has been cast out. The judge of the earth has come among us: we have judged him and put him on the gallows. "He came unto his own, and his own received him not" (John 1:11 KJV). There is room in our world, it seems, for everything—except God.

Among Christian scholars today, one of the main criticisms of the Apostles' Creed is that it contains no account of the life and ministry of Jesus. The reading of the Gospel stories has always been central to the life of the Christian community. The creed was never intended as a substitute for the four Gospels but only as a guide to the faithful reading of them. Whenever we read Jesus' story we are to keep in mind that he was born of a woman, that he was a flesh-and-blood human being. And when we read his story we are to keep in mind that he wasn't just another human being, but was "God's only Son, our Lord," the living self-expression of God's will. That is what the creed offers: some general guidelines for the faithful reading of the Gospels. The creed doesn't try to include all the details but only to remind us of the larger narrative and to focus our attention on Jesus' identity as divine and human, the Son of God and Mary's son.

Still, it's not quite true that the creed just ignores everything that happens between Jesus' birth and death. In fact, already among the earliest Christians it had become customary to sum up Jesus' whole life under one word: "suffering." We can already see that in the Gospels themselves: "Was it not necessary that the Messiah should suffer these things?" (Luke 24:26). Luke records that Paul summed up Jesus' life in the same way: "It was necessary for the Messiah to suffer" (Acts 17:3). By the time of the later New Testament writings, the word "suffering" has become a convenient formula for referring to the whole story of Jesus' life and death: "he suffered" (Heb 2:18).

This abridgement of Jesus' story is no substitute for the unbroken rhythm of reading and rereading the testimony of the four Gospels. But it is a tried-and-true safeguard against certain kinds of misreading. When ancient people heard the gospel they were tempted to think of Jesus as a supernatural spirit, untouched by physical life. For them, it was especially important to be reminded that Jesus is a human Lord who "suffered in the flesh" (1 Pet 4:1).

Christians today might be more tempted by the allure of a triumphalist faith, or by a distorted gospel that promises worldly satisfactions and success. But we are baptized into the way of a suffering Lord who lays on his followers not a crown but a cross. We will share Christ's glory, yes—to the extent that we also share in his sufferings (Rom 8:17).

UNDER PONTIUS PILATE

I T IS SO EASY TO forget what the Christian faith is really about. We might slip into the assumption that it is a kind of philosophy, a comprehensive view of life and the world. Debates with atheists are often carried out on this level. We give the impression that Christianity has to be cleverer than atheism if it is to be true. Or we might assume that the Christian faith is essentially a religious doctrine, a set of accurate beliefs about God. Scholars and students are especially vulnerable to this assumption. We start out trying to get a clearer understanding of our beliefs, and before long we have come to feel that those beliefs, if they are to be true, have to be flawlessly integrated into a theological system.

There is some truth in all this. But such approaches become misleading whenever they give the impression that Christianity is essentially a theory. If Christianity is a theory, then salvation is ultimately an intellectual matter. It is about getting rid of the wrong ideas and acquiring the right ones.

The Apostles' Creed is concerned with doctrine. The ancient catechism was meant to help believers get a clear outline of the teaching of Scripture. There are some under-lying doctrinal patterns in the creed: belief in God as Father, Son, and Holy Spirit; and belief in creation's goodness, its redemption, and its final glorification. Still, it's important to notice that the creed isn't a list of concepts and ideas. At the center of the creed is a story, or at least the summary of a story. We are meant to take our bearings not just from doctrine but from history: from a sequence of events that occurred in a particular time and place.

That's how one of history's most dubious characters, Pontius Pilate, finds his way into the creed. He enters the creed "like a dog into a nice room," as the twentieth-century theologian Karl Barth put it.[22] The name of Pontius Pilate is a historical anchor. It prevents us from turning the Christian faith into a set of general truths about the world. It reminds us that the gospel is not an idea but a fact.

The baptismal confession centers on a name: the name of Jesus. And in case we start to think that "Jesus Christ" is a theoretical concept, the creed adds a second name: "Jesus— the one who suffered under Pontius Pilate." Pontius Pilate is there to remind us that God has acted at a particular moment in human history. The salvation of the world can be dated. Certain people were there when it happened.

The heart of Christianity is not an idea but a brute fact. Not a theory but a particular human life. Not a general prin-ciple but a person with a name: Jesus, who suffered under Pontius Pilate.

Because Jesus himself is at the center, the continuous read-ing of the four Gospels is the central spiritual discipline of the Christian life. The story of Jesus is read whenever believers assemble. In the sacraments of baptism and the Lord's Supper we participate communally in Jesus' story, remembering and repeating the events of his life through a liturgical reenactment. In prayer we repeat verbatim the words that Jesus taught his followers to say: "Our Father ..." (Matt 6:9–13). When we serve the marginalized, the poor, and the oppressed, we are not just following a general principle of compassion but are giving a fresh dramatic performance of the script of Jesus' life. In a sermon on the love of the poor, the fourth-century preacher Gregory of Nazianzus appealed to his congregation:

> While we may, let us visit Christ, let us heal Christ, let us feed Christ, let us clothe Christ, let us welcome Christ, let us honor Christ. ... Since the Lord of all will have mercy and not sacrifice ... , let us offer to him through the poor who are today downtrodden.[23]

It is as if each new believer becomes another character in the gospel story. Each one has a part to play. Jesus still lives, and his story still continues in the lives of his followers. The church calendar, too, is just an elaborate way of remembering and repeating Jesus' story year after year. We read the Gospels not only with our minds but also with our lives.

Really there are as many unique performances of the story of Jesus as there are believers. But each one remains accountable to the history narrated in the four Gospels. We all respond differently to Jesus' story, but the story itself does not change. The same Jesus, born of Mary and condemned by Pilate, is always at the center. All the church's practices and institutions are ultimately attempts to respond to that person. All the mysteries of faith are rooted in the events of history. That is why one of history's villains, Pontius Pilate, lives in the memory of the church and will be confessed until the end of the world whenever a person is baptized into the way of Jesus.

WAS CRUCIFIED

IN THE ROMAN EMPIRE, CRUCIFIXION wasn't only about death. It was about public disgrace. The problem with getting yourself crucified wasn't just that it would kill you but that it would humiliate you at the same time. Modern readers of the New Testament might assume that the worst thing about crucifixion was the physical suffering. But in a culture of honor and shame, the pain of the soul—humiliation—can be even worse than the pain of the body.

The psalms of Israel often lament over the experience of humiliation. Psalm 79 describes the sack of Jerusalem by a neighboring army:

> O God, the nations have come into your inheritance;
> they have defiled your holy temple;
> they have laid Jerusalem in ruins.
> They have given the bodies of your servants
> to the birds of the air for food,
> the flesh of your faithful to the wild animals
>   of the earth.
> They have poured out their blood like water
> all around Jerusalem,
> and there was no one to bury them.

(Ps 79:1–3)

This list of horrors culminates in the worst fate of all: public disgrace.

> We have become a taunt to our neighbors,
> mocked and derided by those around us.
>
> (Ps 79:4)

It is as if to say: we have been butchered—and, what's worse, humiliated! Jesus went to his death reciting a psalm of humiliation:

> My God, my God, why have you forsaken me? ...
> I am a worm, and not human;
> scorned by others, and despised by the people.
> All who see me mock at me;
> they make mouths at me, they shake their heads.
>
> (Ps 22:1, 6–7)

To be crucified was to be cast out of the human community, rejected by God and the world. It was literally a fate worse than death.

The humiliation of Jesus' death made a deep impression on his early followers. Quoting an early Christian hymn, Paul describes the whole life of Jesus as a descent into humiliation and disgrace. "He emptied himself, taking the form of a slave"; he "humbled himself and became obedient to the point of death—even death on a cross" (Phil 2:7–8). Jesus descended to the lowest rung on the social ladder. He became a slave and died a slave's death. Though he possessed the highest honor, he embraced the worst disgrace.

The world was saved by Jesus' shame: that is the scandalous message of the cross.

Jesus' followers were the first people in the history of the world to describe humility as a virtue. Paul reminds the Philippian believers that they ought to have the "same mind" as Christ (Phil 2:5), renouncing honor and becoming like slaves in service to one another. In ancient Roman culture, the whole purpose of life was to acquire honor and to shun whatever might diminish one's reputation. To be humble was the worst thing that could happen to a person. Yet the earliest Christians scorned pride and elevated humility. Paul calls himself a "slave of Jesus Christ" (Rom 1:1), as if such slavery were the highest honor in the world.

The message of a humble Lord was a shocking thing to hear in the ancient world. Yet today if anyone is asked whether it's better to devote one's life to self-aggrandizement or to service, most would admit that a life of service is better. The message of the cross has inverted the ancient values of honor and shame. Jesus' shocking claim that it is better to serve than to be served (Mark 10:45) is accepted today as if it were plain common sense. We take it for granted that nurses and carers deserve special respect, and that the poor and powerless have a special dignity.

Because, today, the virtue of humility is taken for granted, we no longer feel the original scandal of the gospel. We are no longer offended by Jesus' shame. But it was his shameful death that passed judgment on the world's moral order and laid bare a new order of righteousness. Up has become down; down has become up. In Jesus, God

> has brought down the powerful from their thrones,
> and lifted up the lowly;
> he has filled the hungry with good things,
> and sent the rich away empty.

(Luke 1:52–53)

DIED, AND
WAS BURIED

C HRISTIANS CONFESS THAT THE DEATH of Jesus is the
turning point of history. The New Testament authors
have many different ways of describing the meaning of that
death. Through his shameful death, Jesus attains the highest
honor (Phil 2:6–11). By succumbing to mortality he makes
human nature immortal (1 Cor 15:42–57). His death is the
world's life (Rom 5:12–21). It is the darkness that illuminates,
the judgment that does not condemn (John). It is a defeat
that ushers in God's sovereign reign (Mark). It is a termina-
tion that inaugurates a new epoch in history (Luke–Acts).
It is a fulfillment that totally surpasses what was promised
(Matthew). It is a sacrifice that dissolves the entire sacrificial
system from within (Hebrews). It is a violent catastrophe that
triumphs over the violence of human history (Revelation).

These are not exactly straightforward explanations. They
are paradoxical expressions, each pointing back to the brute
fact of Jesus' death without exhausting the meaning of that
event.

Paul's theme of union with Christ was especially important in later Christian teaching about Jesus' death. According
to Paul, Jesus has shared all that is ours so that we may share
all that is his. He shares our poverty and we share his riches (2
Cor 8:9). He stands under the curse that is rightly ours, and
we stand under the blessing that is rightly his (Gal 3:6–14). By
uniting himself with us, he is identified completely with our
sin and we are identified with his righteousness (2 Cor 5:21).
The idea here is not so much substitution as mutual participation: God and humanity are perfectly united in the person
of Jesus so that each partakes of all that belongs to the other.

About a hundred years after Paul, the second-century
theologian Irenaeus developed the same logic by arguing
that we could not have been redeemed unless every aspect
of our human condition was embraced by the Son of God:

> He did not reject human nature or exalt himself above
> it. ... Becoming an infant among infants, he sanctified
> infants; becoming a child among children, he sancti-
> fied those having this age ... ; becoming a young adult
> among young adults, he was an example for young
> adults and sanctified them to the Lord. ... Lastly, he
> came even to death so that he might be "the Firstborn
> from the dead," himself "holding primacy in all things"
> (Col 1:18), the Author of life, prior to all and going
> before all.[24]

The Son of God heals our nature by joining it to himself.
Human nature is changed by this union. Mortality joins

hands with immortality. The grave becomes the beginning of life.

The mysterious connection between birth and death was explored by Gregory of Nyssa in a fourth-century address to new believers preparing for baptism. Gregory pointed out that Jesus would not really have shared our nature if he had not also shared its limits. Everyone comes into the world through the womb and departs into the tomb. And so the Son of God embraced our humanity at these extreme limits. In Gregory's words:

> The birth makes the death necessary. He who had decided to share our humanity had to experience all that belongs to our nature. Now human life is encompassed within two limits, and if he had passed through one and not the other, he would only have half fulfilled his purpose. ... Our whole nature had to be brought back from death. Thus he stooped down to our dead body and stretched out a hand, as it were, to one who lay prostrate. He approached so near death as to come into contact with it.[25]

Because, in Jesus, God has fully shared our condition, there is no human experience that can alienate us from God. Every affliction is an opportunity to identify with Jesus, to "suffer with him so that we may also be glorified with him" (Rom 8:17). Even dying becomes another way of following Jesus and of identifying with him. We die differently because the Son of God has touched our frail mortality and has drawn it into the wider context of his life. We die differently because we know that "neither death, nor life ... will be able to separate us from the love of God in Christ Jesus our Lord" (Rom 8:38–39).

Each one of us approaches the day of our death. But there is someone waiting for us there: Jesus, the Lord of life, who meets us at all life's crossroads, at the beginnings and ends of all our ways.

HE DESCENDED INTO HELL; ON THE THIRD DAY HE ROSE AGAIN FROM THE DEAD

"I F I MAKE MY BED in Sheol, you are there" (Ps 139:8). The message of the Bible is that death is not the end. Death does not defeat God's promise. Death is not separation from God. In Jesus, God has dwelt among the dead. God has touched the very limits of our nature, from birth to death, in order to sanctify us and to unite us to God. The Living has embraced the dead. Death has been subsumed by life.

Several of the New Testament authors describe Jesus' death as a descent into the world of the dead. "When he ascended on high he made captivity itself a captive," after having first "descended into the lower parts of the earth" (Eph 4:8–9). He "went and made a proclamation to the spirits in prison," and then went "into heaven and is at the right hand of God" (1 Pet 3:18–22). Christ's word is proclaimed among the dead. His name is confessed "under the earth," among the dead (Phil 2:9–11). The dead are not lost forever. They are not condemned to silence. In Jesus, "the dead will hear the voice of the Son of God, and those who hear will live" (John 5:25). Because of him, the emptiness of death has been filled with God's fullness.

Eastern Orthodox iconography is especially attentive to this aspect of Christian hope. In Orthodoxy, the icon of the resurrection portrays a glorified Christ standing over the broken doors of hell. Beneath his feet, the chains and locks that have held the dead are all broken. The doors of hell have come unhinged. The grave has been emptied. An old man and an old woman are depicted on either side of Christ. They are Adam and Eve. Christ has seized them by the wrists and raised them up from the shadowy underworld.

Jesus descends into hell because that is where we have fallen. The fourteenth-century English writer Julian of Norwich put it like this:

> For Jesus is all who shall be saved and all who shall be saved are Jesus. ... For he went into hell, and when he was there he raised up out of the deep deepness the great root of those who were truly knit to him in high heaven.[26]

The Son of God has taken our nature to himself. He allows our fallen nature to drag him down. He descends to the very abyss of the human condition. He traces our plight right

back to the root and takes hold of us there. He embraces our humanity at the point of its total collapse into nonbeing.

Because he shares our nature he is able to fall with us into death; because he is the Son of God he is able to fill death with his presence so that the grave becomes a source of life. In Christ, the dead are united to God and are alive in the strength of that union. The resurrection is not just an isolated miracle that happens to Jesus. It is something that happens to us—to Adam and Eve, to me, to the human family. As Jesus rises, the whole of humanity rises with him.

In the ancient church, the message of Christ's triumph over death produced some peculiar attitudes toward the dead. Believers would assemble for prayer in tombs. They would worship Christ among the bones of the dead. Believers would raise the bodies of martyrs in the air and parade them through the streets like trophies. At funerals they would gaze lovingly on the dead and sing psalms of praise over their bodies. Such behavior shocked their pagan neighbors. According to Roman law, the dead had to be buried miles away from the city so that the living would not be contaminated. But Christians placed the dead right at the center of their public gatherings. The earliest church buildings were really just big mausoleums erected over the remains of the martyrs. The tombs of the saints were, in the words of John Chrysostom, "tombs with life, tombs that give voice."[27]

When new believers were preparing for baptism, they would gather in the presence of the dead, and there they would receive instruction in the ancient catechism. Even today the Apostles' Creed makes the most sense when you imagine the words echoing among the bones of the cata-combs. The creed is marked everywhere by an unflinching acceptance of the facts of human mortality, coupled with a straightforward confidence in the ultimate triumph of life—a triumph that has already happened once and for all in the person of Jesus.

Where others see only defeat, Jesus' followers see a paradoxical victory. Where others see only contamination, we see the sanctification of human nature. Where others see only darkness and despair, we see broken gates. Where others see an end, we see new beginnings. Death is serious: but not as serious as life. It has been placed in a wider context of meaning. We bury our dead under the sign of the cross. We lay our bones to rest not in horror but in peace. The dominant sound at a Christian funeral is not mourning but the singing of praise.

Death is no longer the ultimate power in this world. In the ancient church, the martyrs were seen as a special proof of that. In the fourth century, Athanasius compared the martyrs to children who play with a lion in the desert:

> If you see children playing with a lion, don't you know that the lion must be either dead or completely powerless? In the same way ... when you see Christ's believers playing with death and despising it, there can be no doubt that death has been destroyed by Christ and that its corruption has been dissolved and brought to an end.[28]

In the death and resurrection of Jesus, death itself was altered. And now, says Athanasius, "we no longer die as those condemned but as those who will arise."[29]

By nature we are all on the way from birth to death. But by grace we are traveling in the opposite direction. The Christian life is a mystery that moves from death to birth. At the beginning we are baptized into Christ's death; and at the end we are born into the life of the resurrection. We are born as though dying; we die as those who are being born.

Where, O death, is your victory?
Where, O death, is your sting?

(1 Cor 15:55)

HE ASCENDED INTO HEAVEN AND IS SEATED AT THE RIGHT HAND OF THE FATHER

T HE DUALISTIC SECTS OF THE second century had a dis-taste for some parts of the Gospel tradition, including the stories of Christ's ascension (Mark 16:19; Luke 24:51; Acts 1:9–11). Marcion's edited version of the Gospel of Luke had omitted both the birth narrative and the ascension. This was because Marcion imagined a spiritual, disembodied savior, and he forced the Scriptures to conform to that vision. Other teachers claimed that Christ ascended spiritually, leaving his physical body behind. In such doctrines, the body is believed to be evil; the material world is consigned to ruin; salvation is about escaping the misery of this world. Jesus himself (so it was said) wanted nothing to do with physical life in this world; he came to bring enlightenment and to liberate the human spirit from its bondage to the world of creation.

It was against such teaching that the early Christians proclaimed a gospel of Christ's bodily incarnation, bodily suffering, bodily death, bodily resurrection, and bodily ascension. The faith of the ancient church was not about spiritual escape but about the redemption and transfiguration of human life in its fullness, including the life of the body. As Irenaeus said it in the second century, the Son of God "did not reject human nature or exalt himself above it," but united himself with our nature in order to unite us to God.[30]

When the New Testament writers speak of the ascension, they are not describing Jesus' absence but his sovereign presence throughout creation. He has not gone away but has become even more fully present. His ascent "to the right hand of the Father" is his public enthronement over all worldly power. No scriptural passage is quoted so often in the New Testament as Psalm 110:1:

> The LORD says to my Lord,
> "Sit at my right hand
> until I make your enemies your footstool."

The earliest Christians proclaimed that Jesus had been enthroned as the universal Lord and messiah. The exalted Christ has "entered his glory" (Luke 24:26; 1 Tim 3:16). From now on, "all things are subject" to his authority (Phil 3:21; Heb 2:8). Because he is ascended, his life is universally available. His loving authority extends over the whole creation and is present wherever believers assemble (Eph 1:20–23). He "has gone into heaven and is at the right hand of God, with angels, authorities, and powers made subject to him" (1 Pet 3:22).

So the ascension is not meant to make us wonder where Jesus has gone. Instead it ought to elicit the psalmist's question,

> Where can I go from your spirit?
> Or where can I flee from your presence?
>
> (Ps 139:7)

In a painting by the Australian Aboriginal artist Shirley Purdie, the ascension of Jesus is shown not as a flight into the sky but as a triumphant ascent into the red earth. He "ascends down," so to speak, into the land—not fleeing our world but entering into its depths in order to exercise his loving authority over (and within) the whole creation.[31] That is a profound depiction of the New Testament understanding of the ascension. Because Jesus has ascended, he is even nearer to us and to all things. "In him all things hold together, ... and through him God was pleased to reconcile to himself all things" (Col 1:17–20).

And through our union with Christ, we share also in his ascension. The lives of believers are now forever located "in Christ," as Paul so often says. When Jesus ascends to the Father, he takes our humanity with him. To quote Irenaeus again, because Jesus has ascended we also "ascend through the Spirit to the Son, and through the Son to the Father."[32] In Jesus, our nature has taken up residence in the presence of God.

HE WILL COME
TO JUDGE
THE LIVING
AND THE DEAD

T O JUDGE IS TO DISCRIMINATE, to separate one thing from another. The Gospel of John portrays Jesus as the light of the world. The same light shines on everyone, but there are different ways of responding to it. Some walk gladly into the light while others screw their eyes shut and remain in darkness. "And this is the judgment, that the light has come into the world, and people loved darkness rather than light" (John 3:19). That is what it means for Jesus to bring judgment. It is not that he is gracious to some and angry toward others. Jesus is "full of grace and truth" (John 1:14), but grace itself divides those who encounter it.

When the ancient Christians talked about divine judgment, they were careful to avoid the impression that there are two different gods, a god of wrath and a god of grace. That line of thinking would lead straight to the theological nightmares of Gnosticism. For Christians, there is no division within God. "God is light and in him there is no darkness at all" (1 John 1:5). The one face of God is revealed in Jesus.

Some early Christian teachers suggested that heaven and hell might in fact be the same place. Isaac the Syrian, a monk and preacher of the seventh century, argued that all people are ultimately brought into the presence of divine love. But "the power of love works in two ways": it is a joy to some but a torment to others.[33] Teachers sometimes witness a similar phenomenon in the classroom. The same class can be a delight for one student and a torment for another. One is excited; the other is bored. Both students are in the same place, and both are listening to the same teacher. But one is in heaven and the other is in hell. That is how Isaac the Syrian imagines the world to come: not as two different places but as two different ways of responding to the love of God. "Those who are punished in hell," Isaac writes, "are scourged by the scourge of love. For what is so bitter and vehement as the punishment of love?"[34]

The judgment that Christ brings, moreover, is not just a division between two kinds of people. When Christ's light shines into our lives, it creates a division within ourselves. None of us is entirely good or entirely bad. Each of us is a mixture. The bad grows up in our lives like weeds among the wheat, and the two are so closely entwined that in this life we can't easily tell the difference (Matt 13:24–30). Sometimes our worst mistakes turn out to produce good fruit. And sometimes we discover that our virtues have produced unforeseen collateral damage. Our lives are not transparent to ourselves. We cannot easily tell where the bad ends and the good begins.

So it is a comfort to know that one day someone else will come and lovingly separate the good from the bad in our lives. The confession that Christ will come as judge is not an expression of terror and doom. It is part of the good news of the gospel. It is a joy to know that there is someone who understands all the complexities and ambiguities of our lives. It is a joy to know that this one—the only one who is truly competent to judge—is "full of grace and truth" (John 1:14). He comes to save, not to destroy, and he saves us by his judgment.

The fourth-century writer Gregory of Nyssa composed an imagined dialogue with his older sister Macrina—"my teacher," as he liked to call her. The dialogue discusses the body, the soul, and the resurrection. It depicts divine judgment as a painful but necessary purification in which each person is finally set free to respond fully to the love of God:

> The divine judgment ... does not primarily bring punishment on sinners. ... It operates only by separating good from evil and pulling the soul toward communion in blessedness. It is the tearing apart of what has grown together which brings pain to the one who is being pulled.[35]

Jesus will come to judge the living and the dead. That will be the best thing that ever happens to us. On that day the weeds in each of us will be separated from the wheat. It will hurt—no doubt it will hurt—when our self-deceptions are burned away. But the pain of truth heals; it does not destroy. On our judgment day we will be able for the first time to see the truth of our lives, when we see ourselves as loved.

ARTICLE III

I believe in the Holy Spirit,
the holy catholic church,
the communion of saints,
the forgiveness of sins,
the resurrection of the body,
and the life everlasting.
Amen.

O GOD, in these last days you have sent your Holy Spirit upon all people, and you have bound your people together in the unity of that same Spirit. Help us to walk by your Spirit and not to gratify the desires of the flesh, so that we, who in Christ Jesus have crucified the desires of the flesh, may manifest the fruits of the Spirit in all that we do. This we ask in the power of the Holy Spirit, who with you and the Son is worshiped and glorified. **AMEN.**

I BELIEVE IN
THE HOLY SPIRIT

THE STORY OF THE BIBLE begins with the Spirit brooding over the abyss, ready to bring forth creation out of nothing (Gen 1:2). And at the turning point of the ages we find the Spirit brooding over the womb of a virgin (Luke 1:35). The Spirit rests on Mary's body in order to bring forth the new Adam, the beginning of a new creation.

The language of the creed reminds us that the work of this creative Spirit is not yet finished. The same Spirit is now brooding over the whole human race, bringing forth a new human community in the image of Christ.

One of the great themes of the Bible is the unity of the human family. In the garden of Eden, God makes a man and a woman, a miniature society imprinted with God's own image. And the Bible ends with depictions of a future city where people from every tribe and tongue will live together in a perfect harmony of praise (Rev 7:9).

In Genesis, the fall brings about a tragic disordering of human relationships. There is a curse now at the heart of the relation between man and woman, as well as between parents and children. The relation between humans and the rest of creation is likewise blighted (Gen 3:14–19). God's creation is divided. Each human being is a fragment torn loose from the whole.

This grim assessment of human fallenness culminates in the story of Babel (Gen 11:1–9). Here, human beings have begun to use their collective life to mock God. And so God divides their language, making it impossible for them to work together. They can no longer share a common world or articulate a common good. They cannot form a coherent society. Each group is a mere splinter of humanity, all scattered across the cursed earth, exiled and alone.

But with the coming of Jesus, the story of Babel is reversed. When the Spirit descends on the frightened company of Jesus' followers, they all begin to speak in different languages. The multicultural crowd outside is astonished to find that each one's language is being spoken by a band of Galileans. They ask, "How is it that we hear, each of us, in our own native language?" (Acts 2:1–13).

The Pentecost story shows the undoing of the fall through the creation of the Christian community. There is now a new human society in which all the old divisions are torn down. That is what happens when the Spirit is present. The Spirit fulfills the Creator's original plan by bringing forth a universal community whose boundaries are as wide as the world. The Spirit broods over the chaos of human nature, lovingly piecing the fragments back together so that together we form an image of the Creator.

Paul notes that the presence of the Spirit is marked by heightened individuality as well as a deeper communal belonging. The Spirit fuses unity and diversity by bringing "many gifts" together in "one body" (1 Cor 12:12–31). We become more truly ourselves as the Spirit broods over us and as our lives are knit together with other lives and stories.

In this way the Spirit broods over each of Christ's followers, renewing the human race one life at a time and drawing all into a common family. Basil, a great fourth-century Cappadocian pastor and social reformer, explained it like this: the Spirit "is like a sunbeam whose grace is present to the one who enjoys it as if it were present to that one alone, yet it illuminates land and sea and is mixed with the air."[36] There is nothing more personal, and more universal, than the Holy Spirit.

THE HOLY
CATHOLIC CHURCH

A T BAPTISM EACH BELIEVER PROCLAIMS that the church is "catholic." The word simply means universal. It means that there is only one church because there is only one Lord. Though there have been many Christian communities spread out across different times, places, and cultures, they are all mysteriously united in one Spirit. Each local gathering of believers is a full expression of that mysterious catholicity.

The church is catholic because it is a microcosm of a universal human society. In the waters of baptism, all the old social divisions are made irrelevant. The church includes every kind of person: rich and poor, male and female, Jew and gentile, slave and free (Gal 3:26–28). Whatever defined a person before is relativized by the new defining mark of membership in the company of Jesus' followers. The thirteenth-century Italian theologian Thomas Aquinas explained that the message of Jesus is universal "because no one is rejected, neither lord nor servant, neither male nor female."[37] There is no social barrier that could exclude a person from inclusion in this body. The boundaries of the church are as wide as the human race.

Further, the church is catholic because it preaches a catholic message. The gospel is not addressed to one particular social class or ethnic group. It is addressed to every imaginable human being. There is nobody in the world for whom the message of Jesus could be irrelevant. One of the most unusual aspects of the Christian faith is its translatability. The other great monotheistic traditions, Judaism and Islam, place a high value on preserving the divine message in its original language, whether Hebrew or Arabic. But right from the start, the Christian movement was marked by translation. Jesus himself spoke Aramaic, but the four Gospels all translated his teaching into vernacular Greek so that the message would be available to as many readers as possible. Within a remarkably short time the Christian movement had taken root in many different cultures, each one reading and proclaiming the gospel message in its own tongue. The message of Jesus is a catholic message.

The message of the gospel is also "catholic" in the way it responds to the human plight. The deepest human needs are addressed in the gospel. The message of Jesus doesn't just speak to a special part of life—the moral or spiritual part, for example. It speaks to the whole person, body and soul, individual and social. It is a catholic message because it embraces the whole person in a word of grace and truth. The gospel is as broad and deep as human life itself. It is a catholic word because it speaks to the whole human condition.

But there is an even more radical dimension of Christian catholicity. The greatest barrier that divides human beings from one another is not culture or language or class. The greatest barrier is death. It splits the human family into the two classes of the living and the dead. All other social divisions are petty compared to this great division. All human beings are powerless before this fundamental boundary. But in the resurrection Jesus has stepped across the barrier and restored communion between the living and the dead. He has formed one family that stretches out not only across space but also across time. The body of Christ is the most inclusive community imaginable because it includes not only those who are now living but also all believers who have ever lived.

The message of the gospel is directed not primarily to individuals but to this new community. God's plan of salvation all along has been to create one human society as the bearer of the divine image. In that sense, the church isn't just the way people respond to salvation; the church *is* salvation. The church is what God has been doing in the world from the beginning. It is a representative microcosm of what God intends for the whole human family.

That is why every division between believers is a denial of the gospel. A Christian community is catholic to the extent that it is always uniting. Wherever we identify a line of division within the human family, the risen Jesus calls us to step across that line in the power of the Spirit. For "there is one body and one Spirit, just as you were called to the one hope of your calling, one Lord, one faith, one baptism, one God and Father of all" (Eph 4:4–6).

THE COMMUNION
OF SAINTS

S OMETIME IN THE SECOND CENTURY, a Greek philosopher named Celsus wrote a book attacking the Christian
faith. Nearly a hundred years later, the great Egyptian scholar
Origen was asked to reply to Celsus's criticisms. Origen duti-
fully composed a big book that is perhaps still the finest work
of Christian apologetics ever written. But before launching
into his defense of the faith, Origen pointed out that the way
of Jesus doesn't really need any defense. He wrote:

> Jesus is always being falsely accused, and there is never
> a time when he is not being accused. ... He is still silent
> in the face of this and does not answer with his own
> voice. But he makes his defense in the lives of his gen-
> uine disciples, for their lives cry out the real facts and
> defeat all false charges.[38]

Jesus wrote no books. He established no institutions. He did
not lay down the right answers to moral questions. He did
not seem particularly interested in founding a new religion.
He was the author not of ideas but of a way of life. Everything

Jesus believed to be important was entrusted to his small circle of followers. What he handed on to them was simply life. He showed them his own unique way of being alive—his way of living, loving, feasting, forgiving, teaching, and dying—and he invited them to live the same way.

Becoming a Christian is not really about institutional membership or about adopting a system of ideas. To become a Christian is to be included in the circle of Jesus' followers. I am washed with the same bath that Jesus and all his followers have had. I get to share the same meal that Jesus shared with his followers. Four of Jesus' followers left written records of what he said and what he was like, and I get to spend my life continually pondering those four accounts. I read them not because I am studying ideas about Jesus but because I am studying *him*. I want everything in my life, right down to the smallest and most disappointing details, to enter somehow into communion with the life of Jesus.

I share the holy bath and the holy meal, and I read the holy stories, because I am seeking Jesus. But when I do these things I am also seeking myself. I want to find myself among the circle of Jesus' followers. I want to be wherever Jesus is—and he is in the company of his friends. I want my whole life to be "hidden with Christ in God" (Col 3:3). I want my life's small story to be tucked into the folds of Jesus' story.

When this happens, my life acquires a meaning beyond itself. I begin to see myself as part of a great company, an ever-widening circle of people who have handed their lives over to the pattern of Jesus' life. This great company of disciples seems to speak with one voice, to breathe with one

Spirit, to cry "Abba, Father!" with one unceasing prayer (Rom 8:15–16).

The Fourth Gospel ends by telling us that it has offered only a glimpse of Jesus. If everything Jesus did was written down, "the world itself could not contain the books that would be written" (John 21:25).

Perhaps, at the end of the age, the Total Gospel will be read out and will be found to contain everything—every life, every story, every human grief and joy, all included as episodes in the one great, infinitely rich story of Jesus and his friends. The world itself is too small for such a book. Life and death are too small for the communion of saints.

THE FORGIVENESS
OF SINS

T HE CONFESSION OF THE FORGIVENESS of sins was a relatively late addition to the creed. The earliest baptismal confessions spoke simply of "the Holy Spirit, the holy church, and the resurrection of the flesh."

But a dramatic debate arose among fourth-century believers about the nature of sin and forgiveness. Christians in those days were still subjected to periods of persecution under the Roman emperors. In 303 the emperor Diocletian ordered that the property of Christians was to be seized, their books burned, and their places of worship destroyed. All Christian leaders were to be imprisoned. Only those who sacrificed to the Roman gods would be released. Some Christians were martyred. But martyrdom was always the exception. Countless frightened Christians—including, of course, many clergy—came out to make the sacrifices. The emperor even permitted the Christians to sacrifice en masse, making it as easy as possible for them to renounce their faith.

By offering public sacrifice to the Roman gods, such Christians had effectively renounced their baptism. But before long things returned to normal, and Christianity was again tolerated as part of Rome's pluralistic empire. Predictably, the apostate believers, known as "traitors," soon came back to church as if nothing much had happened.

This situation created a pastoral crisis for many congregations. What is to be done with believers who have renounced their baptism? Can they be accepted back into the faith? Is there a public way of marking their reentry into the church? Should they be baptized a second time? Or should they be permanently excluded from participation in the Christian community?

Even more awkward was the question about clergy who had made the pagan sacrifices. When ministers of Christ invalidate their faith, does it mean that their ministry has been invalid all along? What if you had been baptized by a minister who later renounced his faith? Would you need to get baptized again by someone else?

These were difficult questions. It was a time of intense soul-searching for many believers. Through this struggle over the "traitors," the deepest questions of Christian identity came sharply into focus. What is it that makes you a follower of Christ? And what can you do if you have strayed from Christ's path? Is the Christian community a church of the pure (as some called it), or can struggling, weak, uncertain souls also find a place within that community?

The fourth-century crisis led eventually to clear answers to these questions. Christian teachers argued that the church includes everyone who confesses Jesus and receives baptism. It is not only for the pure and the spiritually successful.

Failures in discipleship—even dramatic public failures—do not exclude a person from the grace of God. As Augustine insisted in one of his many sermons against spiritual elitism: "We must never despair of anyone at all."[39] When backslidden believers return to the faith, they don't need to be rebaptized. They simply need to show, through a changed way of life, that they are trying to take their baptism seriously. There is no need to be baptized more than once, since that would imply that we need to be forgiven more than once. The forgiveness of sins has taken place once for all in the death and resurrection of Jesus.

These conclusions were so important that the ancient church began to include "the forgiveness of sins" as part of the baptismal confession. In 381 the Nicene Creed was expanded to include the statement "we acknowledge one baptism for the forgiveness of sins."

A church that takes its stand on the forgiveness of sins can never be a church of the pure. It will always be a community that is patient and understanding toward the timid and the imperfect. Whenever a judgmental, elitist spirit enters into the Christian community, we need to hear again the confession: "I believe in the forgiveness of sins."

We believe that we stand not by our own achievements but by the achievement of Jesus' death and resurrection. We believe that the spiritually strong and the spiritually weak are both sustained by the same forgiving grace. We believe that we rely solely on grace, not only in our worst failures but also in our best successes. We believe that if ever we should turn away from grace, if ever our hearts grow cold and we forget our Lord and become unfaithful to his way, he will not forget us. His faithfulness is deeper than our faithlessness. His yes is stronger than our no. In a seventh-century sermon on God's mercy, Isaac the Syrian said:

> As a handful of sand thrown into the great sea, so are the sins of all flesh in comparison with the mind of God. And just as a strongly flowing stream is not obstructed by a handful of dust, so the mercy of the creator is not stemmed by the [sins] of his creatures.[40]

THE RESURRECTION
OF THE BODY

FROM START TO FINISH, the creed affirms the value of the material world. In opposition to rival systems of thought that denigrate matter and the body, the ancient catechism confesses God as the maker, redeemer, and sanctifier of this world. The life of the flesh is not alien to God. It is God's creature and the object of God's loving intentions.

The first part of the creed proclaims God as the creator of all things, not only of the spiritual world but of the material world too: "maker of heaven and earth."

The second part of the creed confesses that the Son of God has become part of this world by taking human nature to himself. Ancient gnostic teachers viewed the bodies of women with the utmost horror; but for Christians, the womb of a woman is the sacred venue of the divine action in this world. All God's intentions for creation come into focus here: "conceived by the Holy Spirit, born of the Virgin Mary." And the Son of God suffers in the flesh. He is crucified. He dies. He is buried. He is raised in the flesh and continues to share our nature in the glory of the resurrection.

The third part of the creed confesses that God's Spirit remains present in the midst of this world. Believers share in the power and presence of the Holy Spirit. The Spirit does not live on some higher plane but is here with us. The Spirit "befriends the body"[41] so that the life of the resurrection begins to appear already in our ordinary lives. And the life that we anticipate now, in the Spirit, is the life that we also await with eager hope.

Belief in bodily resurrection is one of the controlling undercurrents of the New Testament. Yet the nature of the resurrection is hardly ever addressed directly. The Gospel accounts never try to depict the resurrection itself. Mark's account does not even include a depiction of the risen Jesus: the tomb is empty, and it is left to the reader to understand why (Mark 16:1–8).[42] The other Gospels depict the risen Jesus, but not the event of resurrection itself (Matt 28; Luke 24; John 20). The tomb is already empty when the disciples get there. The resurrection has occurred in secret. It has happened—where? In the tomb? In hell? In eternity? Wherever and however it happened, the event has already occurred. That is why the disciples are faced with a decision, whether to believe or not.

The closest the New Testament comes to explaining the resurrection is Paul's discussion in 1 Corinthians 15. His argument is that we too will rise in the same way that Christ is risen. But we don't have any clear picture of what a resurrection looks like. So Paul tries to explain it using the image of a seed (1 Cor 15:35–49). The body now is like a seed, and the life of the resurrection is like the tree. There is an unimaginable difference between the seed and the tree. They do not look alike. You would not be able to guess the appearance of the tree by looking at the seed. Yet their identity is the same. In the same way, Paul says, our mortal bodies will be planted and will be raised immortal in Christ. Paul calls this "a mystery" (15:51). In the coming life we will be the same identical persons that we are now—yet unimaginably different. "We will all be changed, in a moment, in the twinkling of an eye" (15:51–52).

In this passage Paul explains the meaning of the resurrection by not-explaining it. He points to the mystery of the seed and the tree and offers that mystery as an explanation. He leads our minds right to the edge of what can be grasped or imagined.

So what are we really claiming to believe when we say that we believe in the resurrection of the body? In a third-century sermon,[43] Origen noted that the baptismal confession does not speak of "the resurrection of bodies" but "the resurrection of the body"—singular. Perhaps, he suggests, what is raised up on the last day will not be individuals but the body of Christ, a single person that incorporates the whole of humanity with Jesus at its head. Origen's line of reasoning is based partly on Ezekiel's vision of the valley of dry bones. What the prophet sees in this vision is not a multitude of individual resurrections but one corporate resurrection of "the whole house of Israel" (Ezek 37:11). In the same way, Christian hope is never just hope for myself. It is a social hope. It is hope for humanity. The only future that I may legitimately hope for is a future that also includes my neighbor.

As his sermon continues, Origen goes a step further. He says that if Jesus is the head, then he must be waiting for his body to assemble. It is as if Jesus' resurrection were still incomplete. "His joy waits," Origen says, until the whole body of humanity has been raised. If all the world were redeemed except one person, there would still be something missing in the joy of Jesus. He would continue to wait. The festivities would be on hold. He would not yet drink the cup of the kingdom.

If God's intention is to bring forth a single redeemed body, then the eternal joy of the life to come depends, in some measure, on each of us. The joy of Jesus is on hold until we take up our place with him. That is the remarkable conclusion that Origen reaches in his sermon.

This still leaves us no closer to being able to form a clear picture of the life of the world to come. So what do Christians hope for? Perhaps it is enough to say that Christian hope is a social and therefore an embodied hope, and that this hope centers on communion with the person of Jesus. We learn these things not by speculating about the afterlife but by contemplating the risen Jesus and accepting by faith the things that are revealed in him. Most of all, what we know about Jesus is that he is the *philanthropos,* the lover of humanity. And so the life that we await will be a life of love.

AND THE LIFE
EVERLASTING

T HERE IS NOTHING ESPECIALLY APPEALING about the thought of living forever. The Argentine writer Jorge Luis Borges tells the story of a man who drinks from a river of immortality and becomes immortal. But without death, life lacks definition; it doesn't mean anything. One day the man learns of another river that can take immortality away. And so for centuries he wanders the earth and drinks from every spring and river, seeking to end the curse of endless life. "Death," writes Borges, "makes men precious and pathetic; their ghostliness is touching; any act they perform may be their last."[44]

You cannot make life better just by increasing its quantity. What matters most is quality. It's perhaps regrettable that our English version of the creed speaks of "the life everlasting"— as if life just goes on and on for an indefinitely long time. A better translation would be "eternal life." The creed uses an expression that is found frequently in the New Testament, especially in the Gospel of John. For John, "eternal life" is about quality, not quantity. It is a quality of life that believers experience already when they attach themselves to Jesus. "Whoever believes in the Son has eternal life" (John 3:36). "Anyone who hears my word and believes him who sent me has eternal life" (John 5:24).

John does not really define this special quality of life, except by saying that it is identical with Jesus himself. The Son of God is the one who is truly and fully alive. All other living things are alive through him (John 1:3–4). "Eternal life" can even be used as a title for Jesus. He is called "the eternal life that was with the Father" (1 John 1:2). When we get close enough to this personal life source, we begin to share his quality of life. We too become truly and fully alive. "And this is eternal life, that they may know you, the only true God, and Jesus Christ whom you have sent" (John 17:3).

So when we confess that we believe in eternal life, we're not talking about the duration of life but about a relationship. In the person of Jesus, we find ourselves drawn into a quality of life that is so rich that it can only be described as eternal. Jesus says, "I came that they may have life, and have it abundantly" (John 10:10).

When lovers embrace, they feel sometimes that time has stopped and that the whole world is smaller than the space of their small room. An intense experience of love can alter our ordinary perceptions and seem to lift us beyond the limits of space and time. That is why so many poets and philosophers speak of the "eternal" quality of love. And it is why every experience of love has something tragic about it too: we feel that we have transcended time, yet we know it cannot last. Love is fragile and fleeting. Time reaps everything away in the end.

Perhaps eternal life is something like that intense experience of love, but without the shadow of tragedy. When we experience life in its fullness, death is rendered obsolete. Jesus says, "I am the resurrection and the life. Those who believe in me, even though they die, will live, and everyone who lives and believes in me will never die" (John 11:25–26). Jesus is so truly and fully alive that, to him, even death is really another way of being alive. When we find our way to the living source of life, to Jesus himself, we discover that death is not really death anymore. Even in death our relationship to Jesus is not broken. Death becomes another place where we can go to find him. Wherever we go, he waits to meet us there.

In the thirteenth century, Francis of Assisi composed his famous hymn, "The Canticle of the Sun."[45] Francis sees everything in the light of God's love, and so he sees every creature as a friend. He sings praise to Brother Sun and Sister Moon, Brother Fire and Sister Water. And after spreading his joy over the whole creation, he turns to "Sister Death" and greets even her as a friend. Francis has forgotten how to be afraid. He has found his way to the source of life. He meets Jesus everywhere, even in death, and so he never really dies but only enters more deeply into life.

The lovers embracing in their room forget that time is passing or that the outside world exists. Fleetingly, they rise above time to an eternal moment. What would it mean for the whole of life to be caught up in such a moment? Perhaps we would not even notice that death had been overcome. We would be too preoccupied by life and love. Irenaeus describes eternal life as a kind of blessed forgetfulness. One day, he says, believers will share so fully in the life of God that "they will forget to die."[46]

AMEN

I HAVE BEEN TRYING IN THESE pages to explain the faith of the Apostles' Creed. But I have only scratched the surface. Every line of the creed reaches down into the mystery of the gospel. We are dealing here with words of faith—words whose meaning cannot be fully comprehended, even though a coherent vision of the world rises into view as we say them. No mind has yet grasped the creed in all its fullness, just as "no one has yet breathed all the air."[47]

So it is strange that we end the creed by pronouncing a solemn "amen." To say amen to the creed is to sign my name to it. I confirm the truth of this: I authorize it: amen. Yet we barely fathom what we are saying in the creed. How could anyone have the power to say amen to all this?

A friend told me once that he always crosses his fingers when he gets to the line about the virgin birth. I replied, "What? You mean the rest of the creed is so easy that you can say it with uncrossed fingers? Does the rest of it make perfect sense to you? Do you mean to say that you can verify the truth of everything else—creation, incarnation, resurrection, the last judgment—all except the virgin birth?"

Is there anyone who never feels a flicker of doubt when they contemplate the mysteries of faith? Can anyone really say the amen with all their heart? Isn't it really here, at the last word of the creed, that we ought to cross our fingers? Shouldn't we end the creed by saying: "Oh boy, I hope so!" How can anyone have the audacity to say "Amen"?

When Paul wrote to the church at Corinth, he said:

> As surely as God is faithful, our word to you has not been "Yes and No." For the Son of God, Jesus Christ, whom we proclaimed among you … was not "Yes and No"; but in him it is always "Yes." For in him every one of God's promises is a "Yes." For this reason it is through him that we say the "Amen," to the glory of God.
>
> (2 Cor 1:18–20)

The whole creed is about God's action, God's agency, God's initiative. Even at the end, when we pronounce the amen, we are drawing not on our own resource but God's. We are participating in the action of Jesus, who looks into the face of God and sees all God's ways and works, and says: "Yes! Amen!" When we say the creed, we echo his mighty and eternal amen with our own small, hopeful voices.

And so we're back where we started: with the mystery of the "I" that speaks in the creed. Who is this "I"? Whose voice is it that says "I believe" and then pronounces the authoritative "amen"?

The trend in many churches today has been to replace the "I" with the communal "we." The assumption is that it's individualistic to say "I" and that switching to the plural helps to foster a sense of community and corporate identity. Thus the creed is amended—corrected?—to say, "We believe." In the same way, hymns are sometimes updated to reflect the preference for the communal "we."

Interestingly, the early Christians had exactly the opposite view. In an exposition of Psalm 121, Augustine argued that the "I" is the proper symbol of corporate worship, while the use of "we" is individualistic:

> Let [the psalmist] sing from the heart of each one of you like a single person. Indeed, let each of you be this one person. Each one prays the psalm individually, but because you are all one in Christ, it is the voice of a single person that is heard in the psalm. That is why you do not say, "To you, Lord, have we lifted up our eyes," but "To you, Lord, I have lifted up my eyes." Certainly you must think of this as a prayer offered by each of you on his or her own account, but even more you should think of it as the prayer of the one person present throughout the whole world.[48]

Augustine's point is that the church is not a collection of atomistic individuals. It's not just a matter of many different voices joining together to sing a psalm or say the creed. Rather, the church speaks with one voice. It is intensely personal when I say "I believe." I say the creed as if the words applied to me alone. But beneath and within and around my own personal "I," I hear the surge of a greater voice. There is a corporate "I" in which my own voice participates. This corporate "I" is the body of Christ—which really means Christ himself as the unifying head of a new human society. In Augustine's view it is ultimately Christ who prays and sings and declares the amen. "All the members of Christ, the body of Christ diffused throughout the world, are like a single person asking God's help, one single beggar, one poor suppliant. And this is because Christ himself is that poor man, since he who was rich became poor."[49]

In the same way, the faith that we proclaim at baptism is ultimately the faith of Jesus himself. He is the one who truly turns to God and trusts in God fully. In baptism we are immersed into his faith. We are included in his unique relationship to God. When we say "I believe" we are speaking in him, just as it is really his voice speaking in us by the Holy Spirit when we cry out "Abba, Father." We participate in Jesus' own response to God when we confess and pray and join our voices to his amen.

In the Gospels, Jesus often begins his sayings with the striking preface: "Amen, amen, I tell you ..."[50] He alone has the authority to pronounce the amen. He says the amen not in agreement to anyone else's word but as an expression of his own authority. His word is truth, not because it meets any external criteria of truthfulness but because he is himself the standard against which all other claims to truth are measured. It is he who looks into the depths of God and tells us what he sees. His word is Yes and Amen. In fact, the book of Revelation goes so far as to name him "the Amen, the faithful and true witness" (Rev 3:14). In him the amen to God has become personified.

And so at the end of the creed we join our voices to his—what else could we do?—and allow ourselves to be caught up in Jesus' own response to God. "I believe … Amen!" And all to the glory of God—Father, Son, and Holy Spirit.

ENDNOTES

For *The Apostles' Creed*

1. Irenaeus, *Against the Heresies* 1.10.1.
2. Hippolytus, *On the Apostolic Tradition*, 133–36.
3. Irenaeus, *Against the Heresies* 1.10.1.
4. Irenaeus, *On the Apostolic Preaching* 1.1.7.
5. Using the distinction of J. L. Austin in *How to Do Things with Words*.
6. Augustine, *Confessions* 6.5.7.
7. Augustine, *Sermon* 118.1.
8. Athanasius, *Against the Pagans* 29.
9. Gregory of Nazianzus, *Oration* 31.7.
10. Gregory of Nazianzus, *Oration* 29.16.
11. Athanasius, *On the Council of Nicaea* 24.
12. Tertullian, *Against Praxeas* 10.
13. Augustine, *Exposition of Psalm* 58.1.10.
14. Sarah Coakley, *Powers and Submissions*, 37.
15. See Adolf von Harnack, *Marcion: The Gospel of the Alien God*.
16. Gregory of Nyssa, *Catechetical Oration* 7; in *Christology of the Later Fathers*.
17. Gregory of Nyssa, *Fourth Homily on Ecclesiastes* 335.11.
18. Hippolytus, *Commentary on Daniel* 4.11.
19. Origen, *On First Principles* 2.6.6.
20. Jacob of Serug, *On the Mother of God* 50–51.
21. Lewis Carroll, *Through the Looking Glass*, chapter 5.
22. Karl Barth, *Dogmatics in Outline*, 108.
23. Gregory of Nazianzus, *Oration* 14.40.
24. Irenaeus, *Against the Heresies* 2.22.4.
25. Gregory of Nyssa, *Catechetical Oration* 32.

26. Julian of Norwich, *Revelations of Divine Love*, chapter 51.

27. John Chrysostom, *Homily on Saint Eustathius* 4; in *The Cult of the Saints*.

28. Athanasius, *On the Incarnation* 29.

29. Athanasius, *On the Incarnation* 10.

30. Irenaeus, *Against the Heresies* 2.22.4.

31. The painting, titled "Ngambuny Ascends," is discussed in Rod Pattenden, "Seeing Otherwise: Touching Sacred Things," 24–25.

32. Irenaeus, *Against the Heresies* 5.36.2.

33. Isaac the Syrian, *Homily 28*.

34. Isaac the Syrian, *Homily 28*.

35. Gregory of Nyssa, *On the Soul and the Resurrection* 84.

36. Basil, *On the Holy Spirit* 9.22.

37. Thomas Aquinas, *Sermon-Conferences of St. Thomas Aquinas on the Apostles' Creed*, 129.

38. Origen, *Contra Celsum*, 4.

39. Augustine, *Exposition of Psalm* 36.2.11.

40. Isaac the Syrian, *Homily 51*.

41. Eugene F. Rogers, *After the Spirit*, 70.

42. Assuming that the shorter ending of Mark's Gospel is authentic.

43. Origen, *Homily 7 on Leviticus*.

44. Jorge Luis Borges, "The Immortal," in *Collected Fictions*, 192.

45. The most popular English version is William Henry Draper's paraphrase, "All Creatures of Our God and King."

46. Irenaeus, *Against the Heresies* 5.36.2.

47. Gregory of Nazianzus, *Oration* 30.17.

48. Augustine, *Exposition of Psalm* 122.2.

49. Augustine, *Exposition of Psalm* 39.28.

50. Often translated "truly, truly" or "very truly" in English Bibles.

THE LORD'S PRAYER

Wesley Hill

OUR FATHER IN HEAVEN,

I hallowed be your name,

II your kingdom come,

III your will be done,

  on earth as in heaven.

IV Give us today our daily bread.

v Forgive us our sins

   as we forgive those who sin against us.

vi Save us from the time of trial

vii and deliver us from evil.

   For the kingdom, the power,

   and the glory are yours

   now and forever.

AMEN.

INTRODUCTION

"Your Father in Secret"

A T THE CENTER OF JESUS' Sermon on the Mount in the Gospel of Matthew, He offers to His disciples a model for prayer. This would not have seemed at all unusual to Jesus' followers. Many teachers who attracted crowds in Palestine, like Jesus did, were expected to pass on their insights about how best to beseech God, and Jesus wouldn't have raised any eyebrows by conveying His. In the Gospel of Luke, for instance, Jesus' disciples are the ones who prompt His instruction: "Lord, teach us to pray, as John [the Baptist] taught his disciples" (11:1).

What would have been surprising to the crowd listening to Jesus that day was the *way* Jesus spoke about prayer. He rejected the ostentatious style of prayer with which His listeners would have been familiar. Instead, He emphasized how uncomplicated prayer should be:

> And whenever you pray, do not be like the hypocrites; for they love to stand and pray in the synagogues and at the street corners, so that they may be seen by others. Truly I tell you, they have received

> their reward. But whenever you pray, go into your
> room and shut the door and pray to your Father who
> is in secret; and your Father who sees in secret will
> reward you. When you are praying, do not heap up
> empty phrases as the Gentiles do; for they think that
> they will be heard because of their many words. Do
> not be like them, for your Father knows what you
> need before you ask him. (Matt 6:5–8)

With these words, Jesus dismisses at a stroke the unusual
prayers of the experts in the Jewish law as well as the elabo-
rately theatrical models of the pagan gentile world. There's no
need for pretentious displays, Jesus insists. Prayer shouldn't
be calculated to impress, whether one is seeking to attract
the attention of God or other people. Why? *Because God
doesn't* need *our prayer*. In effect, Jesus says: God isn't looking to have His arm twisted or to be cajoled or bargained
with or manipulated. God doesn't require a flawless recita-
tion of certain phrases, as if He were poised to fly into a
rage in the absence of the right formula or performance. No,
Jesus says, God is "your Father," and He already is disposed
favorably toward you. "Before they call I will answer, while
they are yet speaking I will hear" (Isa 65:24). Go find a quiet
place where you can relax, Jesus seems to say. Unclench your
fists. Breathe deeply. Let your heart rate decrease. Know that
you're already bathed in the Father's love, and ask simply for
what you need, in the assurance that the One to whom you're
speaking is already cupping His ear in your direction. *That's*
what prayer should be.

It's no wonder, then, that when Christian liturgies intro-duce the Lord's Prayer in the context of worship, they often use a formula like this: "And now as our savior Christ has taught us, we are bold to say ..." We can, in other words, give up all our anxious efforts to pacify, convince, or haggle with God. We can trade in that performative style of prayer for one that is more homely and familial. As former Archbishop of Canterbury Rowan Williams writes: "We have the nerve to call God what Jesus called him, because of the Spirit we share with Jesus as a result of being baptized, 'immersed' in the life of Jesus."[1] What Jesus—and later Paul, following in His footsteps—offers to believers is a picture of a God who is eager, indeed, delighted to hear prayer. Unlike human fathers, who are often engrossed in their smartphones and have to have their attention captured in some creative way by their children, God is already and always attentive to His children. It is with that in mind that Jesus says to His disciples, "Pray then in this way ..." (Matt 6:9).

T HE LORD'S PRAYER, OFTEN CALLED the *Pater Noster* (Latin for "Our Father"), is a kind of template, a "Here, try it this way" sort of prayer. It's a model for approaching God with childlike confidence that He will hear. Depending on who you ask, it is composed of six or seven petitions, the first three focused on God's holy character and rule and the latter three or four concerned with invoking God's help in some way.[2] In what follows, we will inch our way through each petition, drawing on the writings of the church fathers, the Protestant Reformers, and more recent Orthodox,

Catholic, and Protestant theologians and preachers to draw out the significance of Jesus' words for Christian prayer today.

Above all, I want to show that the Lord's Prayer is first and foremost about Jesus Himself. Each petition is not only His instruction to His followers about how they are to pray. More fundamentally, each petition is a window into Jesus' own life of prayer—His reliance on and manifestation of the One He called Father. As Dale Allison has put it, "Jesus embodies his speech; he lives as he speaks and speaks as he lives."[3] The Lord's Prayer is a portrait of Jesus Christ—the One who addresses God as Father, who sanctifies God's name, who announces and bears God's healing reign, who submits to God's will, who gives His flesh as daily bread for the life of the world, who provides for the forgiveness of sins through His death on the cross and thus inducts His followers into a lifestyle of forgiveness, and who ultimately delivers believers from the power of death and the devil. Jesus embodies and enacts the prayer He taught His followers to pray.[4] Jesus is "the invisible background of every one of [the Lord's Prayer's] petitions"—all of them are arrows that point toward Him, though He isn't mentioned by name in any of them.[5]

A BRIEF WORD ABOUT TRANSLATION AND inclusive language. I have chosen to use the English Language Liturgical Consultation's 1988 translation of the Lord's Prayer as the primary text that I will comment on here. But I will also reference the familiar King James Version (how could I do otherwise?) as well as newer versions, such as Sarah Ruden's arresting translation.[6] I will also reference, on occasion, my own reading of the Greek versions found in the Gospels of Matthew and Luke.

I have also decided to retain masculine pronouns for God throughout, though I explain at the end of chapter 1 why this must not be understood in a literal way, as if God were male. I also follow the time-honored practice of capitalizing divine pronouns ("He," "His"), in part to signal my belief that while "He" may appropriate our masculine language for His self-communication, God transcends our creaturely categories, and we should not suppose that God's employment of our language is anything other than analogical.[7]

INVOCATION

Our Father in heaven

ALMIGHTY AND EVERLASTING GOD, you are always more ready to hear than we to pray, and to give more than either we desire or deserve. Pour down on us the abundance of your mercy, forgiving us those things of which our conscience is afraid and giving us those good things for which we are not worthy to ask except through the merits and mediation of Jesus Christ, your Son, our Lord, who lives and reigns with you and the Holy Spirit, one God, now and forever. **AMEN.**

OUR FATHER
IN HEAVEN

T HE GOD OF THE BIBLE creates simply by *speech*. "Let there be light" are God's first spoken words in the book of Genesis (1:3). And unlike the creation myth of ancient Babylon, no feminine consort attends as God utters the world into existence.[8] This creation-by-speaking, as Israel's prophets later underscored, may be pictured with our imagery of fatherhood:

> O LORD, you are our Father;
>> we are the clay, and you are our potter;
>> we are all the work of your hand. (Isa 64:8)

God is the One who gives the world its being, and in that sense God may be said to "Father" it. But at the same time, God's fatherhood is unlike any fatherhood we know on earth. The Old Testament's use of "Father" for the God of Israel is only a metaphor for God's relationship to His chosen people.[9]

Perhaps the word "only" isn't quite right, though. True, God is not a Father in the way that human fathers are. God, who radically transcends our creaturely categories, is not male (nor is God female, for that matter), and God is not biologically procreative in a human sense. Yet, for all that, the God of Israel chooses the metaphor of fatherhood as one of the prime symbols of His relationship to His people: "I have become a father to Israel, and Ephraim [the northern kingdom] is my firstborn" (Jer 31:9). The Jewish people look back to their deliverance from bondage in Egypt as the moment that sealed their relationship to God as their Father. God had told Moses to say this to Pharaoh, the recalcitrant king of Egypt: "Thus says the LORD: Israel is my firstborn son. I said to you, 'Let my son go that he may worship me' " (Exod 4:22–23). In one of the most beautiful passages of Isaiah, the prophet writes: "You, O LORD, are our father; our Redeemer from of old is your name" (63:16). And, perhaps most poignantly of all, Jeremiah records God's lament over wayward Israel and Judah, borrowing the imagery of a child wounding a father with their rejection:

> I thought
>   how I would set you among my children,
> and give you a pleasant land,
>   the most beautiful heritage of all the nations.
> And I thought you would call me, My Father,
>   and would not turn from following me. (3:19)

Despite all this, however, there remains throughout the Old Testament a certain reserve about the father metaphor for God.[10] There are nearly half a million words in the Hebrew Bible, yet God is only portrayed as a father some fifteen times.[11] It is almost as if these rare instances of the God of Israel being called (or calling Himself) "father" are place-holders, awaiting some unforeseen future revelation that will cause them to take on a new resonance.

W HEN WE TURN TO THE New Testament, we immediately notice: gone is the reserve of the Old Testament when it comes to calling God "Father." If you were to tally how many times Jesus uses that name for God, the total would reach approximately 65 by the time you finished the Gospel of Luke and over 170 by the time you reached the end of the Gospel of John. Clearly, something new and surprising is afoot.

Jesus claims on several occasions in the Gospels to enjoy an unprecedented intimacy with God, and in these moments His calling God "Father" is especially prominent. "All things have been handed over to me by my Father; and no one knows the Son except the Father, and no one knows the Father except the Son and anyone to whom the Son chooses to reveal him," Jesus says (Matt 11:27). In the Gospel of John, Jesus' language is even stronger: "The Father and I are one" (10:30). And then, in the intimacy of prayer, on the eve of His crucifixion, Jesus exclaims, "So now, Father, glorify me in your own presence with the glory that I had in your presence before the world existed" (John 17:5). It took the church long centuries to plumb the implications of these cryptic words. Eventually, however, their significance could not be denied. What Jesus obliquely indicated in parables and symbolic gestures, the church has come to confess in clear, convicted prose.

From and to all eternity, God is one—but not in such a way that God is solitary. That's what Christians confess when they recite the Nicene Creed. Jesus Christ, the only Son of God, is "eternally begotten of the Father, God from God, Light from Light, true God from true God, begotten, not made, of one Being with the Father." The God Christians worship has no rivals but nor is He, for that reason, impersonal. Unfathomably, God exists *in* and *as* relationship. God the Father has a Son, whom He "begets"—here the creed uses the normal, if slightly archaic, word for human procreation. But this "begetting," this birthing, of the Father's Son does not happen in the way that human births do. It isn't physical, and it doesn't happen at any datable moment: contrary to an early Christian heresy, there was never a time when the Son was not. The Son's being begotten from His Father is, as the creed insists, eternal. Before and beyond all worlds (our time-bound language reaches its limits here), God is born from God but in such a way that there is only one God.[12] And as Father and Son fill and possess each other with something like sheer, radiant bliss, they do so in the love and delight of the Holy Spirit, who, like the Father and the Son, is eternal, without beginning or end, but who also—we reach the limits of language—is breathed out and given identity, we might say, by the Father and the Son together.

This is the ultimate origin of Jesus' teaching that God is Father. God has never *not* been the Father. His Son has never *not* been the Son. And their mutual love, the Spirit, has never begun nor ever ceased to bind them together in unbreakable communion. This mystery is part of what Jesus starts to disclose when He instructs His disciples to call God "Father."

T HE FIRST WORDS OF THE Lord's Prayer, then—"Our Father in heaven"—are remarkable because Jesus calls God "Father," expressing a breathtaking intimacy with the One who had rescued Israel from Egypt. Those first words of the prayer are even more remarkable because with them, *we* are invited to address God in the same way that Jesus does. God is Father eternally, and Israel, too, in its memory of God's saving acts on its behalf, had known God by that name. But Jesus' words—His use of the plural possessive pronoun "our" is the key—beckon us to take our place alongside Him, looking up to Him as our older brother (Heb 2:10–18), entering into, partaking in, and emulating His relationship to God. For Him, that relationship has always been. He has never *not* enjoyed the privilege of communion with His Father. But for us, even those of us who have been born into God's covenant people, that relationship happens by enticement, as we are wooed into a new redemptive closeness with God through Jesus.[13] As Karl Barth puts it,

> Jesus Christ, who is the Son of God, who has made himself our brother and makes us his brothers and sisters ... takes us with him in order to associate us with himself, to place us beside him so that we may live and act as his family and as the members of his body. ... Jesus Christ invites us, commands us, and allows us to speak with him to God, to pray with him

his own prayer, to be united with him in the Lord's Prayer. Therefore he invites us to adore God, pray to God, and praise God with one mouth and one soul, with him, united to him.[14]

Barth is building on what St. Paul wrote shortly after Jesus' resurrection. Paul insists that Christians are those who have the boldness—there's that word again—to take on their lips Jesus' own address to God. We "receive adoption as children. And because you are children, God has sent the Spirit of His Son into our hearts, crying, 'Abba! Father!' " (Gal 4:5–6). Later, in his powerful Letter to the Romans, Paul would write similarly: "When we cry, 'Abba! Father!' it is that very Spirit bearing witness with our spirit that we are children of God" (8:15–16). We are tagalongs, you might say, taking advantage of the closeness Jesus enjoys with His Father. As the prophet Zechariah long ago predicted, people "from nations of every language shall take hold of a Jew, grasping his garment and saying, 'Let us go with you, for we have heard that God is with you' " (8:23). Indeed, God is with Jesus, and we do grasp our older brother's garment, begging Him to take us with Him to the Father. And He does.

WHAT DOES IT MEAN THAT Jesus tells us to pray to our Father "in heaven"? Heaven, as the Bible describes it, is not a far-off place in some distant galaxy. It is not a place at all in the sense we usually use that term, which makes it hard to talk about for people who cannot imagine existing without taking up space. Rather, "heaven" is a word that allows us to speak about God's nearness and availability without pinning Him down to a specific geographical address. Because God's life is not bodily, He is not limited by the categories of time and space that mark our human existence. God is not part of "the metaphysical furniture of the universe."[15] The earliest version of the Lord's Prayer, the one that goes back to Jesus himself, probably didn't have the phrase "in heaven." Luke's version says simply, "Father, hallowed be your name" (11:2). But Matthew adds it, perhaps in order to ward off any misunderstanding that God is a creaturely Father. Jesus' God is defined "over and against father gods, gods who beget the world."[16] The One whom Jesus calls "Father" is a *heavenly*, not an *earthly*, Father. As usual, it may be that the poet says it best:

> Our Father, You who dwell within the heavens—
> but are not circumscribed by them.[17]

BEFORE WE LEAVE THE OPENING address of the Lord's Prayer, we should pause to reflect on how, millennia after Jesus first bequeathed it to His followers, this prayer has become difficult for some of us to pray in ways that Jesus' first disciples could never have foreseen. Calling God "Father" is painful for many believers today because a long history of patriarchy (a social system—the only one most of us have ever known—in which men wield primary power and privilege) and fatherly abuse have robbed the term of much of its intended comfort. Feminist theologians have pointed out that we can easily toggle between thinking that God is beyond gender, but we call Him "Father" because that is what the Bible authorizes, and thinking that we call God "Father" because God *is* male. The former is what Christianity has always taught, but the latter is what many Christians seem to *hear*. And that, feminist thinkers rightly warn us, is dangerous.

Can anything be said in response to this? Other than lamenting and redoubling our commitment to work for social justice, Christians should also regularly reflect on and preach about how God's fatherhood must always and only be understood through His unity with His self-giving Son. Any picture of God as "Father" that leads us to think in terms of domination and cruelty rather than of humble service and unending love is not a true understanding of the God and Father of our Lord Jesus Christ, "who loved [us] and gave himself for [us]" (Gal 2:20).

Theologian Sarah Coakley has insisted that feminists not only *can* but *must* call God "Father" in order to help the church see that patriarchal interpretations of God's fatherhood aren't at all the best readings of what the Lord's Prayer is about. By adhering tenaciously to the conviction that "the *true* meaning of 'Father' is to be found in the Trinity," Christian feminists today may, through praying the Lord's Prayer, teach the rest of us why it isn't a charter for male domination.[18]

PETITION I

Hallowed be your name

HOLY GOD, your name is unlike any other name. Show us your divine majesty and mercy, that we may honor your name in worship, cling to it in times of trouble, and proclaim it boldly to the world. This we ask in the holy name of Jesus Christ, who lives and reigns with you and the Holy Spirit, one God, now and forever. **AMEN.**

HALLOWED BE
YOUR NAME

W E ARE USED TO THINKING of the ancient Greek and Romans gods by their names: Apollo, Dionysus, and so on. Their personalities—and hair-trigger tempers—are vivid and reliably tempestuous. Unlike them, Israel's God seems elusive, even inscrutable. Erich Auerbach, reflecting on the story in Genesis in which God comes to the patriarch Abraham and asks the unthinkable of him, notices the strangeness of God of the Bible by comparison with the Greek deities:

> He does not come, like Zeus or Poseidon, from the Aethiopians, where he has been enjoying a sacrificial feast. Nor are we told anything of his reasons for tempting Abraham so terribly. He has not, like Zeus, discussed them in set speeches with other gods gathered in council ... unexpected and mysterious, he enters the scene from some unknown height or depth and calls: Abraham![19]

To put it bluntly, the God of the Bible is beyond our categories of comprehension.

Despite His distance from the likes of Zeus or Apollo, Israel's God also has a personal name that He discloses to human beings. Near the beginning of the book of Exodus, we find this exchange between God and Moses, on the eve of Moses' journey back to Egypt to reunite with his ancestral people and lead them to freedom:

> Moses said to God, "If I come to the Israelites and say to them, 'The God of your ancestors has sent me to you,' and they ask me, 'What is his name?' what shall I say to them?" God said to Moses, "I AM WHO I AM." He said further, "Thus you shall say to the Israelites, 'I AM has sent me to you.' " God also said to Moses, "Thus you shall say to the Israelites, 'The LORD, the God of your ancestors, the God of Abraham, the God of Isaac, and the God of Jacob, has sent me to you':
>
> > This is my name forever,
> > and this my title for all generations. (Exod 3:13–15)

This English translation makes it hard to see, but the God of Israel's proper name lies behind "LORD," that word usually printed in all-capital letters in English Bibles. It is sometimes written out as "Yahweh" (or, in some older versions, "Jehovah"). Following ancient Jewish custom, English Bibles do not print this holy name, instead substituting a title, "Lord" (meaning "Master" or "Sovereign").

The divine name is a sort of pun. Its four Hebrew letters—
yod, heh, waw, heh (Hebrew has no vowels)—are almost the
same letters used in the earlier mysterious sentence, "I AM
WHO I AM." But even more noteworthy is that this "name" of
God doesn't seem to clarify much of anything about God's
character or personality. According to Pope Benedict XVI,
it is, paradoxically, "a name and a non-name at one and
the same time."[20] In some mysterious way, God seems to
be saying to Moses, "You may call Me by name, but do not
make the mistake of thinking that you thereby *comprehend*
Me. I am *free* to be Who I will be. My name means … I exist."

God's name, in other words, signifies His sheer transcen-
dence—He is not like other gods, much less a mortal creature.
Yet equally, it underscores His immanence—His nearness and
availability to those who call out to Him. As one Jewish com-
mentator put it, "God's pronouncement of His own Name
indicates that the Divine Personality can be known only to
the extent that God chooses to reveal His Self, and it can be
truly characterized only in terms of itself, and not by analogy
with something else."[21] God is God, with or without us. God
doesn't need our assistance or support; rather, God gives us
our existence. But, at the same time, God chooses not to be
God without us. He offers His name to Moses. God makes
a covenant with the people of Israel and promises to answer
when they call. God lets Himself be known.

T HROUGHOUT THE OLD TESTAMENT, God is concerned
that His name not be misunderstood. What would other

nations think if the Lord, who had given Israel permission
to call Him by name, suddenly reneged on His commitment
to them? "For my name's sake I defer my anger," God says
through the prophet Isaiah, "for the sake of my praise I
restrain it for you, so that I may not cut you off" (Isa 48:9).
God is acting to preserve His reputation: "For my own sake,
for my own sake, I do it, for why should my name be profaned? My glory I will not give to another" (Isa 48:11).

So it comes as a complete shock when, centuries later,
God *does* give His name to another. That gift is described
by St. Paul:

> Therefore God also highly exalted [Christ Jesus]
>   and gave him the name
>   that is above every name. (Phil 2:9)

From henceforth, after Jesus' resurrection from the dead,
people will call Him by the name of "Lord"—the same name
that God had given to the people of Israel to call *Him* by. How
this unimaginable gift could be given was one of the most
unsettling and exciting mysteries that the earliest Christians
had to ponder.

But the plot thickens even more. Elsewhere in his let-
ters to young churches, Paul also names the quickening,
empowering, gracious presence of God moving among
believers—God's own Spirit—with the same personal name.
"Now the Lord of whom [the book of Exodus] speaks is the
Spirit" (2 Cor 3:17 REB). The name with which God named
Himself to Moses—the same name that God handed over to
Jesus as a crowning honor after Jesus' shameful death and

resurrection—is also the name of the Spirit at work in the churches.

The only way this unthinkable trifold sharing of the one, holy divine name is conceivable is if Jesus and His—God's—Spirit are united to God in such a way that their mutual sharing of the same name isn't really "sharing," as we think of it, at all. Jesus and the Spirit must be so internal to God's identity, God's own life, that they are rightly called by the name of God. In giving the Son and the Spirit His name, the Father identifies Himself with Jesus Christ and the Holy Spirit in the most intimate way possible.[22] The Father says, in effect, "This is my Son. He, together with the Holy Spirit, is one with me. Listen to him" (see Matt 3:17; 17:5). It's no surprise, then—though it is breathtaking—when the Gospel of Matthew ends with a mention of a singular *name*: "the name of the Father and of the Son and of the Holy Spirit" (28:19).

THE WORD "HALLOW" MEANS TO "honor" or "make uncommon"—to "make something special," as we might say in contemporary English. According to Simone Weil, when we ask God to "hallow" His name, "we are asking for something that *exists* eternally, with full and complete reality, so that we can neither increase nor diminish it, even by an infinitesimal fraction."[23] God's name *is already* uncommon, regardless of whether we acknowledge it or not.

That name has been uttered in love by the Father, His Son, and their Spirit from before all worlds. To pray for God's name to be hallowed is to ask God to preserve and display this mysteriously radiant reality. It is to ask God to keep before the eyes of the world this drama of divine majesty and mercy so that we can continue to speak it back to God in worship and cling to it in times of desperation.

We may think, for instance, of a Christian like Polycarp, one of the earliest Christian martyrs. In the second century, faced with the demand that he hallow the emperor of Rome as "Lord" and "Savior," Polycarp refused and said, "For eighty-six years I have been serving [Jesus Christ], and he has done me no wrong. Indeed how can I blaspheme my king who saved me?"[24] Closer to home, we may think of a Christian like Kevin Harris formerly of the Marin Foundation, who, when he was living in Chicago's Boystown neighborhood, grew concerned about the damage done when his fellow Christians led many lesbian and gay people to believe that God's message for them was only one of judgment. The Marin Foundation started the "I'm Sorry" campaign, in which Christians attended LGBT pride parades and apologized for not communicating more clearly the message of God's love and mercy for all sinners without exception.[25] The Marin Foundation's initiative might be seen as protecting God's name—upholding God's reputation by acting in ways that emphasize His love.

Through costly actions like these, Christians show their reverence for the divine name that is always and already holy. Clifton Black connects God's own hallowing of His name and our reverencing it in response: "God's self-consecration kindles in us the yearning to revere the Almighty as God alone deserves."[26] As we meditate on God's eternal holiness, we may begin to ask ourselves: What words and actions on our part are fitting complements to this reality?

PETITION II

Your kingdom come

HEAVENLY FATHER, your kingdom is not of this world. Give us eyes to see and ears to hear, so that we may recognize and embrace your kingly rule in our lives, which is good news for the poor, freedom for prisoners, sight for the blind, and liberty to those who are oppressed; this we ask in the name of Jesus the King. **AMEN**.

YOUR KINGDOM COME

IN CONTEMPORARY ENGLISH, THE WORD "kingdom" primarily denotes a place. A king's kingdom is the land over which he rules. But when Mark the Evangelist wanted to sum up the way Jesus started His earthly ministry, he used these words:

> Now after John was arrested, Jesus came to Galilee, proclaiming the good news of God, and saying, "The time is fulfilled, and the kingdom of God has come near; repent, and believe in the good news." (1:14–15)

The Greek word that Mark and the other Gospel writers use to summarize Jesus' message—*basileia*—is probably better translated with a word that indicates *activity*. A word like "rule," "reign," or even "kingship" is closer to the original meaning of *basileia*—which means that when Jesus says "the kingdom of God has come near," He is proclaiming that God is asserting His rule in the world in and through Jesus' ministry. Jesus is heralding the fact that God—like a king who has been abroad and absent from his native land—finally is returning to take back His throne. Jesus is announcing a sort of re-cor-onation. The God we might have thought was silent, never to be heard from again, is back on the scene and ready to rule.

But what *kind* of rule will it be? Coronations can be ter-rifying. The enthronement of a new king or leader can make one queasy with dread. If you've never had to fear when a new prime minister, president, or monarch comes into power, then you have lived a life of rare privilege. For many people in the world—throughout history and also presently, even in the modern West—the passing of power to a new ruler is a matter of gnawing anxiety.

A scene from the end of *The Godfather*—one of the most haunting pieces of cinema I've ever seen—captures this fear well. The protagonist, Michael Corleone, stands near the bap-tismal font in an ornate Catholic church for his nephew's christening. As the camera lingers on his stoic facial expres-sion and elegant suit, the scene cuts to a series of assassina-tions that Michael has orchestrated, which are happening at the very same time as the service of baptism. It turns out that Michael has arranged to become the kingpin of the New York mob, and he is ascending to his throne by means of a blood-bath. The cost of his rule is the death of anyone who stands in his way. The agonizing, devastating final scene of the film shows him being crowned, as it were, as "Don Corleone"—the new monarch of terror.

This fictional story is haunting enough, but similar stories happen in real life all the time. Dictators trample on human dignity to ascend their thrones. Terrorists seize the reins of power. Evil overlords who care nothing for the poor or the sick take control of governments and kingdoms, and the citizens consequently fear for their lives. Coronations, for much of the world, are occasions of uncertainty, worry, and alarm.

Perhaps that same worry and alarm was stirred up in the hearts of Jesus' hearers when He preached. His message about God's reign would have conjured up all the churning emotions that coronations usually conjure up: the trembling uncertainty about how severe the new king's reign would be, the nagging apprehension that the king might demand of them what they aren't able to give, the dread of what wars the king might lead them into. This is the way things go with kings in our world. Perhaps Jesus' hearers would have remembered the words of the prophet Samuel:

> These will be the ways of the king who will reign over you: he will take your sons and appoint them to his chariots and to be his horsemen, and to run before his chariots; and he will appoint for himself commanders of thousands and commanders of fifties, and some to plow his ground and to reap his harvest, and to make his implements of war and the equipment of his chariots. He will take your daughters to be perfumers and cooks and bakers. He will take the best of your fields and vineyards and olive orchards and give them to his courtiers. He will take one-tenth of your grain and of your vineyards and give it to his officers and his courtiers. He will take your male and female slaves, and the best of your cattle and donkeys, and put them to his work. He will take one-tenth of your flocks, and you

shall be his slaves. And in that day you will cry out
because of your king. (1 Sam 8:11–18)

The world of first-century Judea was sadly familiar with
this sort of kingly script. The Jews of Palestine were used to
ambitious would-be rulers rising through the ranks by means
of betrayal and intrigue and nighttime assassinations. They
were familiar with the story of Julius Caesar's stabbing. They
knew the way that plot unfolds.

But God's now-arriving rule doesn't follow the usual pattern, according to Jesus. God's reign spells liberation for
Israel, not coercion. God taking up His crown means the
dawning of a new era of deliverance, not domination. When
Jesus wants to point His hearers to the telltale signs of God's
kingship bursting onto the scene, He says things like this:
"But if it is by the finger of God that I cast out the demons, then
the kingdom of God has come to you" (Luke 11:20). Where
you see people being delivered from oppression, in other
words, *there* you see God's reign in action. Jesus made His
followers into emissaries of God's saving rule; "he sent them
out to proclaim the kingdom of God and to heal" (Luke 9:2).
Where you see healing and the restoration of what sin and
death have disfigured, *there* you see God's kingship displayed.

That is what Jesus teaches His followers to cry out for:
"Your kingdom come" means "Father, make Your healing reign
more and more tangible and visible in our world. Let Your
rule assert itself ever more concretely in the places where
sickness and evil still seem to have the upper hand."

J ESUS ALSO TEACHES HIS FOLLOWERS to pray "Your kingdom come" because—we must not evade this uncomfortable truth—God's rule is not yet visible in the way we long for it to be. God's reign, Jesus says,

> is like a mustard seed, which, when sown upon the ground, is the smallest of all the seeds on earth; yet when it is sown it grows up and becomes the greatest of all shrubs, and puts forth large branches, so that the birds of the air can make nests in its shade. (Mark 4:31–32)

Or, as He puts it in another place, "The kingdom of heaven is like yeast that a woman took and mixed in with three measures of flour until all of it was leavened" (Matt 13:33). God's rule is breaking into the world in Jesus' ministry—but not in such a way that it can be readily identified by the unaided human eye. We can discern it by faith, but we don't yet *see* it in the way that we will someday.

One illustration that modern Bible interpreters use to describe the mysterious already-but-not-yet nature of God's reign is the distinction between "D-Day," the operation whereby the Allied forces in World War II secured a foothold in France in 1944, and "V-E Day," or "Victory in Europe Day," which came some eleven months later when Nazi Germany offered its unconditional surrender.[27] Historians looking back now recognize that the war was effectively won when the Allies landed on Normandy's beaches. The D-Day invasion hearkened the end of the Nazi regime, even though the death camps kept running and many more lives of combatants and civilians alike were lost before Germany's surrender in May of the following year.

It's as though we live between two similarly momentous days. We look backward to the life, death, and resurrection of Jesus as the moment when God's rule showed itself to be unconquerable—theological D-Day, we might call it. In a very real way, God's conquest of His rebellious world was achieved when His Son left His tomb behind on Easter morning. Yet suffering continues, and we go on longing for an end that isn't yet public and universal. In this time between the times, as we await Christ's coming in glory, we who have caught the vision of the way the war will end, we "who have the first fruits of the Spirit, groan inwardly while we wait for adoption, the redemption of our bodies" (Rom 8:23). We know that God will one day do for us and for His whole creation what He did for Jesus in raising Him from the dead, but for now, in the meantime, we weep and wait. And that is why we continue to pray, "Your kingdom come," meaning, "Father, let us see, in the present, more and more signs that the war You have won against the powers that corrupt and enslave Your world is nearing its consummation. Give us more tangible previews of that great day when death will be swallowed up in victory. Help us see that Jesus' resurrection isn't just a one-off event but will sweep us along in its wake so that we will share in His transformation."

"We are waiting," says Karl Barth, "until Easter becomes for the world a general event."[28]

PETITION III

Your will be done
on earth as in heaven

GRACIOUS GOD, you will only what is good and acceptable and perfect. Heal our bent and wandering wills, and teach us perfect obedience, that we may love your will above our own by imitating Christ, who submitted to your will by giving up his life for us; in his name we pray. **AMEN**.

YOUR WILL BE DONE ON EARTH AS IN HEAVEN

I N THE TIME IT HAS TAKEN me to compose this sentence, two children have died from malaria, around a dozen children under the age of five have passed away from hunger, and over one hundred babies around the world have been killed in the womb. It reminds me of a line from the end of *The Private Patient* by P. D. James: "If the screams of all earth's living creatures were one scream of pain, surely it would shake the stars."[29] The image is haunting—a terrible choir of pain, God's ears bombarded by the screams of agony of His creation.

If God's own life consists of the sheer bliss of love shared by Father, Son, and Spirit, the mismatch between that reality and all these horrors is unconscionable—and the third petition of the Lord's Prayer forces us to confront that. When we pray, "Your will be done, on earth as in heaven," we are aware of how God's will is *not* being done in our world. We are asking God to overcome this contradiction, to act in such a way that life on earth increasingly resembles the peaceable and joyous life of God, of heaven.

In petitionary prayer, we set ourselves against what seems "normal." If a world filled with cancer, AIDS, sex slavery, rapacious greed, and toxic waste seems to us like "just the way things are," then petitionary prayer invites us to imagine a different world—the world as God meant it to be and will ultimately make it, a world in which those things are profoundly abnormal. To pray "Your will be done" is to adopt an appropriate distress over the world as it exists now and to hold on to the conviction that God will even now begin to change the world. As theologian David Wells puts it,

> Petitionary prayer only flourishes where there is a twofold belief: first, that God's name is hallowed too irregularly, His kingdom has come too little, and His will is done too infrequently; second, that God Himself can change this situation. Petitionary prayer, therefore, is the expression of the hope that life as we meet it, on the one hand, *can* be otherwise and, on the other hand, that it *ought* to be otherwise. ... To pray declares that God and His world are at cross-purposes.[30]

So as we pray for God's reign to become more fully visible, as we ask for God's perfect heavenly wholeness to come on earth as well, we are asking for the aftershocks of the fall to be quieted, declaring, "Let your glory be over all the earth" (Ps 57:5). We are, in effect, taking our stand against the world as it is now and asking for more and more foretastes of the world as it will be when the kingdom of God is finally consummated.[31]

B UT HOW DOES THAT HAPPEN? How does God respond to our asking for His will to be done on earth as in heaven? In order to answer that question, once again we have to see how Jesus demonstrates in His own life what it means to pray His prayer.

On the eve of His crucifixion, Jesus prays in the way He had earlier instructed His disciples to pray: "My Father, if it is possible, let this cup pass from me; yet not what I want but what you want. ... My Father, if this cannot pass unless I drink it, your will be done" (Matt 26:39, 42). In Greek, the wording of the Lord's Prayer and the wording of Jesus' anguished cry in the garden are identical (compare Matt 6:10 with 26:39, 42). And the way that prayer is answered, of course—the way the Father's will comes to be done on earth, in that hour—is that Jesus is *not* rescued from His fate. He is arrested, tried, bound, scourged, and crucified. This doesn't look like the peace of heaven dispelling the darkness of the earth so much as the reverse.

What should we make of that? More pointedly, how ought Jesus' prayer in Gethsemane to shape our understanding of God's will coming to be done on earth? Just so: in a world marked by sin and death, for the will of God—the wholeness, life, and love of God—to take root on earth requires the vanquishing of that sin and death. It won't do to say that God is only found in moments of obvious health, beauty, and joy. God must also be at work in suffering, in darkness, in torment, because the triumph of God's love can be assured only if God confronts the horror we've made of the world, bears it, and removes it. Only if the will of God mysteriously includes Jesus' death on a cross can the will of God be guaranteed. All other solutions would be mere Band-Aids, putting off the inevitable confrontation by papering over it. If the heavenly will of God is to be enacted on a sin-scorched earth, then it must also be the will of God for Jesus to enter fully into the pain of that earth. The way to God's will being done lies *through* Jesus' suffering, not through its avoidance. Only by entering into and overcoming the world's evil can Jesus usher in the healing we pray for.

The will of God that is done in heaven is clearly the perfect, eternal love of Father, Son, and Spirit, unmarred by any suffering or dying. What is less intuitive—but what Gethsemane and, later, Calvary force us to notice—is that the will of God is also the way of the incarnate Lord into the far country of *our* suffering and dying, where He is mocked, spit upon, strung up, and left to suffocate. *That* is what it looks like for the will of God to be done on earth as it is in heaven because *that* is the only way our earth can be saved.

P ERHAPS HERE IS AS GOOD a place as any to pause and ask what we mean when we say that *we* petition *God*. If the Christian tradition is right to call God unchanging, then what sense does it make to ask God to act in accord with our prayers? Is it the case that our asking for God's kingdom to come and will to be done on earth is what moves God to usher in the kingdom and assert His will?

Martin Luther was one of many Christians who saw clearly that the point of petitionary prayer is not to try to convince God to do something He otherwise would not do.

Luther insisted that instead, asking for God's kingdom and will to be made manifest—which they would be, regardless of our efforts—is about stretching our hearts so that we may learn to desire truer, greater realities. As C. S. Lewis says in the stage play and film *Shadowlands*, "I pray because I can't help myself. I pray because I'm helpless. I pray because the need flows out of me all the time, waking and sleeping. It doesn't change God. It changes me."[32]

PETITION IV

Give us today
our daily bread

ALMIGHTY AND EVERLASTING GOD, you fed the
Israelites in the wilderness with bread from heaven,
and you have given us the spiritual food of your Son,
Jesus Christ. Give us all we need this day, and make
our hearts generous so that we may be signs of your
kindness to all we meet, in the name of Jesus Christ,
the bread of life. **AMEN.**

GIVE US TODAY
OUR DAILY BREAD

A FTER THE REFORMER MARTIN LUTHER DIED, his friends who came to his room to remove his corpse found a note he had scrawled sometime in his final days: "We are beggars, that is true."[33]

With those scribbled phrases, Luther summed up his own hard-won theological perspective on what it means to be a human being: we are all utterly dependent on divine grace alone. Our supposed merits are insufficient to win us any favor with God. But Luther's final sentence also expresses one of the chief themes of the Lord's Prayer: far from being self-sustaining, we are needy creatures, reliant on energy from a source outside ourselves if we are to go on living. We are like beggars, whose only hope for food and shelter is the compassion of Another.

When Jesus teaches us to pray "Give us today our daily bread," He is first of all training us to see ourselves in a certain way in relation to God. To the surprise of His status-conscious disciples, He insists, "Truly I tell you, unless you change and become like children, you will never enter the kingdom of heaven" (Matt 18:3). If there is one fact that is obvious about children, it is their *dependence*. Unless a parent or guardian provides milk for a baby, the infant will die. According to Jesus, that remains our true condition into our adulthood, whether we are conscious of it or not. Were God to withdraw His nourishment from us, we would not just slowly shrivel but immediately cease to exist.

A professor of mine described the Christian doctrines of creation and divine providence with the analogy of a plugged-in TV. If someone were to unplug the TV's cord, it isn't the case that the characters on screen would gradually fade, their words and gestures growing more and more sluggish until the screen went dark altogether. Rather, as soon as the TV's connection to its source of power is cut off, the images cease to flicker. The TV has no electricity of its own; it projects its images only by constant connection to its electrical feed. We likewise are dependent on God's *continual* "upholding all things by the word of his power" (Heb 1:3 KJV). That's why the Lord's Prayer includes the word "today." It is not enough for God to kick-start the process of sustaining human beings and then sit back like a parent retreating into a book while the children race off to attempt some task or play by themselves. On the contrary, we rely on God's provision each moment of our lives.

And we shouldn't overlook the fact that Jesus teaches us to request that provision. Nineteenth-century Anglican priest and theologian F. D. Maurice recommended that wealthy, well-fed Christians in particular should ponder this petition during Lent, the forty days leading up to Easter during which many believers fast from certain luxuries, culinary or otherwise. Some Christians, says Maurice,

> are apt to mock God when they speak these solemn words ["Give us today our daily bread"], apt to take food and every other blessing as if it were their right of which no power in heaven or earth except by sheer injustice can deprive them. Something which shall tell them of dependence, some secret reminiscence, insignificant to others, that all things are not their own; some hint that there are a few million creatures of their flesh and blood who cannot call any of these things their own, is needful for them.[34]

Those well-nourished Christians who stop eating meat during Lent, says Maurice, "are desiring to recollect that it is a good which He *bestows*."[35] They are trying, in other words, to pray "Give us today our daily bread" with more sincere humility, recognizing that God does not owe them food but may nonetheless be pleased to supply it. Voluntarily going without bread for a while will help you realize how much you need it and how little power you yourself have to guarantee that you'll always have it.

JESUS HIMSELF MODELS THE POSTURE of dependence on God that He commends to His followers. (This is our recurring theme. As Karl Barth puts it, "The Commander … embodies the command."[36]) Each petition of the Lord's Prayer is a window onto Jesus' character and actions before it is instruction for us.

After being baptized in the Jordan River in solidarity with repentant Israel and while abstaining from food in the wilderness before launching His public ministry, Jesus experienced the gnaw of hunger and knew what it meant to depend on God for His survival. "He ate nothing at all during those days, and when they were over, he was famished," says Luke's Gospel (4:2). While His stomach was empty, the devil appeared to Jesus and proposed that He perform a miracle of converting desert rocks into warm loaves, but Jesus spurned the suggestion. "It is written, 'One does not live by bread alone,' " He replied, invoking the story of God supplying the Israelites with manna (Luke 4:4, quoting Deut 8:3). Refusing to assume the rebel posture of self-reliance, Jesus told His tempter that He would wait for His Father to give Him bread on His own terms.

This was, after all, the point of the story that Jesus alluded to. Having escaped slavery in Egypt, the people of Israel found themselves tempted again and again to forget their sheer dependence on God for their freedom. No sooner had they made it through the middle of the sea without so much as getting their feet damp than they built an altar to a self-made god. As soon as they remembered the abundance they had left behind, they were inclined to perceive God as having cheated them. This is why God directly—without waiting for the process of seeding, harvesting, threshing, and baking to produce bread—gave manna to the Israelites. According to the passage Jesus quoted, Moses instructs the people: "He humbled you by letting you hunger, then by feeding you with manna, with which neither you nor your ancestors were acquainted, in order to make you understand that one does not live by bread alone, but by every word that comes from the mouth of the LORD." Through His obedience, Jesus enacts His own prayer. He demonstrates what it looks like to trust in the manna-giving God, the One He called "Father."

IN JOHN 6, JESUS ONCE again talks about the Old Testament story of manna in the wilderness. Disputing with Him, the religious leaders of Judea challenge Jesus to perform some certifying gesture: "What sign are you going to give us then, so that we may see it and believe you?" They go on (helpfully, they must suppose) to suggest the kind of thing they have in mind for Jesus to do: "Our ancestors ate the manna in the wilderness; as it is written, 'He gave them bread from heaven to eat.' " They seem to say that Jesus should act like Moses, calling down food from the skies and causing water to gush out of rocks.

Mysteriously, though, when He answers them, Jesus leaps from the story His opponents cite, a story of God's miraculous care in the past, to the immediate present: "Very truly, I tell you, it was not Moses who gave you the bread from heaven, but it is my Father who gives you the true bread from heaven. For the bread of God is that which comes down from heaven and gives life to the world" (John 6:30, 31, 32–33). And then, in case they miss the point, He spells out what He means:

> I am the bread of life. Your ancestors ate the manna in the wilderness, and they died. ... I am the living bread that came down from heaven. Whoever eats of this bread will live forever; and the bread that I will give for the life of the world is my flesh. (John 6:48–51)

Manna is sustaining only for so long, Jesus insists. Bread can keep human beings alive but not for forever. For eternal life, stronger, more substantial bread is needed—and that bread is His own life, offered for human consumption. Jesus promises, "Those who eat my flesh and drink my blood have eternal life, and I will raise them up on the last day; for my flesh is true food and my blood is true drink" (John 6:54–55).

When we come back to the Lord's Prayer after hearing Jesus' discourse on the bread of life and His flesh given to the world for eating, it becomes hard not to see Jesus *Himself* as the daily bread He encourages us to pray for. In her meditations on the Lord's Prayer, Simone Weil says simply, "Christ is our bread."[37] This explains why the churches of both the East and West pray the Lord's Prayer just before the distribution of Communion. The priest consecrates the bread and wine, asking the Holy Spirit to sanctify them so that they might be the body and blood of Christ for the faithful. As worshipers go up to receive these gifts, they receive at the same time the answer to their prayer moments earlier: "Give us today our daily bread."

In the Eucharist, Jesus puts Himself in our hands so we know exactly where to find Him.[38] In that moment, we don't have to wonder whether God is for us. We *know* He is because we've just tasted His provision. He gives us His Son—His life-giving flesh.

PETITION V

Forgive us our sins as we forgive those who sin against us

MERCIFUL GOD, you are slow to anger and abounding in steadfast love. Forgive us the wrongs we have done, and give us strength to forgive those who have wronged us, so that we may bear with one another in love, and maintain the unity of the Spirit in the bond of peace. In the name of Jesus Christ, whose death has brought reconciliation. **AMEN.**

FORGIVE US OUR SINS AS WE FORGIVE THOSE WHO SIN AGAINST US

ONE OF MY FRIENDS TELLS a story about taking his uncle to an Episcopal church for the first time. Each Sunday, prior to receiving Communion, worshipers in Episcopal churches say these words: "Most merciful God, we confess that we have sinned against you in thought, word, and deed ..." My friend's uncle, seeing those words in the prayer book, squirmed uncomfortably. Later, he told my friend: "Should we really expect *everyone* to confess that they've sinned that week? That's what having a prayer of confession suggests— that every single one of us needs to acknowledge some sin. But what about those Christians who have gained victory over sin already? Surely they shouldn't be forced to confess what isn't true."

Without entering into the complicated history of ideas like "victorious Christian living" or "entire sanctification," I am struck by what my friend's uncle saw so clearly. By having a confession of sins as part of the church's regular liturgy, the Episcopal Church is indeed making the assumption that everyone attending church that morning needs to make that confession. Where I differ from my friend's uncle is in thinking that this practice, far from being problematic, simply expands on what Jesus encouraged in the church when He gave the Lord's Prayer to His disciples. "Pray then in this way," He said to His followers—all of them—who had gathered on the hillside to hear His sermon (Matt 6:9). Included were these words: "Forgive us our sins as we forgive those who sin against us."

Elsewhere in the New Testament, we're warned of the danger of pretending that we're somehow above the need for regular forgiveness. The First Letter of John imagines that some of its hearers might be deluded about their complicity in evil prior to their baptism: "If we say that we have not sinned, we make [God] a liar, and his word is not in us" (1 John 1:10). But a more subtle danger lurks alongside this one. Other believers, honest about their prior guilt and confident of their new status as God's children, may claim present innocence while admitting to past failures. But the apostle is equally insistent that this won't do. "If we say that we have no sin," 1 John says, changing the verb tense, "we deceive ourselves, and the truth is not in us" (1:8). Whatever the Epistle of 1 Peter means when it says that "whoever has suffered in the flesh has finished with sin" (4:1), it shouldn't be read as inviting us to think of ourselves as beyond the need for daily mercy and pardon. The Articles of Religion that helped form the theology of Anglican churches speaks about sin like a disease that is passed on genetically, one that even baptism does not heal all at once: "This infection of nature doth remain, yea in them that are regenerated."[39] It would seem that by encouraging His disciples to regularly say, "Forgive us our sins," Jesus is the ultimate originator of this unblinking view of human frailty.

T HE FACT THAT WE PRAY "Forgive us our sins" not just once at our baptism but again and again says some-thing significant about the nature of sin. For many of us, the word "sin" conjures up childhood memories of stealing a cookie when we were told not to or of messages we heard in adolescence from youth pastors about the wickedness of cer-tain kinds of sex. "Sin," we may think, is a word preachers use to try to inoculate us against the appeal of forbidden pleasures. And yet it would seem that Jesus expects even those who have been able to rise above certain bad habits, like stealing cookies or cheating on one's spouse, to go on praying, "Forgive us our sins." This suggests that what the Lord's Prayer is referring to is something deeper, wider, more pervasive, and intractable than individual peccadilloes or improvable behaviors. To return to the language of the liturgy, Jesus appears to be encouraging a view of sin as "what we have done and ... what we have left undone."[40] It won't do to think of sin as something I've been able to rise above through sheer dint of hard work, while on the other hand, you are still mired in it. Nor is it sufficient for me to congratulate myself on having stolen no cookies or having had no illicit sex this past week and therefore count myself freed from the obligation on Sunday to pray the fifth petition of the Lord's Prayer.

Augustine of Hippo was someone who understood sin's true depths better than most. In order to illustrate why we all must think of ourselves as sinners, even if we've made enormous progress in developing habits of virtue and godliness, Augustine pointed to the heart of God's law, the command that Jesus described as the greatest: "You shall love the Lord your God with all your heart, and with all your soul, and with all your mind" (Matt 22:37, quoting Deut 6:5). It is certainly the case, Augustine admitted, that many Christians do love the Lord their God. But can any of us say that we love God with *all* our heart, with *all* our soul, with *all* our minds?[41] Like a relentless therapist, Augustine won't let us dissemble. Which one of us can say with a straight face that we are withholding none of our devotion and loyalty from God? And, in any case, even if we could say that, we still haven't reckoned with the second great commandment: "You shall love your neighbor as yourself" (Matt 22:39, quoting Lev 19:18). If by some miracle we were able to love God with the entirety of our being, experience demonstrates that even the best of us aren't able to love those around us with the same deference, understanding, and magnanimity that we reserve for ourselves. This is why the liturgy insists that we pray before each Eucharist: "We have not loved you with our whole heart. We have not loved our neighbors as ourselves. We are truly sorry, and we humbly repent."[42]

Once you adopt this deeper and darker view of human corruption, it becomes harder to hold on to any religious pride—and, by the same token, harder to look down on others as somehow worse off than yourself. We're circling around the Christian doctrine of original sin, vividly described by Francis Spufford as the conviction that committing actual murder is in the same family of actions as "telling a story at a dinner party at the expense of an absent mutual friend, a story which you know will cause pain when it gets back to them but you tell it anyway, because it's just very, very funny." One of these things may take a life, and the other may take a piece of a soul, but both are motivated by "a certain self-pleasing smirk," and in that way, both are devastating to both perpetrator and victim.[43] It's *that* which we're praying God to release us from when we ask, "Forgive us our sins."

ONE OF THE TROUBLING THINGS about the fifth petition of the Lord's Prayer is the way it seems to make God's forgiving us contingent on our forgiving others. That's at least how many Christians have interpreted the relationship between the two halves of the petition. "Forgive us our sins as we forgive those who sin against us" means, in many minds, "Forgive us our sins *because* we forgive those who sin against us." The Protestant Reformers, especially, worried about the kind of spirituality that this interpretation promotes. In their experience, people who came to God with their supposedly virtuous actions and tried to use them as bartering chips to get God to dispense mercy were often secretly living in terror of God. If you approach God asking for forgiveness and supplying your own efforts at forgiving others as the basis for why God should grant your request, chances are you're a deeply fearful believer, expecting God to cast you out of sight if you don't display a worthy enough track record. Martin Luther was fond of pointing out if you think that your generosity toward others is somehow going to get you off the divine hook, then it isn't really generosity. Only actions that are motivated by love, rather than self-preservation, can be truly generous. If your need to bolster your own righteousness is your motivation for forgiving and serving other people, then your efforts at forgiveness and service are more about you than they are about the people you're supposedly interested in caring for.

But John Calvin suggests that there is another way to read the fifth petition of the Lord's Prayer. In the lovely exposition that he provides in book 3 of his *Institutes of the Christian Religion*, Calvin first points out the problem we've been discussing:

> We must note that this condition—that [God] "forgive us as we forgive our debtors" [Matt. 6:12]—is not added because by the forgiveness we grant others we deserve his forgiveness, as if [our forgiveness] indicated the cause of [God's forgiveness].[44]

Calvin had been gripped by the Pauline insight that God's forgiveness is never conditioned by our actions to say otherwise. On the contrary, we are made capable of forgiving others through God's having first forgiven us. The order is crucial. As Paul wrote, "Be kind to one another, tenderhearted, forgiving one another, as God in Christ has [already] forgiven you" (Eph 4:32).

So, says Calvin, we must look for another way to under-stand the Lord's Prayer:

> By this word the Lord intended partly to comfort the weakness of our faith. For he has added this as a sign to assure us he has granted forgiveness of sins to us just as surely as we are aware of having forgiven others, provided our hearts have been emptied and purged of all hatred, envy, and vengeance.[45]

In other words, Calvin says, Jesus isn't offering a *condition* for our receiving God's forgiveness so much as He is offering an *illustration* of what God's disposition toward us is really like. Think about the times when you have actually extended for-giveness to someone who hurt you. Remember the stirring in your gut when your spouse or your sibling brokenheartedly acknowledged the way they were in the wrong, the way they neglected you, humiliated you, or stabbed you in the back. Recall the surge of compassion that you experienced when you said out loud to them, "I forgive you. I don't hold this against you, and it's not going to keep me from continuing to love you." *That*, says Calvin, is what Jesus wants you to hold in your mind as you pray to God to forgive you because God's forgiveness is *that* wonderful, only more so.

In Luke's Gospel, just after He offers the Lord's Prayer to His disciples, Jesus says:

> Is there anyone among you who, if your child asks for a fish, will give a snake instead of a fish? Or if the child asks for an egg, will give a scorpion? If you then, who

are evil, know how to give good gifts to your children, how much more will the heavenly Father give the Holy Spirit to those who ask him! (Luke 11:11–13)

It may be that the so-called condition attached to the fifth petition of the Lord's Prayer means to say no more than this: "If you then, who are prone to nurse petty grudges, know how to extend forgiveness to your friends when the time comes, how much will your heavenly Father forgive you when you ask Him!"

I N THE LITURGY, JUST BEFORE we pray the Lord's Prayer, we hear the words Jesus spoke on the night of His betrayal. Taking the chalice of wine in His hands, He said, "Drink this, all of you: This is my blood of the new covenant, which is shed for you and for many for the forgiveness of sins." A few moments later in the liturgy, we pray, "Forgive us our sins," and we know in that moment, because of Jesus, that God will.

PETITION VI

Save us from
the time of trial

ALMIGHTY AND MERCIFUL FATHER, your Son,
Jesus Christ, was tempted as we are, yet without sin.
Teach us to be joyful in hope, patient in affliction, and
persistent in prayer, that our faith may be proven
genuine, resulting in praise and glory and honor at the
revelation of Jesus Christ, who lives and reigns with
you and the Holy Spirit, one God, now and forever.
AMEN.

SAVE US FROM THE TIME OF TRIAL

Pope Francis made headlines around the world when he suggested in a TV interview that it might be time to change the wording of the Lord's Prayer. Speaking of the sixth petition of the prayer, familiar to English speakers in the King James Version as "Lead us not into temptation," the pope said:

> It is not a good translation because it speaks of a God who induces temptation. I am the one who falls; it's not [God] pushing me into temptation to then see how I have fallen. A father doesn't do that, a father helps you to get up immediately. It's Satan who leads us into temptation, that's his department.[46]

On the one hand, the pope seemed to make a good point. In Christian theology, God is never understood as the origin of evil. James rules that out in no uncertain terms: "No one, when tempted, should say, 'I am being tempted by God'; for God cannot be tempted by evil and he himself tempts no one" (1:13). Human beings often project our own cruel or foolish

inclinations onto God, imagining that God, like us, sometimes lures others into sin just for the fun or meanness of it.
But the God we see in Jesus Christ isn't like that. God is the
One who rescues us from sin, who makes us long for holiness and goodness—not the One who incites us to go against
the grain of His loving will. James again: "One is tempted by
one's own desire, being lured and enticed by it" (1:14). We
aren't tempted by God.

And yet, on the other hand, the Bible does feature numerous stories in which God, like a metalsmith, applies pressure
on His people to refine their faith and obedience, to make
it stronger and more durable. The most famous example is
the binding of Isaac, in which God subjects His covenant
partner Abraham to the utmost test of loyalty: "After these
things God tested Abraham. He said to him, 'Abraham!' And
he said, 'Here I am.' He said, 'Take your son, your only son
Isaac, whom you love, and go to the land of Moriah, and
offer him there as a burnt offering on one of the mountains
that I shall show you'" (Gen 22:1–2). Isaac, it turns out, is
spared the knife, but not before his father's heart has been
put through the furnace. Abraham's faith endures—"Now I
know that you fear God, since you have not withheld your
son, your only son, from me" (Gen 22:12)—but not because
the Lord has exempted him from the ultimate trial.

God's testing is central to the way He relates to Israel in
the Old Testament. At key junctures in Israel's life with God,
God brings it about that His people are laid on the anvil.
"Prove me, O LORD, and try me; test my heart and mind,"
prays the psalmist (26:2), and the Lord does. A story like

Abraham's, being asked to offer up his beloved son Isaac to God, is one that invites us, too, to reflect on our own dark nights of the soul and to ask how God might be sifting our faith to uncover its mettle.[47] Whatever else the petition "Lead us not into temptation" means, it cannot mean that God will spare us the searing heat of the refiner's fire. When those moments come, we should be prepared to say with Shadrach, Meshach, and Abednego, "If our God whom we serve is able to deliver us from the furnace of blazing fire and out of your hand, O king, let him deliver us. But if not, be it known to you, O king, that we will not serve your gods" (Dan 3:17–18).

WHAT, THEN, DOES IT MEAN for us to petition God to save us from the time of trial? The best clue lies in following the occurrences of the word we translate as "temptation" or "trial" in English. The Greek word that lies behind these English words is *peirasmos*. The verbal form of it appears in the Gospel of Matthew just after Jesus has been baptized in the Jordan River. Like Israel emerging from their journey through the Red Sea, Jesus immediately goes into the wilderness. Matthew puts it this way: "Then Jesus was led up by the Spirit into the wilderness to be tempted by the devil" (4:1). At least two details are crucial for us to notice. First, we should observe that the Spirit of God doesn't prevent Jesus from facing temptation. On the contrary, the Spirit is the One who leads Jesus toward it. Like Job in the Old Testament, Jesus faces extreme testing precisely in and through God's providence. Far from being aloof or unaware as Jesus enters the wastelands of Judea to face His tempter, God arranges for His passage.

But, second, God is not the one doing the tempting. That is the devil's business. The Spirit may be the superintendent of the play, but He doesn't assume the role of the villain who appears on stage with Jesus.

The Greek word *peirasmos* shows up yet again in Matthew's Gospel toward the very end of the narrative. Just after Jesus has celebrated His final supper with His disciples, He and they depart for the garden of Gethsemane. When they arrive, Jesus exhorts His disciples, "Stay awake and pray that you may not come into the time of trial [*peirasmos*]" (26:41). Although the disciples may not know it, we know that this will be the darkest night of Jesus' life. All of human evil is converging on that garden, circling like a vulture above Jesus' head. Jesus says to His enemies, "This is your hour, and the power of darkness" (Luke 22:53). That "hour" ends with Jesus being arrested, to the shock of His disciples; later that night, facing an unjust trial; and, hours later, being nailed to a cross and left to suffer the curse of death.

At both the beginning and the end of His earthly ministry, Jesus faces the truest, deepest form of temptation or trial. He burrows into temptation's depths and breathes the suffocating atmosphere of trial as He prays in Gethsemane and, ultimately, dies on the cross. And He does it alone. As Hans Urs von Balthasar puts it, "Jesus prays *in* the *peirasmos*, whereas the disciples pray to be preserved *from* it."[48] The disciples may be there beside Jesus in the garden and, more distantly, on Calvary's hill, but they are not there in the furnace of temptation *with* Jesus. They are onlookers but not full participants. They witness Jesus' temptation and agony, but they do not—they cannot—bear it in the way that He does.

This should affect the way we pray this particular petition of the Lord's Prayer. We pray, "Save us from the time of trial" or "Lead us not into temptation," depending on the translation. Reading these words in the context of the entire gospel, we can see immediately that God intends to answer— has *already* answered—this prayer. We will be saved from the time of ultimate trial, sheltered from it and spared from ever experiencing its true horrors, because there is One who already has experienced those horrors in our place. Because Jesus was not saved from temptation, we are.

Whatever temptations God permits us to endure, we may be confident that they are never punitive. The New Testament does teach that believers will go through times of tribulation (and we can verify that teaching empirically: think of the persecuted church around the world today, illustrated horrifically by the Coptic martyrs beheaded in Libya in 2015 by ISIS operatives[49]). The First Letter of Peter warns us away from any shock at God's refusal to spare us such times: "Beloved, do not be surprised at the fiery ordeal [*peirasmos*] that is taking place among you to test you, as though something strange were happening to you" (4:12). God permits His children to be hammered on the anvil of suffering "so that the genuineness of your faith—being more precious than gold that, though perishable, is tested by fire—may be found to result in praise and glory and honor when Jesus Christ is revealed" (1:7).[50] We may pray to be spared the most intense forms of such testing, but either way, we can now endure in the certainty that all trials are permitted only for our good. Jesus has already gone into the furnace's fiery depths and, by His redemptive alchemy, transformed its hellish flames into burnishing purifiers. In the words of Karl Barth, "God has already done what we ask him."[51]

PETITION VII

And deliver us from evil

ALMIGHTY GOD, through the death of Christ you have delivered us from the power of death and the devil. Give us faith that is firm, hope that is steadfast, and love that abides, so that we may be kept blameless at the coming of Jesus Christ, who sits at your right hand and who, with the Holy Spirit, is worshiped and glorified. **AMEN.**

AND DELIVER
US FROM EVIL

IN THE MIDDLE OF THE Rwandan civil war of the early
1990s, over the course of a mere one hundred days, almost
a million members of the Tutsi community were murdered
with machetes and rifles. It took the rest of the world time to
come to grips with what had happened and eventually face
its own complicity insofar as it had done nothing to stop the
horror. When Canadian general Roméo Dallaire arrived as
commander of the UN Assistance Mission to try to achieve
a ceasefire, he witnessed firsthand the bloody hundred days:
"In Rwanda I shook hands with the devil. I have seen him, I
have smelled him and I have touched him."[52] Confronted with
neighbors invading the homes of neighbors, raping and hack-
ing them to pieces, we can't rely on abstract tropes about sin
being present in every human heart. We need to speak about
the demonic, about Satan. That is what Dallaire understood
as he gaped at the piles of Tutsi corpses and witnessed the
indifference of his fellow Westerners.

Jesus taught His followers to pray for deliverance from *the*
evil—that is, the *one* who is evil, the ancient adversary of God,

who, in the words of John Chrysostom, "wages against us an implacable war."[53] It's for this reason that some translations render this petition "Save us from the Evil One," with capital letters. "Evil has a definite physiognomy," as the liberation theologian Leonardo Boff puts it.[54] The Jesuit priest Alfred Delp, who was involved in a plot to assassinate Adolf Hitler, commented on the seventh petition from his Nazi prison cell: "There is not only evil in this world, there is also the evil one; not only a principle of negation but also a tough and formidable anti-Christ."[55] What we need to be rescued from isn't just the devices and desires of our own wayward hearts, as real and dangerous as those are, but also the malevolence of a personal being bent on our suffering.

In speaking this way, Jesus is in line with the entirety of the Bible. It may not in every place be as clear that the devil himself is in view, but the Bible everywhere speaks of evil not simply as pervasive but as *personal*. As early as the third chapter of Genesis, the origin of Adam and Eve's rebellion is depicted as a reasoning, speaking serpent (3:1). Job's torments are traced back to the instigation of a mysterious "accuser" (literally "the satan," in 1:6). The prophet Daniel is visited by an angel who reports a battle with "the prince of the kingdom of Persia" (10:13); Paul warns his converts that they must be prepared to contend "against the rulers, against the authorities, against the cosmic powers of this present darkness, against the spiritual forces of evil in the heavenly places" (Eph 6:12). Peter, likewise, tells his readers, "Like a roaring lion your adversary the devil prowls around, looking for someone to devour" (1 Pet 5:8). In the apocalyptic vision that closes the Bible's storyline, the defeat of ultimate evil is described like this: "And the devil who had deceived [the nations] was thrown into the lake of fire and sulfur" (Rev 20:10). And, above all, the New Testament portrays Jesus as having constantly to contend against a mighty and wily foe: "No one can enter a strong man's house and plunder his property without first tying up the strong man" (Mark 3:27). Scripture, in short, "has a penchant for personifying evil."[56] And when Jesus encourages His disciples to pray, "Deliver us from evil," it is most likely that it is this *personal* evil to which He refers.

Bdrop UT CAN MODERN WESTERN PEOPLE, who are skeptical of the efficacy of witchcraft and spiritualism, follow Jesus on this point? One of the fascinating developments in recent science, both in the hard sciences as well as the social sciences, has been the focus on how human beings are at all times at the mercy of powers greater than themselves. Contrary to sunny notions of free will and self-expression, we all are shaped by powers as small as microscopic biochemical forces, some of which are microbial interlopers in our bodies, to those as large as inherited notions of what constitutes acceptable gender performance.

Think, for instance, of how racism makes itself manifest in a society. Older generations of white Americans may have more readily thought, "So long as I am paying my black employee a fair wage and greeting her warmly each day, I'm not a racist." But racism operates more covertly and insidiously than that. In a recent experiment, for instance, a sociologist asked participants to stare at a screen on which a series of black and white faces flashed. These images appeared and disappeared so quickly that the viewers were not even consciously aware of having seen them. Immediately after seeing a black or white face, the participants were then shown a picture of a gun or a tool. These images were quickly removed from the screen but not quite as quickly as the facial images, so as to allow the participants to register having seen them. It turned out that when participants viewed a black face followed by a tool, they were more apt to remember the tool as having been a gun than they were when the image of a tool followed that of a white face. The racialized tendency to associate black faces with a violent weapon, the sociologist concluded, "requires no intentional racial animus, occurring even for those who are actively trying to avoid it."[57] People are, in a very real way, enslaved to something outside of their control. As one theorist has put it, racism has "a life of its own."[58]

So modern Western minds actually might be catching up with the inspired wisdom of Scripture rather than the other way around. Evil is not just what we *do*, but—more hauntingly—it is what we *suffer*, what we are mired in and encrusted with. And if that is the case, we are unable to extricate ourselves from it by any direct action. No amount of good intentions—to return to our example from above—can cause a white person to disassociate black skin from the threat of harm. The prince of racism—and of so many other forms of evil—hinders even the most virtuous white people from ending their own racist habits of mind by sheer decision. Stronger medicine is needed. And that is what Jesus urges us to pray for: we must, in the end, appeal to God to deliver us from the grip of the Evil One. Christians who worship whiteness don't just need education; we need exorcism.

T HE NEW TESTAMENT RUSTLES WITH the news that God *already* has delivered us from the Evil One. Consider these words from the early Christian sermon that we know as the Letter to the Hebrews:

> The children of a family share the same flesh and blood; and so [Jesus] too shared ours, so that through death he might break the power of him who had death at his command, that is, the devil; and might liberate those who, through fear of death, had all their lifetime been in servitude. (2:14–15 NEB)

Making our mortal human nature His own, the Son of God died in order to defeat the Evil One who wielded death as a weapon. As the Orthodox liturgy says, He is "trampling down death by death."[59]

Or consider this from the First Letter of John: "The Son of God was revealed for this purpose, to destroy the works of the devil" (3:8). Or this, from the letter of Paul to the Colossians: Christ "disarmed the rulers and authorities and made a public example of them, triumphing over them in [the cross]" (2:15). Somehow, by dying, Jesus has rendered the devil impotent, denuding him of his ability to win the war he wages against human beings. There are different ways of thinking about how Jesus achieved this, and the New Testament uses a variety of different pictures or metaphors to help us see the full scope of His triumph over the Evil One. But the point all the images are seeking to drive home is that a decisive victory was secured in and through the events of Jesus' crucifixion and resurrection—a victory that sealed evil's fate once and for all, guaranteeing its final demise.

When we pray "Deliver us from evil," we are asking to be able to see, enjoy, and live in accord with what is true but still largely unseen in the present. We know that Jesus has already secured our final release from the Evil One, but we still sense evil's nearness and taste its effects. The victory of Jesus is real but not currently as visible as it one day will be. And so, in confidence but also in trembling and with tears, we pray for the final, public, irreversible experience of celebrating the defeat of the regime of our Enemy.

DOXOLOGY

For the kingdom, the power,
and the glory are yours
now and forever.
Amen.

ALMIGHTY AND EVERLASTING GOD, all your
works praise you and give you thanks. Grant us the
life of your word by the might of your Spirit, that we
may show the glory of your kingdom and speak of your
power and that all people might know your mighty acts
and majesty; through Jesus Christ our Lord, who lives
and reigns with you and the Holy Spirit, one God, now
and forever. **AMEN**.

FOR THE KINGDOM, THE POWER, AND THE GLORY ARE YOURS NOW AND FOREVER. AMEN.

ONE OF THE GREAT SLOGANS of the Protestant Reformation, made famous by Martin Luther's Wittenberg colleague and friend Philipp Melanchthon, goes like this: "To know Christ is to know his benefits."[60] Melanchthon's point was to stress that Christians shouldn't be too interested in bare facts about Jesus Christ. It isn't enough, for example, to know where He was born, or in what year, or how He preexisted the incarnation, or how His divine and human natures are in a mysterious personal union. As Melanchthon says, "Unless you know why Christ put on flesh and was nailed to the cross, what good will it do you to know merely the history about him?"[61]

Melanchthon was worried about a coldly scientific approach to knowing Christ that seemed to him to be represented by the theologians of his day. In place of that approach, he stressed that Christ is rightly known when we hear a preacher say aloud in church, "Almighty God in His mercy has given His Son to die for you and for His sake forgives you all your sins."[62] *That* is when we really *know* Christ—when we trust in Him for salvation and hear His words of assurance announced to us.

But in our day, we are especially vulnerable to a different error than the one Melanchthon tried to correct. For so long in Western theologies, we have focused most of our attention on all that we believe Christ provides for us—a clean conscience, say, or a restored marriage, a renewed work ethic, a reconciled community, the promise of justice and healing for the creation, and so on—that we have tended to forget the *aim* of all Christ's benefits: that we ultimately would be, as the hymn puts it, "lost in wonder, love, and praise."[63] Yes, pearly gates and golden streets will be lovely, but the point of all this heavenly imagery is to help us see that God Himself will be the Christian's eternal delight.[64]

When Pope Benedict XVI published the first volume of his trilogy of books on the life of Jesus, he introduced it with an arresting question: "What did Jesus actually bring, if not world peace, universal prosperity, and a better world? What has he brought?" What indeed? Surveying the sorry state of our world, we can sympathize with the Jewish philosopher Martin Buber's remark to one of his Christian friends on the eve of World War II: "We [Jews] know more deeply, more truly, that world history has not been turned upside down to its very foundations—that the world is not yet redeemed. We *sense* its unredeemedness."[65] So are we to conclude that Jesus effected no change in the world's situation, that His mission was a failure? Benedict XVI says no: "What has [Jesus] brought? The answer is very simple: God. He has brought God."[66] All of Jesus' life was oriented toward one goal: bringing human beings into a restored relationship with God so that they can behold God's glory forever, bathed in His radiant light and reflecting His worthiness back to Him in praise and adoration.

I T IS GOD IN HIMSELF who pervades the final lines of the Lord's Prayer. If we have been praying in the previous few petitions for God to meet our needs for sustenance, forgiveness, and deliverance, our attention shifts in the final doxology as we simply attend to God's might and majesty. The incomparable King James Version renders it this way, capturing the way the Greek manuscripts foreground the divine pronoun: "For Thine is the kingdom, and the power, and the glory, for ever. Amen." Yes, God's kingly reign is for our benefit, and all His power is marshaled for the purpose of doing us good. But something more is in view here. The point isn't so much for us to ask God for more things but for us to realize that God transcends our limits and frustrations and that our saying so befits His splendor. Sarah Ruden puts it this way:

We can expect to be saved from the devil because of this deity we invoked already, but now [at the end of the Lord's Prayer] there is more of the deity: he has not only a kingdom but power and glory. ... God is not just an entity coming into manifestation, invisible in the sky but with a name to be blessed, a kingdom to arrive, and a will to be enacted. His kingdom, power, and glory simply *are*, now and through eternity.[67]

This is what the final praise in the Lord's Prayer means to direct us toward: there is coming a time when we will have no more need to ask God for bread, for absolution, or for rescue. All of our tears will have been wiped away, death will have been finally defeated, and the earth and its people will be at peace and thriving. When that time comes, in the words of an old hymn,

> Hope shall change to glad fruition,
> Faith to sight, and prayer to praise.[68]

Petitions will not be necessary in God's future. We will cease asking God to supply our needs, since we will be entirely satisfied. All that will remain is to praise God—to enjoy His benevolent reign, to rejoice in what His power has achieved, and to see His glory. "Let it be so," which is what "Amen" amounts to, is the only appropriate response to these promises.

CODA

Praying the Lord's Prayer with Rembrandt

W HEN I MOVED INTO A HOUSE by myself after living in community for several years, one of the first things I did was order a framed print of Rembrandt van Rijn's *Return of the Prodigal Son*, the Dutch painter's memorialization of Jesus' parable of the runaway child and the forgiving father (Luke 15:11–32). I had read Henri Nouwen's pastoral meditation on Jesus' story and the painting, and it had moved me deeply.[69] I wanted to use the painting much as Nouwen had—as a daily reminder that I, a lost son, was beloved by a compassionate Father.

For a while the print hung over the fireplace in my living room. But then I moved again, and I decided to place it in a more private part of the house, on the wall space just above the kneeler that I often use to pray. Now, whenever I bend my knees and rest my elbows on the wooden shelf, my eyes are almost level with the back of the son. I can look up slightly to focus on the Father's hands on the son's shoulders, and I can look into the Father's face.

Nouwen describes Rembrandt's memorable image so well:

> I saw a man in a great red cloak tenderly touching the shoulders of a disheveled boy kneeling before him. I could not take my eyes away. I felt drawn by the intimacy between the two figures, the warm red of the man's cloak, the golden yellow of the boy's tunic, and the mysterious light engulfing them both. But, most of all, it was the hands—the old man's hands—as they touched the boy's shoulders that reached me in a place where I had never been reached before.[70]

It's taken a couple of years for me to realize how much looking at this print hanging over my kneeler has affected the way I pray, too. In particular, I think, it's changed the way I pray the Lord's Prayer. Now, whenever I recite it, as often as not I'm looking at Rembrandt's image while I do. Each line has taken on new resonance.

Our Father, who art in heaven, hallowed be Thy name. To pray for the reverencing and uplifting of the Father's name is to pray that *this* welcoming, forgiving Father—the Father whose hands gently rest on His lost son's shoulders—be more widely known, seen for the compassionate Father that He is, and worshiped as the Giver of extravagant mercy. To pray for *this* Father's name to be hallowed is to pray that more lost sons and daughters find themselves kneeling under that gracious gaze.

Thy kingdom come, thy will be done on earth as it is in heaven. To pray for *this* Father's kingdom to come and *this* Father's will to be done is to pray for a reign of mercy, kindness, humility, and profligate divine generosity. It is to pray that debts would be remitted, rebellion ended with homecoming, and banquets held for the dissolute and the self-righteous alike. It is to pray not for the iron-fisted rule of a tyrant but for the self-giving reign of a Father who loves.

Give us this day our daily bread. To pray for regular sustenance from *this* Father is to pray to One who was ready to serve the best meat to a son who had already burned through half the family inheritance. To pray to *this* Father for daily bread is to receive not only the staples of life but also a filet mignon, not only water but also the best vintage. It is to receive abundance, lavishness, and generosity "immeasurably more than all we can ask or conceive" (Eph 3:20 NEB).

And forgive us our trespasses as we forgive those who trespass against us. To pray for forgiveness from *this* Father is to pray to One who leaps up and sprints toward us—throwing dignity to the wind—to offer us forgiveness before we have even been able to blubber our request for it. To pray for *this* Father's forgiveness is to barely get the words out before realizing we've been clothed with the finest garments the house has to offer. To pray for our trespasses to be forgiven is to feel already this Father's warm tears as they drip down on our scabbed head.

And lead us not into temptation but deliver us from evil. To ask *this* Father to "deliver us from evil" is to pray to One whose hands and cloak provide shelter for us. Nouwen again: "With its warm color and its arch-like shape, [the Father's cloak] offers a welcome place where it is good to be. … But as I went on gazing at the red cloak, another image, stronger than that of a tent, came to me: the sheltering wings of the mother bird." To pray to *this* Father for protection is to pray to One whose character Jesus embodied when He wept, "Jerusalem, Jerusalem! ... How often have I desired to gather your children together as a hen gathers her brood under her wings, and you were not willing!" (Matt 23:37).

For thine is the kingdom, and the power, and the glory, for ever and ever. Amen. To praise the kingship, the dominion, and the splendor of *this* Father is to praise the kingship of humility, the noncoercive dominion of nurturing love, and the radiant splendor of stooping and touching and embracing. To praise *this* Father "for ever and ever" is to acknowledge that such self-giving divine love is the fount of creation and redemption in eternity past and will be the theme of the lost son's songs into eternity future.

To pray the Our Father with Rembrandt and Jesus' Father in view is to find yourself praying it in a way you hope never to stop.[71]

ENDNOTES

For *The Lord's Prayer*

1. Rowan Williams, *Meeting God in Paul* (London: SPCK, 2015). In the lecture given at Canterbury Cathedral in April of 2012 that was transcribed and edited for this volume, Williams used the word "cheek" after "nerve" which captures the idea memorably (Merriam-Webster gives "self-assurance" as one definition of "cheek").

2. Augustine, counting "Save us from the time of trial" and "Deliver us from evil" as two petitions, saw seven parts in the Lord's Prayer, while Origen, John Chrysostom, Gregory of Nyssa, and others collapsed those petitions into one, comprised of negative and positive counterparts. Although I think the latter position is more likely to be true to the Gospels' intent, I will follow Augustine in treating the negative and positive parts of the sixth petition separately.

3. Dale C. Allison, *The Sermon on the Mount: Inspiring the Moral Imagination* (New York: Crossroad, 1999), 22.

4. Allison, *The Sermon on the Mount*, 22.

5. Helmut Thielicke, *The Prayer that Spans the World: Sermons on the Lord's Prayer* (London: James Clarke, 1965), 22.

6. Sarah Ruden, *The Face of Water: A Translator on Beauty and Meaning in the Bible* (New York: Pantheon, 2017), 122–24.

7. Compare R. W. L. Moberly's remarks in his *Old Testament Theology: Reading the Hebrew Bible as Christian Scripture* (Grand Rapids: Baker Academic, 2013), 5.

8. In the Enuma Elish, the world is birthed from the intermingling of the fresh waters, portrayed as a god named Apsu, with the oceanic saline waters, the goddess Tiamat. See W. G. Lambert, *Babylonian Creation Myths* (Winona Lake, IN: Eisenbrauns, 2013), 3.

9. Robert G. Hamerton-Kelly, "God the Father in the Bible and in the Experience of Jesus: The State of the Question," in J. B. Metz, E. Schillebeeckx, and M. Lefabure, eds., *God as Father?* (New York: Seabury, 1981), 97.

10. Paul Ricoeur, "Fatherhood: From Phantasm to Symbol," in *The Conflict of Interpretations: Essays in Hermeneutics* (Evanston, IL: Northwestern University Press, 1974), 490–91. I am indebted to Janet Martin Soskice's reading of Ricoeur's essay in her essay "Calling God 'Father' " in *The Kindness of God: Metaphor, Gender, and Religious Language* (Oxford: Oxford University Press, 2007), 74–80.

11. See Deut 32:6; 2 Sam 7:14; 1 Chr 17:13; 22:10; 28:6; Pss 68:5; 89:26; Isa 63:16; 64:8; Jer 3:4, 19; 31:9; Mal 1:6; 2:10. On other occasions in the Old Testament, God is depicted in fatherly imagery but without the word "father" being used; see Exod 4:22–23; Deut 1:31; 8:5; 14:1; Ps 103:13; Jer 3:22; 31:20; Hosea 11:1–4; Mal 3:17. Other Jewish texts that were read and studied in the time of Jesus use "father" for God too: see, for instance, the *Qiddushin* tractate of the Babylonian Talmud, 36a; *Exodus Rabbah* 46.4.

12. The Council of Toledo (AD 675) puts it this way: "We must believe that the Son was not made out of nothing, nor out of some substance or other, but from the womb of the Father (*de utero Patris*), that is, that he was begotten or born (*genitus vel natus*) from the Father's own being." See Jacques Dupuis, ed., *The Christian Faith in the Doctrinal Documents of the Catholic Church* (New York: Alba House, 1982), 102–6.

13. "Our Father, you who are in heaven. ... With these words God wants to entice us, so that we come to believe he is truly our Father and we are truly his children, in order that we may ask him boldly and with complete confidence, just as loving children ask their loving father" (Martin Luther, *The Small Catechism*).

14. Karl Barth, *Prayer*, fiftieth anniversary edition (Louisville: Westminster John Knox, 2002), 22–23.

15. Stanley Hauerwas, *With the Grain of the Universe: The Church's Witness and Natural Theology* (Grand Rapids: Brazos, 2001), 28.

16. Janet Martin Soskice, *Kindness of God*, 76.

17. Dante Alighieri, *The Divine Comedy*, 11.1–2.

18. Sarah Coakley, *God, Sexuality, and the Self: An Essay "On the Trinity"* (Cambridge: Cambridge University Press, 2013), 327, 324.

19.　Erich Auerbach, *Mimesis: The Representation of Reality in Western Literature*, trans. by Willard R. Trask (Princeton: Princeton University Press, 1953), 8.

20.　Benedict XVI, *Jesus of Nazareth: From the Baptism in the Jordan to the Transfiguration* (New York: Doubleday, 2007), 143.

21.　Nahum Sarna, *Exploring Exodus: The Origins of Biblical Israel* (New York: Schocken, 1986), 52.

22.　Christopher R. Seitz, *Figured Out: Typology and Providence in Christian Scripture* (Louisville: Westminster John Knox, 2001), 143–44.

23.　Simone Weil, *Waiting for God*, trans. Emma Craufurd (New York: Harper, 1973), 217.

24.　*Martyrdom of Polycarp* 9.3.

25.　Andrew Marin, *Love Is an Orientation: Elevating the Conversation with the Gay Community* (Downers Grove, IL: IVP, 2009), chapter 8. For more on the Marin Foundation's "I'm Sorry" campaign, see http://www.themarinfoundation.org/get-involved/im-sorry-campaign/.

26.　C. Clifton Black, *The Lord's Prayer*, Interpretation (Louisville: Westminster John Knox, 2018), 97.

27.　The classic statement is in Oscar Cullmann, *Christ and Time: The Primitive Christian Conception of Time and History* (Philadelphia: Westminster, 1964), 84.

28.　Barth, *Prayer*, 39.

29.　P. D. James, *The Private Patient: A Novel* (New York: Vintage, 2009), 349.

30.　David Wells, "Prayer: Rebelling Against the Status Quo," *Christianity Today* (November 1979), 32–34.

31.　This paragraph and parts of the following section are adapted from Wesley Hill, "Praying the Lord's Prayer in Gethsemane," *First Things*, April 2, 2015, https://www.firstthings.com/blogs/firstthoughts/2015/04/praying-the-lords-prayer-in-gethsemane.

32.　William Nicholson, *Shadowlands: A Play* (New York: Penguin, 1990).

33.　Timothy George, *Theology of the Reformers*, rev. ed. (Nashville: Broadman & Holman, 2013), 105.

34.　F. D. Maurice, *The Lord's Prayer: Nine Sermons Preached in the Chapel of Lincoln's Inn*, fourth edition (London: Macmillan, 1861), 59, italics removed.

35.　Maurice, *The Lord's Prayer*, 59, italics added.

36. Karl Barth, *Church Dogmatics* II.2, §38.2.

37. Weil, *Waiting for God*, 220.

38. I'm indebted to my colleague David Yeago for this insight.

39. "Article IX: Of Original or Birth Sin," in *The Book of Common Prayer* (New York: The Church Hymnal Corporation, 1979).

40. "A Penitential Order: Rite Two," in *The Book of Common Prayer*.

41. Augustine, *On Man's Perfection in Righteousness* 8.19: "For while there remains any remnant of the lust of the flesh, to be kept in check by the rein of continence, God is by no means loved with all one's soul."

42. "A Penitential Order: Rite Two."

43. Francis Spufford, *Unapologetic: Why, Despite Everything, Christianity Can Still Make Surprising Emotional Sense* (San Francisco: HarperOne, 2014), 48.

44. John Calvin, *Institutes of the Christian Religion* 3.20.45.

45. Calvin, *Institutes* 3.20.45.

46. Harriet Sherwood, "Lead Us Not into Mistranslation: Pope Wants Lord's Prayer Changed," *The Guardian*, December 8, 2017, https://www.theguardian.com/world/2017/dec/08/lead-us-not-into-mistranslation-pope-wants-lords-prayer-changed. Subsequently, the wording was officially changed; see Harriet Sherwood, "Led not into temptation: Pope approves change to Lord's Prayer," *The Guardian*, June 9, 2019, www.theguardian.com/world/2019/jun/06/led-not-into-temptation-pope-approves-change-to-lords-prayer.

47. See R. W. L. Moberly, *The Bible, Theology and Faith: A Study of Abraham and Jesus* (Cambridge: Cambridge University Press, 2000), chapter 3.

48. Hans Urs von Balthasar, *Mysterium Paschale*, trans. Aidan Nichols (San Francisco: Ignatius, 2000), 100.

49. The pope of the Coptic Orthodox Church subsequently announced the canonization of the twenty-one martyrs, and an icon written by Tony Rezk depicting crowns descending from heaven onto the martyrs' heads was widely shared on the internet.

50. My interpretation of the sixth petition is indebted to Daniel B. Wallace, "Pope Francis, the Lord's Prayer, and Bible Translation," https://danielbwallace.com/2017/12/12/pope-francis-the-lords-prayer-and-bible-translation/.

51. Barth, *Prayer*, 63.

52. Roméo Dallaire, *Shake Hands with the Devil: The Failure of Humanity in Rwanda* (New York: Carroll & Graf, 2004), xviii.

53. John Chrysostom, Homily 19.10 on Matthew.

54. Leonardo Boff, *The Lord's Prayer: The Prayer of Integral Liberation*, trans. Theodore Morrow (Maryknoll, NY: Orbis, 1983), 115.

55. Alfred Delp, *The Prison Meditations of Father Alfred Delp* (New York: Herder and Herder, 1963), 137.

56. Nicholas Ayo, *The Lord's Prayer* (Lanham, MD: Rowman & Littlefield, 2003 [1992]), 95.

57. B. Keith Payne, "Weapon Bias: Split-Second Decisions and Unintended Stereotyping," *Current Directions in Psychological Science* 15, no. 6 (2006): 287–91.

58. Eduardo Bonilla-Silva, *White Supremacy and Racism in the Post-Civil Rights Era* (Boulder, CO: Lynne Rienner, 2001), 45.

59. From the Paschal Troparion: "Christ is risen from the dead, / Trampling down death by death, / And upon those in the tombs / Bestowing life!"

60. Philipp Melanchthon, *Loci Communes* (1521), dedicatory epistle.

61. Melanchthon, *Loci Communes* (1521), dedicatory epistle.

62. I draw this language from the later *Lutheran Book of Worship* (Minneapolis: Augsburg Fortress, 1978).

63. Charles Wesley, "Love Divine, All Loves Excelling" (1747).

64. Some recent books have emphasized this point helpfully: Hans Boersma, *Seeing God: The Beatific Vision in Christian Tradition* (Grand Rapids: Eerdmans, 2018); Michael Allen, *Grounded in Heaven: Recentering Christian Life and Hope on God* (Grand Rapids: Eerdmans, 2018).

65. Quoted in Jürgen Moltmann, *The Way of Jesus Christ* (Minneapolis: Fortress, 1995), 28.

66. Benedict XVI, *Jesus of Nazareth*, 44.

67. Ruden, *The Face of Water*, 34.

68. Henry Francis Lyte, "Jesus, I My Cross Have Taken" (1824).

69. Henri Nouwen, *The Return of the Prodigal Son: A Story of Homecoming* (New York: Penguin, 1994).

70. Nouwen, *Return*, xx.

71. This coda is adapted from Wesley Hill, "Praying the 'Our Father' with Rembrandt," *Covenant* blog, September 23, 2015, https://livingchurch. org/covenant/2015/09/23/praying-our-father-rembrandt/.

The words of the Lord are pure words,
even as silver that is tried in the furnace,
and as gold that is purified
seven times in the fire.

Psalm 12:6

CATECHISM PRAYERS

Or Collects

We fall into ruts with prayer. We might pray the same written or rote prayer again and again or we might find ourselves saying the same spontaneous prayer or we might not pray at all!

A remedy is to pray the catechism—the Ten Commandments, the Apostles' Creed, and the Lord's Prayer. The catechism provides cues for our prayers, so we don't have to stir up our own words. It also shapes our prayers according to the gospel of God's word: our Lord and Savior Jesus Christ gives us life and forgiveness by his cross and resurrection. Simply pray the very words of the Ten Commandments, the Apostles' Creed, or the Lord's Prayer: take one commandment, one article, or one petition and form it into a prayer of instruction, thanksgiving, confession of sin, and petition.

Below, you'll find twenty-four prayers based on the catechism in conversation with the entire Bible, written by Joey Royal, suffragan bishop of the Anglican Diocese of the Arctic. Consider praying through these prayers for morning or evening prayer or for prayer at meals.

THE TEN COMMANDMENTS

I.

True God, you are a great God and a great King above all gods. You call us to worship you and you alone. Give us strength and wisdom to recognize and reject all false gods, and to devote ourselves, our souls and bodies, to you as a living sacrifice, holy and pleasing to you. This we pray in the name of Jesus Christ, true God and true man. *Amen.*

Psalm 95:3; Romans 12:1

II.

Jealous God, you are great and greatly to be praised. You smash idols and expose the powerlessness of gods who cannot save. Fix our hearts on you and you alone, so that we may flee from idolatry and bow to the one who alone is worthy, Jesus Christ our Lord, to whom every knee will bow and every tongue confess. In his name alone we pray. *Amen.*

Psalm 96:4 (145:3); Ephesians 2:10–11

III.

Lord God, your name is holy, and you have chosen to be known in Christ alone. Instill in us such reverential fear that we will always honor the grandeur of your name, through lives of obedience and worship, in the divine name of Jesus Christ, who with you and Holy Spirit is named, worshiped, and glorified. *Amen.*

Luke 1:49; Psalm 111:9

IV.

Timeless God, you created the day and the night and divided them one from another, and you appointed lights to govern ordinary time and to signify sacred time. Teach us to number our days, to embrace work and rest, and to reject the injustice and idleness arising from the misuse of time, in eager hope of the heavenly rest that awaits us in Jesus Christ, who worked perfect obedience that we may have perfect rest. *Amen.*

Genesis 1:3–4, 14; Psalm 90:12

V.

Heavenly Father, you created us and adopted us in Christ. Give us humility to honor our earthly parents, through whom you brought us into being, by speaking well of them and to them, by caring for them in need, and by forgiving them as you have forgiven us, in the name of Jesus Christ, who has made us sons and daughters through faith, and through whom we have received the Spirit of adoption, by whom we cry "Abba, Father." *Amen.*

Galatians 3:26; Romans 8:15

VI.

Life-giving God, you have formed us from dust and breathed into us the breath of life, and you forbid the unjust taking of life. Make us imitators of Christ, who repaid evil with good, who did not sin in his anger, and who blessed those who cursed him, so that in him we may lay down our lives for others, following the example of him who laid down his life for us. In his name we pray. *Amen.*

Genesis 2:7; Ephesians 5:1–2; 1 Peter 2:23; 3:7;
Romans 12:17; Matthew 5:39; Ephesians 4:27
(Psalm 37:8); Luke 6:28; 1 John 3:16

VII.

Faithful God, you have bound yourself to us as a bridegroom to a bride, and you call us to discipline the desires of the flesh and to flee from youthful lusts. Give us strength to resist temptation so that in any situation, whether single or married, we may be pure and chaste, honoring you in our bodies, in obedience to Jesus Christ, who was tempted in every way we are, yet without sin. In his name we pray. *Amen.*

Romans 8:5–7; Galatians 5:16–17;
2 Timothy 2:22; Hebrews 4:15

VIII.

Gift-giving God, you made heaven and earth and all that dwells therein. Help us to remember that every good and perfect gift is from above, and to pursue godliness with contentment, knowing that we brought nothing into the world and can take nothing out of it, so that, satisfied in your grace, we may avoid all unjust gain, through Christ, in the power of the Holy Spirit. *Amen.*

Psalm 146:6; James 1:17; 1 Timothy 6:7

IX.

Truthful God, your word is truth, and in you there is no shadow of turning. Give us courage to always speak the truth and to reject falsehood, knowing that telling the truth is an act of love, for friends as well as for enemies, so that we may know the truth that sets us free, in Jesus Christ, who, with the Father, is worshiped in Spirit and in truth. *Amen.*

Psalm 119:160; John 17:17;
James 1:17; John 8:31–32

X.

Abundant God, you give us the desires of our hearts when we delight in you. Grant rest to our restless hearts, so that our souls may long for you and you alone, in the name of Jesus Christ, who is our soul's anchor and the desire of all nations, and who, with you and the Holy Spirit, is worshiped, glorified, and treasured as our greatest good. *Amen.*

Psalm 37:4; Psalm 84:2; Hebrews 6:19

THE APOSTLES' CREED

I.

Almighty Father, you have made heaven and earth by the power of your Word, and you have created faith in us by the power of that same Word. Instill in us deep and abiding trust, so that in believing we may come to understand, and in understanding we may more perfectly love you and your Son, Jesus Christ, who, with you and the Holy Spirit, is worthy to be trusted and glorified, now and forever. *Amen.*

Genesis 1:1–3; Psalm 33:6–9; Hebrews 11:3;
2 Peter 3:5; John 1:3; Romans 10:17

II.

Our Lord Jesus Christ, in the virgin's womb you were made flesh for our salvation by the power of the Holy Spirit. Pour upon us that same Spirit, so that faith, hope, and love may be born in us, and that we, like Mary, may be ever receptive to your holy will. This we ask in your holy name. *Amen.*

Luke 1:26–38; John 1:14; Romans 5:5; Titus 3:5–8

III.

Victorious Christ, you died a criminal's death, preached to the spirits in prison, and in great glory burst forth from the tomb. Return us afresh to the cleansing waters of baptism, where we died to sin and were raised to new life, as a participation in the death and resurrection of you, our Lord Jesus Christ who, with the Father and the Holy Spirit, is worshiped and glorified forever and ever. *Amen.*

Philippians 2:8; Matthew 27:27–66 (Mark 15:16–47;
Luke 23:26–56; John 19:2–42); 1 Peter 3:18–22;
Matthew 28:1–8 (Mark 16:1–8; Luke 24:1–12;
John 20:1–18); Romans 6:3–5; Titus 3:5–8

IV.

Our Lord Jesus Christ, you ascended to the Father after forty days, and you promised to your disciples that you will appear a second time to those who eagerly wait for him. Give us minds that are sober and alert, so that when Christ, who is our life, appears, we will also appear with him in glory. We ask this in the name of Jesus the King, who will judge the living and the dead and whose kingdom will have no end. *Amen.*

Luke 24:50–53; Acts 1:6–11; Hebrews 9:28; 1 Peter 5:7;
Colossians 3:4; Luke 1:33; Psalm 145:13

V.

O God, in these last days you have sent your Holy Spirit upon all people, and you have bound your people together in the unity of that same Spirit. Help us to walk by your Spirit and not to gratify the desires of the flesh, so that we, who in Christ Jesus have crucified the desires of the flesh, may manifest the fruits of the Spirit in all that we do. This we ask in the power of the Holy Spirit, who with you and the Son is worshiped and glorified. *Amen.*

Acts 2:17–18 (Joel 2:28–29); Galatians 5:16–24

VI.

Faithful God, you have brought into being a new humanity in Christ Jesus, and you are building us together into a dwelling in which he lives by his Spirit. Strengthen your people, so that we may continue to live in him, as a chosen people, a royal priesthood, a holy nation and God's special possession; that together we may declare the praises of him who called us out of darkness into his wonderful light. *Amen.*

Ephesians 2:22; 1 Peter 2:9

VII.

Radiant God, you spoke to Peter, James, and John while your beloved Son was transfigured on the holy mount, clothed in dazzling white. Incline our hearts to obey your word, that we may escape the corruption that is in the world, and may become partakers of the divine nature, so that the Spirit who raised Christ from the dead will give life to our mortal bodies, and make our bodies imperishable like his, radiant and glorious, who with you and the Holy Spirit is glorified, one God, now and forever. *Amen.*

Matthew 17:1–9 (Mark 9:2–10; Luke 9:28–36);
Psalm 119:112; 2 Peter 1:4; 1 Corinthians 15:53

The Lord's Prayer

I.

Holy God, your name is unlike any other name. Show us your divine majesty and mercy, that we may honor your name in worship, cling to it in times of trouble, and proclaim it boldly to the world. This we ask in the holy name of Jesus Christ, who lives and reigns with you and the Holy Spirit, one God, now and forever. *Amen.*

Psalm 85:9; Acts 4:12

II.

Heavenly Father, your kingdom is not of this world. Give us eyes to see and ears to hear, so that we may recognize and embrace your kingly rule in our lives, which is good news for the poor, freedom for prisoners, sight for the blind, and liberty to those who are oppressed; this we ask in the name of Jesus the King. *Amen.*

John 18:36; Matthew 11:15; Luke 4:18–19 (Isaiah 61:1–2;
Psalm 147:7–8; Isaiah 58:6)

III.

Gracious God, you will only what is good and acceptable and perfect. Heal our bent and wandering wills, and teach us perfect obedience, that we may love your will above our own by imitating Christ, who submitted to your will by giving up his life for us; in his name we pray. *Amen.*

Romans 12:2; Hebrews 5:7–10; 1 John 3:16

IV.

Almighty and everlasting God, you fed the Israelites in the wilderness with bread from heaven, and you have given us the spiritual food of your Son, Jesus Christ. Give us all we need this day, and make our hearts generous so that we may be signs of your kindness to all we meet, in the name of Jesus Christ, the bread of life. *Amen.*

John 6; Matthew 6:11

V.

Merciful God, you are slow to anger and abounding in steadfast love. Forgive us the wrongs we have done, and give us strength to forgive those who have wronged us, so that we may bear with one another in love, and maintain the unity of the Spirit in the bond of peace. In the name of Jesus Christ, whose death has brought reconciliation. *Amen.*

Psalm 86:15; Luke 11:4; Ephesians 4:2-3

VI.

Almighty and merciful Father, your Son, Jesus Christ, was tempted as we are, yet without sin. Teach us to be joyful in hope, patient in affliction, and persistent in prayer, that our faith may be proven genuine, resulting in praise and glory and honor at the revelation of Jesus Christ, who lives and reigns with you and the Holy Spirit, one God, now and forever. *Amen.*

Hebrews 4:15; Romans 12:2; 1 Peter 1:7

VII.

Almighty God, through the death of Christ you have delivered us from the power of death and the devil. Give us faith that is firm, hope that is steadfast, and love that abides, so that we may be kept blameless at the coming of Jesus Christ, who sits at your right hand and who, with the Holy Spirit, is worshiped and glorified. *Amen.*

Colossians 1:23; 1 Thessalonians 5:23; Hebrews 2:14

You crown the year with your bounty.

Psalm 65:11

DAILY BIBLE-READING PLAN

Or Lectionary

THIS DAILY BIBLE-READING PLAN (or lectionary) is ordered around the church year. The church measures its days and seasons by our Lord and Savior Jesus Christ. Because the church year walks through Jesus' life, death, and resurrection, the church year has two center points: Jesus' birth (Advent, Christmas, and Epiphany) and Jesus' death and resurrection (Lent, Easter, and Pentecost). Just as the sun orders our ordinary calendar, Jesus is the sun of the Christian calendar.

Each day has two readings—often, but not always, an Old Testament and a New Testament reading. You can read them together. You could read just one. You could read one in the morning and one in the evening. You could also read them along with the 30-day Psalter (p. 397), in which case you would begin with the psalm readings.

Jesus—in his birth, life, death, resurrection, and ascension—absorbs our days and interprets them according to his life, forgiveness, and salvation. Each day and season focuses on part of the second article of the Apostles' Creed, "I believe in Jesus Christ his only Son our Lord." But every day is filled with all of Christ: "you crown the year with your bounty" (Psalm 65:11).

Advent begins the first Sunday after Thanksgiving
(traditionally, the Sunday nearest November 30, the Feast of St. Andrew).

FIRST SUNDAY IN ADVENT

DAY	1ST READING	2ND READING
Sunday	Jeremiah 33:14–18	Matthew 21:1–9
Monday	Genesis 3:1–24	Matthew 11:25–30
Tuesday	Genesis 9:1–19	Acts 3:22–26
Wednesday	Genesis 22:1–19	Colossians 1:15–29
Thursday	Genesis 49:1–28	Hebrews 1:1–4
Friday	Numbers 24:14–25	Hebrews 2:1–4
Saturday	Deuteronomy 18:15–19	Ephesians 3:1–12

SECOND SUNDAY IN ADVENT

DAY	1ST READING	2ND READING
Sunday	Micah 4:1–7	Luke 21:25–36
Monday	1 Chronicles 17:1–27	Acts 17:16–34
Tuesday	2 Chronicles 7:11–22	1 John 4:9–16
Wednesday	Isaiah 11:1–10	Colossians 1:1–18
Thursday	Jeremiah 23:2–8	Philippians 2:12–18
Friday	Jeremiah 30:1–22	Philippians 3:12–16
Saturday	Jeremiah 33:14–26	Colossians 3:1–11

THIRD SUNDAY IN ADVENT

DAY	1ST READING	2ND READING
Sunday	Malachi 3:1–6	Matthew 11:2–10
Monday	Isaiah 2:1–5	Hebrews 10:35–39
Tuesday	Isaiah 24:21–25:5	Luke 21:5–24
Wednesday	Isaiah 25:6–10	Luke 12:35–39
Thursday	Isaiah 26:1–21	James 5:7–11
Friday	Isaiah 51:1–16	Luke 1:1–25
Saturday	Isaiah 52:1–12	Luke 1:26–38

FOURTH SUNDAY IN ADVENT

DAY	1ST READING	2ND READING
Sunday	Isaiah 40:1–8	John 1:19–28
Monday	Isaiah 40:9–11	Matthew 1:18–25
Tuesday	Malachi 3:1–7	Luke 1:39–45
Wednesday	Malachi 4:1–6	Luke 1:46–56
Thursday	Isaiah 28:14–19	Luke 1:57–66
Friday	Isaiah 7:1–17	Luke 1:67–80
Saturday	Micah 5:1–5	Matthew 1:1–17

CHRISTMAS

DAY	1ST READING	2ND READING
Christmas Day	Isaiah 9:2–7	Luke 2:1–14
December 26	Micah 5:2–4	Luke 2:15–20
December 27	Isaiah 32:1–8	John 1:15–18
December 28	Isaiah 46:3–13	Luke 2:15–20
December 29	Isaiah 49:1–13	Luke 2:22–24
December 30	Isaiah 55:1–13	Luke 2:25–32
December 31	Isaiah 42:1–9	Matthew 2:13–15
January 1	Isaiah 64:1–12	Luke 4:16–21
January 2	Isaiah 61:1–11	Matthew 2:16–18
January 3	Micah 4:1–8	Matthew 2:19–23
January 4	Isaiah 56:1–8	Matthew 3:1–12
January 5	Isaiah 12:1–6	Luke 3:1–9

EPIPHANY

DAY	1ST READING	2ND READING
Epiphany (January 6)	Isaiah 49:1–7	Matthew 2:1–12
January 7	Genesis 1:1–31	Luke 3:10–14
January 8	Genesis 2:1–25	Luke 3:15–20
January 9	Genesis 4:1–26	Mark 1:1–8
January 10	Genesis 5:1–32	Mark 1:9–11
January 11	Genesis 6:9–22	Luke 3:21, 22
January 12	Genesis 7:1–24	Luke 3:23–38

The number of days between Epiphany and the following Sunday varies each year. Follow the reading plan until the First Sunday after Epiphany; then resume below.

FIRST SUNDAY AFTER EPIPHANY

DAY	1ST READING	2ND READING
Sunday	Isaiah 61:1–3	Luke 2:41–52
Monday	Genesis 8:1–22	John 1:29–34
Tuesday	Genesis 11:1–9	John 1:35–42
Wednesday	Genesis 12:1–20	John 1:43–51
Thursday	Genesis 13:1–18	Luke 4:1–13
Friday	Genesis 14:8–24	Mark 1:12–15
Saturday	Genesis 15:1–21	Matthew 4:12–17

SECOND SUNDAY AFTER EPIPHANY

DAY	1ST READING	2ND READING
Sunday	Deuteronomy 18:15–19	John 2:1–11
Monday	Genesis 17:1–22	Matthew 4:18–25
Tuesday	Genesis 18:1–33	Matthew 5:1–9
Wednesday	Genesis 19:1–29	Matthew 5:27–48
Thursday	Genesis 21:1–8	Matthew 6:1–23
Friday	Genesis 24:1–28	Matthew 7:1–14
Saturday	Genesis 24:29–67	Matthew 7:24–29

THIRD SUNDAY AFTER EPIPHANY

DAY	1ST READING	2ND READING
Sunday	Jeremiah 33:6–9	Matthew 8:1–13
Monday	Genesis 25:19–34	Matthew 8:14–22
Tuesday	Genesis 27:1–45	Matthew 8:28–34
Wednesday	Genesis 27:46–28:22	Matthew 9:9–17
Thursday	Genesis 29:1–20	Matthew 9:27–38
Friday	Genesis 31:1–18	Matthew 10:1–16
Saturday	Genesis 32:3–32	Matthew 10:17–11:1

FOURTH SUNDAY AFTER EPIPHANY

DAY	1ST READING	2ND READING
Sunday	Isaiah 43:1–3	Matthew 8:23–27
Monday	Genesis 33:1–20	Matthew 11:11–24
Tuesday	Genesis 35:1–21	Matthew 12:1–21
Wednesday	Genesis 37:1–36	Matthew 12:22–50
Thursday	Genesis 39:1–23	Matthew 13:1–23
Friday	Genesis 40:1–23	Matthew 14:1–36
Saturday	Genesis 41:1–37	Matthew 15:1–20

FIFTH SUNDAY AFTER EPIPHANY

DAY	1ST READING	2ND READING
Sunday	Jeremiah 17:5–10	Matthew 13:24–30
Monday	Genesis 41:38–57	Matthew 15:29–39
Tuesday	Genesis 42:1–38	Matthew 16:1–12
Wednesday	Genesis 43:1–34	Matthew 16:21–28
Thursday	Genesis 44:1–34	Matthew 17:9–27
Friday	Genesis 45:1–28	Matthew 19:1–15
Saturday	Genesis 46:1–34	Matthew 20:17–34

SIXTH SUNDAY AFTER EPIPHANY

DAY	1ST READING	2ND READING
Sunday	Isaiah 61:10–11	Matthew 17:1–9
Monday	Genesis 47:1–31	Matthew 21:10–46
Tuesday	Genesis 48:1–22	Matthew 23:1–39
Wednesday	Exodus 1:1–22	Mark:1:16–45
Thursday	Exodus 2:1–25	Mark 2:1–28
Friday	Exodus 3:1–22	Mark 3:1–35
Saturday	Exodus 4:1–31	Mark 5:1–20

The three weeks before the beginning of Lent are traditionally called the Pre-Lenten Season.

THE THIRD SUNDAY BEFORE LENT (SEPTUAGESIMA)

DAY	1ST READING	2ND READING
Sunday	Jeremiah 1:4–10	Matthew 20:1–16
Monday	Exodus 5:1–23	Mark 5:21–43
Tuesday	Exodus 6:1–13	Mark 6:1–29
Wednesday	Exodus 11:1–10	Mark 6:30–56
Thursday	Exodus 12:1–28	Mark 7:1–30
Friday	Exodus 12:29–42	Mark 8:10–9:1
Saturday	Exodus 13:1–22	Mark 9:2–32

THE SECOND SUNDAY BEFORE LENT (SEXAGESIMA)

DAY	1ST READING	2ND READING
Sunday	Isaiah 55:10–13	Luke 8:4–15
Monday	Exodus 14:1–31	Mark 10:1–31
Tuesday	Exodus 15:1–21	Mark 10:32–52
Wednesday	Exodus 15:22–16:36	Mark 11:1–33
Thursday	Exodus 17:1–16	Mark 12:13–44
Friday	Exodus 19:1–25	Luke 4:14–44
Saturday	Exodus 20:1–23	Luke 5:12–39

*Ash Wednesday is forty days before Easter Sunday (not including Sundays);
it begins the season of Lent.*

THE FIRST SUNDAY BEFORE LENT (QUINQUAGESIMA)

DAY	1ST READING	2ND READING
Sunday	Isaiah 35:3–7	Luke 18:31–43
Monday	Exodus 24:1–25:9	Luke 6:1–35
Tuesday	Exodus 31:18–33:23	Luke 6:33–7:10
Ash Wednesday	Joel 2:12–19	Matthew 6:16–21
Thursday	Exodus 34:1–10	Luke 7:18–8:3
Friday	Exodus 34:27–35	Luke 8:16–56
Saturday	Exodus 40:1–38	Luke 9:1–27

FIRST SUNDAY IN LENT

DAY	1ST READING	2ND READING
Sunday	Genesis 3:1–24	Matthew 4:1–11
Monday	Numbers 3:5–13	Luke 9:28–62
Tuesday	Numbers 10:11–36	Luke 10:1–22
Wednesday	Numbers 11:1–35	Luke 10:38–11:13
Thursday	Numbers 12:1–15	Luke 11:29–36
Friday	Numbers 13:1–25	Luke 11:37–54
Saturday	Numbers 13:26–33	Luke 12:1–34

SECOND SUNDAY IN LENT

DAY	1ST READING	2ND READING
Sunday	Isaiah 45:20–25	Matthew 15:21–28
Monday	Numbers 14:1–45	Luke 13:1–17
Tuesday	Numbers 16:1–22	Luke 14:25–35
Wednesday	Numbers 16:23–50	Luke 15:11–32
Thursday	Numbers 17:1–13	Luke 16:10–18
Friday	Numbers 20:1–29	Luke 17:1–10
Saturday	Numbers 21:1–22:1	Luke 18:1–8

THIRD SUNDAY IN LENT

DAY	1ST READING	2ND READING
Sunday	2 Samuel 22:1–7	Luke 11:14–28
Monday	Numbers 22:2–41	Luke 18:15–30
Tuesday	Numbers 23:1–30	Luke 19:1–40
Wednesday	Numbers 24:1–13	Luke 20:1–21:4
Thursday	Numbers 27:12–23	Luke 21:37–22:38
Friday	Deuteronomy 5:1–33	Luke 22:39–71
Saturday	Deuteronomy 8:1–20	Luke 23:1–25

FOURTH SUNDAY IN LENT

DAY	1ST READING	2ND READING
Sunday	Isaiah 49:8–13	John 6:1–15
Monday	Deuteronomy 9:1–29	Luke 23:26–56
Tuesday	Deuteronomy 10:1–22	Matthew 26:1–35
Wednesday	Deuteronomy 11:1–32	Matthew 26:36–75
Thursday	Deuteronomy 28:1–14	Matthew 27:1–38
Friday	Deuteronomy 28:15–68	Matthew 27:39–66
Saturday	Deuteronomy 34:1–12	Mark 14:1–31

FIFTH SUNDAY IN LENT

DAY	1ST READING	2ND READING
Sunday	Genesis 12:1–3	John 8:46–59
Monday	Jeremiah 2:1–19	Mark 14:32–72
Tuesday	Hosea 13:9–14	Mark 15:1–19
Wednesday	Zephaniah 3:1–8	Mark 15:20–47
Thursday	Micah 3:9–12	John 12:1–19
Friday	Isaiah 66:1–9	John 12:20–50
Saturday	Zechariah 9:1–17	John 13:16–38

HOLY WEEK

DAY	1ST READING	2ND READING
Palm Sunday	Zechariah 9:9–10	Matthew 21:1–9
Monday	Isaiah 50:5–10	John 18:1–18
Tuesday	Jeremiah 11:18–20	John 18:19–40
Wednesday	Isaiah 62:11–63:7	John 19:1–12
Maundy Thursday	Exodus 12:1–14	1 Corinthians 11:23–52
Good Friday	Isaiah 52:13–15	John 18:1–19:42
Holy Saturday	1 Peter 3:17–22	Matthew 27:57–66

EASTER

DAY	1ST READING	2ND READING
Easter Sunday	Isaiah 52:13–15	Mark 16:1–8
Easter Monday	Acts 10:34–41	Luke 24:13–35
Easter Tuesday	Acts 13:26–33	Luke 24:36–48
Wednesday	Haggai 2:20–23	John 20:1–18
Thursday	Zechariah 6:9–15	Luke 24:1–12
Friday	Ezekiel 17:22–24	Luke 24:36–49
Saturday	Isaiah 44:21–28	Mark 16:9–14

FIRST SUNDAY AFTER EASTER

DAY	1ST READING	2ND READING
Sunday	Job 19:25–27	John 10:19–31
Monday	Jonah 1:1–16	John 21:1–25
Tuesday	Jonah 1:17–2:10	John 2:12–25
Wednesday	Jonah 3:1–10	John 3:22–36
Thursday	Jonah 4:1–11	John 4:1–27
Friday	Isaiah 33:2–6	John 4:28–38
Saturday	Isaiah 42:10–17	John 4:39–45

SECOND SUNDAY AFTER EASTER

DAY	1ST READING	2ND READING
Sunday	Ezekiel 34:11–16	John 10:11–16
Monday	Micah 2:12, 13	John 5:1–17
Tuesday	Isaiah 30:19–26	John 5:18–30
Wednesday	Jeremiah 3:11–19	John 5:31–47
Thursday	Ezekiel 34:1–11	John 6:16–29
Friday	Ezekiel 34:12–22	John 6:30–40
Saturday	Ezekiel 34:23–21	John 6:41–59

THIRD SUNDAY AFTER EASTER

DAY	1ST READING	2ND READING
Sunday	Lamentations 3:18–26	John 16:16–23
Monday	Ezekiel 36:1–15	John 6:60–71
Tuesday	Ezekiel 36:16–32	John 7:1–13
Wednesday	Ezekiel 36:33–38	John 7:14–24
Thursday	Haggai 2:2–9	John 7:25–36
Friday	Zechariah 2:1–13	John 7:37–53
Saturday	Zechariah 11:1–17	John 8:1–11

FOURTH SUNDAY AFTER EASTER

DAY	1ST READING	2ND READING
Sunday	Isaiah 12:1–6	John 16:5–15
Monday	Zechariah 12:1–14	John 8:12–20
Tuesday	Isaiah 65:1–7	John 8:21–29
Wednesday	Isaiah 65:8–16	John 8:30–45
Thursday	Jeremiah 8:4–13	John 9:1–13
Friday	Zechariah 8:18–23	John 9:14–34
Saturday	Isaiah 49:22–26	John 9:35–41

Ascension is forty days after Easter Sunday.

FIFTH SUNDAY AFTER EASTER

DAY	1ST READING	2ND READING
Sunday	Jeremiah 29:11–14	John 16:23–30
Monday	Amos 9:8–15	John 10:1–5
Tuesday	Isaiah 4:2–6	John 10:6–10
Wednesday	Isaiah 29:18–24	Matthew 28:16–20
Ascension Day	Acts 1:1–11	Mark 16:14–20
Friday	Micah 7:7–13	Luke 24:50–53
Saturday	Micah 7:14–20	Acts 1:12–26

SUNDAY AFTER ASCENSION

DAY	1ST READING	2ND READING
Sunday	Ezekiel 36:25–27	John 15:26–16:4
Monday	Zechariah 13:7–9	John 10:17–21
Tuesday	Zechariah 14:1–21	John 10:22–31
Wednesday	Isaiah 66:10–24	John 10:32–42
Thursday	Jeremiah 46:27, 28	John 11:1–27
Friday	Isaiah 32:9–20	John 11:28–44
Saturday	Isaiah 57:15–21	John 11:45–57

Pentecost is fifty days after Easter Sunday, commencing the long Pentecost Season, which ends the Saturday before the First Sunday in Advent.

PENTECOST

DAY	1ST READING	2ND READING
Pentecost Sunday	Acts 2:1–13	John 14:15–31
Pentecost Monday	Acts 10:34–48	John 3:16–21
Pentecost Tuesday	Acts 8:14–17	John 10:1–10
Wednesday	Isaiah 45:18–21	Acts 2:37–47
Thursday	Isaiah 45:22–25	John 14:1–22
Friday	Jeremiah 9:23–26	John 15:1–25
Saturday	Isaiah 44:6–8	John 16:31–17:26

TRINITY SUNDAY

DAY	1ST READING	2ND READING
Sunday	Ezekiel 18:30–32	John 3:1–15
Monday	Joshua 1:1–18	Acts 3:1–21
Tuesday	Joshua 3:1–17	Acts 4:1–37
Wednesday	Joshua 4:1–24	Acts 5:1–42
Thursday	Joshua 6:1–27	Acts 6:1–15
Friday	Joshua 8:1–35	Acts 7:1–60
Saturday	Joshua 9:1–27	Acts 8:1–40

SECOND SUNDAY AFTER PENTECOST

DAY	1ST READING	2ND READING
Sunday	Jeremiah 9:23–24	Luke 16:19–31
Monday	Judges 7:1–25	Acts 15:1–41
Tuesday	Joshua 11:1–23	Acts 10:1–33
Wednesday	Joshua 23:1–16	Acts 11:1–30
Thursday	Joshua 24:1–31	Acts 12:1–25
Friday	Judges 2:1–23	Acts 13:1–52
Saturday	Judges 6:1–40	Acts 14:1–28

THIRD SUNDAY AFTER PENTECOST

DAY	1ST READING	2ND READING
Sunday	Isaiah 25:6–9	Luke 14:16–24
Monday	Judges 7:1–25	Acts 15:1–41
Tuesday	Judges 13:1–25	Acts 16:1–40
Wednesday	Judges 14:1–20	Acts 17:1–15
Thursday	Judges 15:1–20	Acts 18:1–28
Friday	Judges 16:4–31	Acts 19:1–41
Saturday	1 Samuel 1:1–28	Acts 20:1–38

FOURTH SUNDAY AFTER PENTECOST

DAY	1ST READING	2ND READING
Sunday	Micah 7:18–20	Luke 15:1–10
Monday	1 Samuel 2:1–21	Acts 21:1–39
Tuesday	1 Samuel 3:1–21	Acts 21:40–22:29
Wednesday	1 Samuel 4:1–22	Acts 22:30–23:35
Thursday	1 Samuel 5:1–12	Acts 24:1–27
Friday	1 Samuel 7:1–17	Acts 25:1–27
Saturday	1 Samuel 8:1–32	Acts 26:1–32

FIFTH SUNDAY AFTER PENTECOST

DAY	1ST READING	2ND READING
Sunday	Isaiah 58:6–12	Luke 6:36–42
Monday	1 Samuel 9:1–27	Acts 27:1–44
Tuesday	1 Samuel 10:1–27	Acts 28:1–31
Wednesday	1 Samuel 12:1–25	Romans 1:1–15
Thursday	1 Samuel 13:1–14	Romans 1:16–32
Friday	1 Samuel 15:1–35	Romans 2:1–29
Saturday	1 Samuel 16:1–23	Romans 3:1–31

SIXTH SUNDAY AFTER PENTECOST

DAY	1ST READING	2ND READING
Sunday	Jeremiah 16:14–21	Luke 5:1–11
Monday	1 Samuel 17:1–58	Romans 4:1–25
Tuesday	1 Samuel 18:1–21	Romans 5:1–6:2
Wednesday	1 Samuel 19:1–24	Romans 6:12–18
Thursday	1 Samuel 20:1–42	Romans 7:1–25
Friday	1 Samuel 22:1–23	Romans 2:1–29
Saturday	1 Samuel 24:1–22	Romans 13:1–7

SEVENTH SUNDAY AFTER PENTECOST

DAY	1ST READING	2ND READING
Sunday	Exodus 20:1–17	Matthew 5:20–26
Monday	1 Samuel 26:1–25	Romans 14:1–15:3
Tuesday	1 Samuel 28:3–25	Romans 14:14–33
Wednesday	1 Samuel 31:1–13	Romans 16:1–27
Thursday	1 Samuel 1:1–27	1 Corinthians 1:10–31
Friday	2 Samuel 5:1–25	1 Corinthians 2:1–16
Saturday	2 Samuel 6:1–23	1 Corinthians 4:6–5:5

EIGHTH SUNDAY AFTER PENTECOST

DAY	1ST READING	2ND READING
Sunday	Jeremiah 31:23–25	Mark 8:1–9
Monday	1 Chronicles 16:1–43	1 Corinthians 5:9–6:20
Tuesday	2 Samuel 7:1–29	1 Corinthians 7:1–40
Wednesday	2 Samuel 12:1–23	1 Corinthians 8:1–13
Thursday	2 Samuel 15:1–15	1 Corinthians 9:1–23
Friday	2 Samuel 16:5–35	1 Corinthians 1:14–33
Saturday	2 Samuel 18:1–13	1 Corinthians 11:1–22

NINTH SUNDAY AFTER PENTECOST

DAY	1ST READING	2ND READING
Sunday	Jeremiah 15:19–21	Matthew 7:15–23
Monday	1 Chronicles 16:1–43	1 Corinthians 5:9–6:20
Tuesday	2 Samuel 7:1–29	1 Corinthians 7:1–40
Wednesday	2 Samuel 12:1–23	1 Corinthians 8:1–13
Thursday	2 Samuel 15:1–15	1 Corinthians 9:1–23
Friday	2 Samuel 16:5–35	1 Corinthians 10:14–33
Saturday	2 Samuel 18:1–13	1 Corinthians 11:1–22

TENTH SUNDAY AFTER PENTECOST

DAY	1ST READING	2ND READING
Sunday	1 Chronicles 29:10–13	Luke 16:1–9
Monday	1 Kings 3:16–28	2 Corinthians 8:1–24
Tuesday	1 Kings 4:22–34	2 Corinthians 9:1–15
Wednesday	1 Kings 5:1–18	2 Corinthians 10:1–18
Thursday	2 Chronicles 3:1–17	2 Corinthians 11:1–18
Friday	1 Kings 8:1–66	2 Corinthians 12:19–13:13
Saturday	1 Kings 7:1–12	Galatians 1:1–24

ELEVENTH SUNDAY AFTER PENTECOST

DAY	1ST READING	2ND READING
Sunday	Jeremiah 7:1–7	Luke 19:41–48
Monday	1 Kings 9:1–28	Galatians 2:1–21
Tuesday	1 Kings 10:1–29	Galatians 3:1–14
Wednesday	1 Kings 11:1–43	Galatians 4:8–20
Thursday	1 Kings 12:1–33	Galatians 5:1–15
Friday	1 Kings 13:1–34	Galatians 6:11–18
Saturday	1 Kings 14:1–31	Ephesians 6:1–9

TWELFTH SUNDAY AFTER PENTECOST

DAY	1ST READING	2ND READING
Sunday	2 Samuel 22:21–29	Luke 18:9–14
Monday	1 Kings 16:29–17:24	Ephesians 6:18–24
Tuesday	1 Kings 18:1–46	Philippians 1:12–2:4
Wednesday	1 Kings 19:1–21	Philippians 2:19–30
Thursday	1 Kings 21:1–29	Philippians 3:1–11
Friday	1 Kings 22:51, 2 Kings 1:17	Philippians 4:1–3
Saturday	2 Kings 2:1–25	Philippians 4:8–23

THIRTEENTH SUNDAY AFTER PENTECOST

DAY	1ST READING	2ND READING
Sunday	Isaiah 29:18–19	Mark 7:31–37
Monday	2 Kings 4:1–44	Colossians 2:1–23
Tuesday	2 Kings 5:1–27	Colossians 3:1–18–4:18
Wednesday	2 Kings 6:1–23	1 Thessalonians 1:1–10
Thursday	2 Kings 6:24–7:20	1 Thessalonians 2:1–20
Friday	2 Kings 8:1–15	1 Thessalonians 3:1–13
Saturday	2 Kings 9:1–37	1 Thessalonians 4:8–12

FOURTEENTH SUNDAY AFTER PENTECOST

DAY	1ST READING	2ND READING
Sunday	Leviticus 18:1–5	Luke 10:23–27
Monday	2 Kings 10:1–36	1 Thessalonians 5:12–28
Tuesday	2 Chronicles 22:1–12	1 Timothy 1:1–20
Wednesday	2 Chronicles 23:1–21	1 Timothy 2:1–15
Thursday	2 Chronicles 24 1–27	1 Timothy 3:1–16
Friday	2 Kings 14:1–29	1 Timothy 4:1–16
Saturday	2 Kings 15:1–38	1 Timothy 5:1–25

FIFTEENTH SUNDAY AFTER PENTECOST

DAY	1ST READING	2ND READING
Sunday	Jeremiah 17:13–14	Luke 17:11–19
Monday	Isaiah 6:1–13	1 Timothy 6:1–21
Tuesday	Amos 7:7–17	2 Timothy 1:1–18
Wednesday	2 Kings 16:1–20	2 Timothy 2:1–26
Thursday	2 Kings 17:1–23	Titus 1:1–16
Friday	2 Kings 18:1–37	Titus 2:1–10
Saturday	2 Kings 19:1–37	Titus 2:15–3:3

SIXTEENTH SUNDAY AFTER PENTECOST

DAY	1ST READING	2ND READING
Sunday	Deuteronomy 6:4–7	Matthew 6:24–34
Monday	2 Kings 20:1–21	Titus 3:8–15
Tuesday	2 Kings 21:1–26	Philemon 1:25
Wednesday	2 Chronicles 34:1–33	Hebrews 1:1–14
Thursday	2 Chronicles 35:20–36:10	Hebrews 2:5–3:6
Friday	Jeremiah 22:1–30	Hebrews 4:14–5:14
Saturday	Jeremiah 25:1–14	Hebrews 6:1–20

SEVENTEENTH SUNDAY AFTER PENTECOST

DAY	1ST READING	2ND READING
Sunday	Deuteronomy 32:39–40	Luke 7:11–17
Monday	Jeremiah 37:1–21	Hebrews 7:1–28
Tuesday	Jeremiah 38:1–28	Hebrews 8:1–13
Wednesday	Jeremiah 32:1–44	Hebrews 9:1–10
Thursday	Jeremiah 39:1–18	Hebrews 9:16–28
Friday	Jeremiah 29:1–23	Hebrews 10:1–34
Saturday	Daniel 1:1–21	Hebrews 11:1–7

EIGHTEENTH SUNDAY AFTER PENTECOST

DAY	1ST READING	2ND READING
Sunday	1 Samuel 2:1–10	Luke 14:1–11
Monday	Daniel 3:1–30	Hebrews 11:17–40
Tuesday	Daniel 4:1–37	Hebrews 12:1–17
Wednesday	Daniel 5:1–30	Hebrews 13:1–25
Thursday	Daniel 5:31–6:28	James 1:1–15
Friday	Ezra 1:1–11	James 2:1–13
Saturday	Ezra 3:1–13	James 2:14–26

NINETEENTH SUNDAY AFTER PENTECOST

DAY	1ST READING	2ND READING
Sunday	Deuteronomy 10:12–21	Matthew 22:34–46
Monday	Ezra 4:1–24	James 3:1–18
Tuesday	Haggai 1:1–15	James 4:1–5:6
Wednesday	Ezra 5:1–17	James 5:12–20
Thursday	Ezra 6:1–22	1 Peter 3:1–7
Friday	Ezra 7:1–28	1 Peter 3:15–22
Saturday	Ezra 8:31–9:15	1 Peter 5:1–5

TWENTIETH SUNDAY AFTER PENTECOST

DAY	1ST READING	2ND READING
Sunday	Isaiah 44:21–23	Matthew 9:1–8
Monday	Nehemiah 1:1–11	1 John 1:1–10
Tuesday	Nehemiah 2:1–20	1 John 2:1–17
Wednesday	Nehemiah 4:1–23	1 John 5:1–3
Thursday	Nehemiah 8:1–18	1 John 5:10–21
Friday	Nehemiah 9:1–38	2 John 1–13
Saturday	Zechariah 8:1–23	3 John 1–14

TWENTY-FIRST SUNDAY AFTER PENTECOST

DAY	1ST READING	2ND READING
Sunday	Isaiah 65:1–2	Matthew 22:1–14
Monday	Isaiah 43:1–13	Mark 4:1–41
Tuesday	Isaiah 41:1–20	Luke 13:18–35
Wednesday	Habakkuk 2:1–4	Matthew 13:31–58
Thursday	Isaiah 63:7–19	Matthew 16:13–20
Friday	Isaiah 64:1–12	2 Corinthians 3:10–4:18
Saturday	Isaiah 5:1–7	2 Corinthians 5:1–21

TWENTY-SECOND SUNDAY AFTER PENTECOST

DAY	1ST READING	2ND READING
Sunday	Hosea 13:14	John 4:46–54
Monday	Micah 6:1–9	Ephesians 1:1–23
Tuesday	Isaiah 58:1–14	Ephesians 2:1–22
Wednesday	Isaiah 59:1–21	Ephesians 4:7–21
Thursday	Jeremiah 31:1–22	Ephesians 4:29–32
Friday	Jeremiah 31:23–40	Ephesians 5:10–14
Saturday	Isaiah 48:1–22	Ephesians 5:22, 23

TWENTY-THIRD SUNDAY AFTER PENTECOST

DAY	1ST READING	2ND READING
Sunday	Deuteronomy 7:9–11	Matthew 18:23–35
Monday	Micah 4:9–5:1	Matthew 18:1–22
Tuesday	Isaiah 49:14–21	Mark 9:33–50
Wednesday	Isaiah 2:10–21	Luke 17:20–37
Thursday	Isaiah 63:1–6	Romans 8:24–39
Friday	Joel 2:1–11	Mark 12:1–12
Saturday	Joel 2:12–27	Matthew 25:14–30

TWENTY-FOURTH SUNDAY AFTER PENTECOST

DAY	1ST READING	2ND READING
Sunday	Isaiah 32:1–8	Matthew 22:15–22
Monday	Joel 3:1–13	1 Corinthians 3:1–23
Tuesday	Joel 3:14–21	Matthew 19:16–30
Wednesday	Obadiah 1–21	Luke 14:12–15
Thursday	Nahum 1:1–14	Mark 13:1–37
Friday	Nahum 1:15–3:19	Romans 9:1–23
Saturday	Isaiah 10:5–27	Romans 10:1–21

TWENTY-FIFTH SUNDAY AFTER PENTECOST

DAY	1ST READING	2ND READING
Sunday	Isaiah 51:9–16	Matthew 9:18–26
Monday	Isaiah 13:1–22	Romans 11:1–33
Tuesday	Isaiah 14:1–27	2 Thessalonians 1:11–2:17
Wednesday	Isaiah 47:1–15	2 Thessalonians 3:1–18
Thursday	Daniel 2:27–45	2 Timothy 3:1–17
Friday	Daniel 7:1–28	2 Timothy 4:1–22
Saturday	Daniel 9:1–27	Matthew 24:1–14

TWENTY-SIXTH SUNDAY AFTER PENTECOST

DAY	1ST READING	2ND READING
Sunday	Isaiah 49:12–17	Matthew 24:15–28
Monday	Daniel 11:36–12:13	Matthew 24:29–51
Tuesday	Ezekiel 38:1–23	Matthew 22:23–33
Wednesday	Ezekiel 39:1–29	1 Corinthians 15:11–50
Thursday	Isaiah 43:14–25	Hebrews 3:7–4:13
Friday	Isaiah 33:17–24	Hebrews 11:8–16
Saturday	Ezekiel 37:1–14	Hebrews 12:18–29

TWENTY-SEVENTH SUNDAY AFTER PENTECOST

DAY	1ST READING	2ND READING
Sunday	Isaiah 40:9–11	Matthew 25:31–46
Monday	Zephaniah 3:9–20	1 Peter 1:1–12
Tuesday	Isaiah 34:1–17	1 Peter 1:13–2:10
Wednesday	Isaiah 35:1–10	1 Peter 4:1–7
Thursday	Isaiah 54:1–17	1 Peter 4:12–19
Friday	Isaiah 60:7–22	2 Peter 1:1–15
Saturday	Isaiah 62:1–12	2 Peter 2:1–22

TWENTY-EIGHTH SUNDAY AFTER PENTECOST

DAY	1ST READING	2ND READING
Sunday	Isaiah 65:17–19	Matthew 25:1–13
Monday	Isaiah 65:17–25	2 Peter 3:1–18
Tuesday	Ezekiel 37:15–28	Jude 1–25
Wednesday	Habakkuk 3:1–19	1 John 2:18–29
Thursday	Isaiah 40:27–31	1 John 3:1–12
Friday	Jeremiah 14:7–9	1 John 3:19–24
Saturday	Malachi 3:7–18	1 John 4:1–8

30-DAY PSALTER

DAY	MORNING	EVENING
1	1–5	6–8
2	9–11	12–14
3	15–17	18
4	19–21	22–23
5	24–26	27–29
6	30–31	32–34
7	35–36	37
8	38–40	41–43
9	44–46	47–49
10	50–52	53–55
11	56–58	59–61
12	62–64	65–67
13	68	69–70
14	71–72	73–74
15	75–77	78
16	79–81	82–85
17	86–88	89
18	90–92	93–94
19	95–97	98–101
20	102–103	104
21	105	106
22	107	108–109
23	110–113	114–115
24	116–118	119:1–32
25	119:33–72	119:73–104
26	119:105–144	119:145–176
27	120–125	126–131
28	132–135	136–138
29	139–140	141–143
30	144–146	147–150

PERMISSIONS

Bible Permissions

Scripture quotations marked (KJV) are from the King James Version. Public domain.

Scripture quotations marked (NASB) are from the New American Standard Bible®, Copyright 1960, 1962, 1963, 1968, 1971, 1972, 1973, 1975, 1977, 1995 by The Lockman Foundation. Used by permission.

Scripture quotations marked (NEB) are from the New English Bible, copyright © Cambridge University Press and Oxford University Press 1961, 1970. All rights reserved.

Scripture quotations marked (NRSV) are from New Revised Standard Version, copyright © 1989, National Council of the Churches of Christ in the United States of America. Used by permission. All rights reserved.

Scripture quotations marked (REB) are from the Revised English Bible, copyright © Cambridge University Press and Oxford University Press 1989. All rights reserved.

Scripture quotations marked (ESV) are from the ESV® Bible (The Holy Bible, English Standard Version®), copyright © 2001 by Crossway Bibles, a publishing ministry of Good News Publishers. Used by permission. All rights reserved.

The English translation of Zechariah's Song, or The Benedictus, on p. xxii is from the International Consultation on English Texts (ICET), © 1998. Used by permission. www.englishtexts.org.

The English translation of Psalm 95:1–7 on p. xxi and Mary's Song, or The Magnificat, on p. xxii is modernized from the 1662 Book of Common Prayer. Public domain.

The epigraphs on pp. x, xvi, 377, 400 and the colophon on p. 407 use the ESV.

The epigraph on p. 366 uses *The New Coverdale Psalter* in *The Book of Common Prayer* (Huntington Beach, CA: Anglican Liturgy Press, 2019, © of the Anglican Church in North America.

Other Permissions

The Harrowing of Hell icon on page 205 is located at St. Andrew Holborn Church in London, England. Used by permission.

Rembrandt's *The Return of the Prodigal Son* on page 354 is located at The State Hermitage Museum in St. Petersburg, Russia. Public domain.

"Coda: Praying the Lord's Prayer with Rembrandt" is adapted from Wesley Hill, "Praying the 'Our Father' with Rembrandt," *Covenant* blog, September 23, 2015, https://livingchurch.org/covenant/2015/09/23/praying-our-father-rembrandt/. Used by permission.

I rejoice at your word
like one who finds great spoil.

Psalm 119:162

SCRIPTURE INDEX

OLD TESTAMENT

NEW TESTAMENT